DATE DUE

MR 13'89			
1-25-91			

THE MAKERS OF ENGLISH HISTORY

Foreword by Asa Briggs
General Editor · Norman Stone

Macmillan Publishing Company
New York

CONTENTS

ENDPAPERS *Elizabeth I carried by her courtiers, attributed to Robert Peake the Elder and painted* c. *1600.*

HALF-TITLE PAGE *Robert Peel on a music title page, 1837.*

TITLE PAGE *Winston Churchill driving past the cheering inhabitants of Metz, France, on 14 July 1946.*

Introduction copyright © 1987 by Norman Stone
Text copyright © 1987 by Weidenfeld & Nicolson Ltd.

Macmillan Publishing Company
A Division of Macmillan, Inc.
866 Third Avenue, New York, N.Y. 10022

Library of Congress Catalog Card Number: 86-12821

Printed and bound in Italy

printing number
1 2 3 4 5 6 7 8 9 10

Library of Congress Cataloging-in-Publication Data

The Makers of English History.
   Bibliography: p.
   Includes index.
   1. Great Britain—Biography.
2. Great Britain—
history.   I. Stone, Norman.
CT774.M35 1987   941
86-12821
ISBN 0-02-931650-2

FOREWORD
ASA BRIGGS

ONE OF THE CHARACTERS portrayed in this fascinating volume described biographers as vultures. They have, indeed, been given many names. Seldom, however, have they failed to attract English readers. The art, and techniques of the biographer have changed over the years, particularly during the last forty years, but English readers have never ceased to demand more biographies. They usually see history in personal terms, and what is hidden from view is treasured more than that which has been openly proclaimed.

Whether or not history can be adequately described, as Thomas Carlyle described it, as 'the essence of innumerable biographies' will doubtless remain a matter of debate. Carlyle, however, was a Scot not an Englishman and, great though his influence was, it is perhaps right that he does not figure in this gallery. Nonetheless, the volume does include a number of Scots and one remarkable Welshman, David Lloyd George. The guide to further reading at the end, selective as it must be, is as essential as the brief chronology; some characters have been far more fortunate in their biographers than others.

It must have been difficult to select the forty-five subjects of the portraits, two of them joint portraits, both from the nineteenth century, for which the most interesting of all guidebooks, that by G.M.Young, is even called 'a portrait'. Only two painters get into this volume – Blake and Turner: Constable is unlucky. Blake, prophet as well as painter, kept others out. Morris is in, Ruskin out. Thomas Telford, after whom an English new town has been named, is preferred to

James Watt, though, like Watt, he was a Scot. James VI of Scotland, who became James I of England, wins a place over his son Charles I, whom many have regarded as a saint and a martyr. Tennyson is preferred to Wordsworth. The only musician is Sullivan, one of the paired subjects; the only architect Wren; the only scientist Newton. There are seven royal portraits, nine of prime ministers. Only one other politician is included – the Earl of Shaftesbury – but he might best be thought of, perhaps, as belonging to a cross-century religious group including John Wyclif and John Wesley. Hannah More belongs to that group also: she is one of only five women, two of them Queens.

No three historians would have agreed on the same list. Yet there would be agreement that all the characters included in the volume were in their different ways and wherever they came from – including Normandy as well as Scotland and Wales – 'makers of English history'. The richness of that history and the diversity of strands within it are apparent throughout these pages; and at many points the complex relationships between that history and the history both of Europe and of the world are revealed. Drake sailed round the world. Wesley took the world as his parish. Shakespeare was a poet for all mankind. Elizabeth preserved England against Philip II of Spain, Pitt against Napoleon, Churchill against Hitler. Oliver Cromwell, chosen to lead in England's only revolution, had as fierce a sense of an English mission as any other character portrayed in the volume. Blake, in many ways a revolutionary, sought the building of

Jerusalem in England's 'green and pleasant land'.

In his introductory essay Professor Norman Stone raises interesting questions about the elusive nature of 'Englishness': among the many means by which it may be explored, the approach followed in this volume – that of the portrait painting of individuals is bound to be revealing. The missing element in the approach relates, of course, to those Englishmen who left no names behind them – among them not only unknown soldiers but unknown workers. Most of the people living before the age of Henry VIII fall into that category. Indeed, before that time the idea of an individual portrait was not part of the pattern of perception. The image of a great king was a standard image. The roots of English individualism have been traced back to this period, but it requires intensive critical scrutiny as well as vivid imagination to bring back to life known as well as unknown individuals. The medieval historian, Professor Powicke, described 'the queer sensation', as he read medieval documents, of the entries suddenly coming alive: 'it is rather like the experience of sitting down in one's chair and finding that one has sat on the cat. These are real people, this casual official letter is telling us, something that really happened, it was written on the impulse of a real emotion.'

This is a very English approach to history, and there is that same sense of 'Englishness' in the work of Bede, which is brought out in the first portrait in this volume. As the author says, Bede not only wrote the first history of the English people but invented the concept of English history. The subject of the last portrait in the volume, Winston Churchill, had as vivid a sense of history and of the importance of preserving it, as Bede did in his own age. After having written his epic history of the Second World War, the fortunes of which he helped to turn, Churchill turned back to more general history and chose as the title of the volumes, conceived before that war began, not *A History of England* but *A History of the English Speaking Peoples*. Of Bede he had this to say, that he

was 'the most effective and almost the only audible voice from the British islands in those dim times', but it was on the role of history in the present and in the future that he was most eloquent. His own *History*, he insisted, was 'not intended to stir a new spirit of mastery or create a model which will favour national ambitions at the expense of world peace. It may be indeed that an inner selective power may lead to the continuous broadening of our thought.'

'Broadening of our thought' is one of the main functions of history, travel through time with as many implications as travel through space. People as well as events are put into perspective: comparisons are invited, judgements called for. The 'ordinary people' are missing from these pages, yet they have fashioned the England in which we live today as much as the politicians have done. Only in recent years, years of the tape recorder, has oral history been able to do justice to them.

Given that the main appeal of published biography is that it reveals what happened in the mind or behind the scenes – a second function of history – it is significant that much clearing away of 'mysteries' is achieved in the pages of this volume. It is up-to-date in its scholarship. One of the characters in the volume, Francis Bacon, in his life of Henry VII wrote of the King that 'his manner of showing things by pieces and by dark lights hath so muffled [his life] that it hath left it almost a mystery to this day.' Fortunately Pepys left a great diary – that is the only reason why he is one of the characters in this volume – and Gladstone, who would have been in the volume if he had never written a diary, left behind a remarkable journal which illuminates aspects of his character and career which would otherwise be very dark. The biographer has many materials with which to work: they have been well used in the forty-five essays which follow.

Asa Briggs
Worcester College, Oxford

INTRODUCTION
NORMAN STONE

THE PEOPLE who have made for the greatness of England – some of them celebrated in these pages – form a fascinating collection. But what is even more extraordinary is that they come from such a small island. When you think that seventeenth-century England contained only about five million people – fewer than modern Sweden or Switzerland – the scale of the achievement becomes astonishing. Inside Europe it was paralleled only by the Dutch, and then just for a couple of generations, when they invented everything from commodity futures to the telescope and floriculture.

So, how did this small island manage to achieve such greatness? No one really knows. Here was a small country with small, even tiny institutions. Take the example of Trinity College, Cambridge: although it was the biggest college in the university, it was and is quite a small place by twentieth-century standards, with about a hundred Fellows and maybe a thousand members in all. But it is very highly concentrated, and its achievements raise it to a world-beating level: more Nobel Prizes, for instance, than France. How do you explain something like this? It is of course partly money. The College was well endowed in the sixteenth century, when Henry VIII abolished the monasteries and diverted some of their money to education, and successive College bursars managed the funds extremely well: in the 1930s, for example, it acquired some semi-bankrupt agricultural land that turned out, two decades later, to be Felixstowe Docks, the only dock in the country that can claim to be prosperous. But these resources were still relatively small in comparison with those of

other institutions, and in the great days of Cambridge science people had to operate on a shoestring. In the 1930s, if you had an experiment going at the Cavendish Laboratory, you still had to leave the building at 6 p.m. because they turned the lights out; and if you wanted to check your results in the evening, after the doors had been locked, you had to climb in over railings and virtually break into the building. If, for an experiment, you needed wood that was of higher quality than the standard-issue boxwood that lay around, you had to get authorization from a committee. Yet, in these circumstances, the Cavendish Laboratory produced, between the 1880s and the 1950s, a whole set of scientific discoveries, including nuclear physics and the beginnings of microbiology, which eluded institutions elsewhere that were much richer.

For centuries England's impact on the world, in virtually all respects, was out of all proportion to its size; and in the later nineteenth century, it took over – for a brief period – a quarter of the land-surface of the world. One way of understanding how this small island managed to achieve such greatness can be answered in terms of biography. In this book we have chosen forty-five people who, in their separate ways, had a prominent part in the making of England, or, after the Union with Scotland in 1707, Great Britain. These short biographical essays vary in character, as they come from various authors, and the people whom they discuss – all the way from the Venerable Bede to Virginia Woolf – do not of course have any kind of definable common character. If there is a quality of 'Englishness', it is utterly elusive. Nevertheless, it is there. As George Orwell remarked in his essay, *The Lion and the Unicorn*, it is a composite of various pictures: the old maid biking to Holy Communion through the mist; the judge in his horse-hair wig; the mildness of the climate and the lushness of the countryside; endless, tiresome and not very important inconveniences which keep out the foreigner, such as the absurd distinction between pubs and cafés, the ridiculous licensing laws and the stodgy food that forms the staple of the British masses.

You cannot *define* 'England', but at least you can *describe* it, which is the forte of historians. It is, in the first place, a country with enormous variations. There is a wider range of accents in the British Isles than anywhere else in the world. True, what used to be called 'BBC English', the standard version, has threatened regional accents, but they still exist in extraordinary profusion: in the world at large, 'English' may even disintegrate, as Latin did, into variants that become separate languages (when they showed the Glasgow film, *Gregory's Girl* in New York, it had to be subtitled because no one could otherwise follow the thick Glasgow accents). Even inside the various regions and separate parts of the United Kingdom, there were huge variations of character – North and South Wales, North and South Yorkshire, the west of Scotland and the east coast.

In continental eyes, English (and here I deliberately exclude the Scots, who are much more 'European' than the English) history is something of a miracle. The 'mix' of public and private was achieved nowhere else in Europe. Here was a state that was strong and reasonably centralized; from the days of Henry II onwards, it developed a common system of law based on precedents, whereas in other countries the law was more or less what some petty tyrant said it should be. On the other hand, it was not a tyrannical state, and monarchs failed again and again if they tried to make it so: Charles I was executed in 1649 after a trial that was actually staged under his own authority, as the 'Crown'. There was, virtually as

far back as it is possible to go in English history, a consciousness of local rights and liberties that other countries regarded as inconceivable. Elsewhere, such liberties were often seen as disastrous. In Germany, for instance, local liberties acquired under the Holy Roman Empire were simply turned, through abuse, into a set of local tyrannies, hundreds of them, which no central power could check.

The political theorist Edmund Burke observed this, and held up England as a model of moderation, with its slow development of institutions and healthy disregard for politics: 'We compromise, we reconcile, we balance.' The country was full of compromise institutions. There was a monarchy that operated by common sense, for instance; Victoria and Albert, the subjects of an essay here, were model sovereigns, in the sense that they behaved in an exemplary way, largely keeping their own likes and dislikes out of politics, and fulfilling a representative function with great dignity (though with neither humour nor charm). Elsewhere on the continent, dynasties were disintegrating.

In the same style, there was a state Church that offered the consolations of religion but without the stifling orthodoxy that made Counter-Reformation Catholicism so offensive to the liberal, enquiring mind. The Church of England was also in continental eyes something of a miracle – pre-Counter-Reformation Catholicism, someone has called it. It was possible to believe in a wide variety of doctrines that elsewhere could never be confined to a single Church; there were extraordinarily beautiful buildings and some highly intelligent, well-meaning clergymen (though also a certain number of snobbish buffoons, such as Vice-Chancellor Cory of Cambridge in the 1840s, who opposed the construction of a railway line to Cambridge on the grounds that it would only encourage the lower classes to go joy-riding on Sundays and was thus 'equally displeasing to the Almighty and to the Vice-Chancellor of the University of Cambridge').

The Church of England was 'Protestant' in the sense that it did not obey the Pope and followed non-Catholic practices over Communion, but equally it did not follow the development of the truly Low Church versions of Protestantism, where presbyteries replaced episcopal authority, and where an almost inescapable trend developed towards endless division and sub-division of quarrelling sects: Quakers, 'Wee Frees', Moravian Brothers and so on. The practices of some of these sects were extraordinarily gloomy: on the Island of Lewis in Scotland some chicken-farmers, even ten years ago, and perhaps still, put the roosters in lobster pots on Sundays so that they and the hens would not defile the Sabbath with malpractice.

I do not wish to run down the small-town, small-scale Protestant, or Puritanical, sects. Their influence in many ways was extremely beneficial. In education, for instance, they were for a long time much better than other Churches, as you can still see from the quite disproportionate numbers of Scots, Welsh and English Dissenters who occupied prominent places in England. The Scots, for instance, acquired a near-monopoly of engineering at the time of the great industrial revolution in the eighteenth and nineteenth century; here, Thomas Telford, the greatest engineer of his time, is an exemplar; and so, too, in another way, was Adam Smith, born near Kirkaldy and responsible for much of modern economics. They were not Calvinists in any meaningful sense, but they owed much to the Scottish Church's promotion of education. Where, in other countries, including England, Churches put up fine buildings and laid on hot dinners, the Scottish Church put up a box, all black and white inside and marked 'Church', and another, smaller box, marked 'school', in which the pastor, taking time from his religious functions, taught.

The long Puritanical tradition in England, starting with Wyclif – here commemorated – and including some of the best Englishmen, with Cromwell, Gladstone and Peel (though the last two had Scottish origins, they were soon 'angl-icanized'), produced a long line of energetic, single-minded men who gave life to the otherwise often sleepy southern and Anglican world. In some other countries this kind of Protestantism could be quite destructive. It seldom brought in more than a minority of the population, because most people found the austerity of its ways altogether repellent and unnecessary, and it could all too easily become a sort of colonizers' religion, as was the case in South Africa, Northern Ireland and to some extent even Canada as well as large parts of the United States. In England herself, this kind of Low Church sectarian élitism did not give rise to anything like the same arrogance as it sometimes did elsewhere. It co-existed with the Church of England, often uneasily, and the synthesis of religions, using the better parts of both sides, was something of a wonder to continentals who were used to the triumphalist ways of Catholic Orthodoxy, or the state-reinforcing habits of the Orthodox Church in Tsarist Russia.

The Anglican strand in English public life has received much criticism for blandness, interference in secular matters, and general laziness over things that matter. But the Anglican vision was responsible for an astonishing amount of public charity, which put this country way ahead of its neighbours for several centuries – including even the sixteenth century, when the Elizabethan Poor Law required local landowners to pay for the upkeep of people less fortunate than themselves. One exemplar of this tradition is recorded here, Lord Shaftesbury, who fought to restrain the ills of 'early capitalism', as successful entrepreneurs began to exploit their work-forces.

Here, through forty-five portraits, we have a composite picture of England: her huge variety, and her strange sameness. We have included men and women of all kinds, patriots, warriors, sailors writers and intellectuals of various sorts (my own favourite being the twisted character, Newton, who overcame his troubles to produce works of genius). Which of these is the outstanding English hero or heroine, is for readers to judge.

BEDE

673–735

IF THERE IS any one individual who can truly be described as 'the maker of English history', it is the Venerable Bede. He not only wrote the first history of the English people, he invented the concept of English history. And, what is most remarkable of all, he did so at a time when there was no such place as England and no such state as the kingdom of England.

Bede lived in an age when Roman Britain had long since been overthrown and its place taken by a fluctuating number of small kingdoms. In the west there were the British (Celtic) kingdoms of the native inhabitants, kindoms such as Strathclyde, Rheged, Gwynedd, Dyfed and Dumnonia. In the east there were the Germanic kingdoms established by the new arrivals of the fifth and sixth centuries: Kent, Sussex, Wessex, Essex, East Anglia, Mercia and Northumbria. Each of these kingdoms had its own traditions and its own ruling dynasty. Each king, in a seemingly endless round of slave hunts and cattle rustling expeditions, did his best to prey upon his neighbours. In a world composed of a number of independent and mutally hostile kingdoms how could anyone possibly conceive of writing a history of the English people? It is not as though the inhabitants of the Germanic kingdoms all thought of themselves as 'English' in language and culture. Some of the inhabitants of some of the kingdoms were, it is true,

Angles, and from their name the word 'English' derives. But others were Saxons, some were Jutes and some were probably Frisians or Swedes. Modern historians have grown accustomed to lumping them all together and calling them Anglo-Saxons. But why should anyone at the time have chosen to write, as Bede wrote, as though they were one people? And even if conceived of, how could this vision of history possibly be put into practice? How to tell not half a dozen or more separate stories, but a single, coherent, readable story? Yet Bede achieved the apparently impossible. And if, after this, Angles, Saxons and Jutes increasingly began to think of themselves as one people – the English – then may it not be that this studious monk had a hand not just in the making of English history but also in the making of the English themselves?

What makes Bede's achievement all the more miraculous is that there can have been few men who have seen less of the world in which they lived than he did. Born in 673, he was entrusted by his parents to the monks at Wearmouth when he was just seven years old. By the time he died on Ascension Day (25 May) 735 he had spent fifty-five years in the monastery and had left it only twice, once to visit Lindisfarne, once to visit York. But what did this matter? He had his mind's eye and he had at his elbow the library of late Roman scholar-

Bede, depicted on a twelfth-century copy of his Life of St Cuthbert.

ship collected by his first abbot, Benedict Biscop, on five trips to Italy. And as Bede himself wrote, 'amid the observance of the monastic rule and the daily task of singing in the choir, it has always been my delight to learn, or to teach, or to write.'

This delight in learning, teaching and writing stayed with Bede right to the end of his life. One of his pupils remembered how 'on the Tuesday before Ascension he found it increasingly difficult to breathe. Despite this he continued cheerfully to teach and dictate all day, saying from time to time "Learn quickly. My Lord may call me soon".' On the last two days of his life he worked with an even greater sense of urgency. 'Take your pen,' he said, 'and sharpen it and write quickly.' Only when the last sentence of the last chapter was written did he call upon his Father to take him to the longed-for joys of heaven. This full lifetime spent learning, teaching and writing meant that he became the greatest scholar of his age in Europe. A late ninth-century author, writing in what we now call Switzerland, described Bede as 'a new sun in the West, ordained by God to illuminate the whole globe'.

His knowledge of the world and of its place in space and time was vast and encyclopaedic. He knew, of course, as all informed contemporaries knew, that the world was round 'like a ball used for playing games' and that he lived within the northern temperate zone. But he also had at his fingertips an immense amount of detailed knowledge, whether of the action of the tides in the Solent or the geography of Palestine, or of the theories of chronology and the measurement of time. This knowledge was to give him an extraordinary perspective on the history of his own island and of his own time.

Despite Bede's assiduous researches he found very few sources for the fifth and sixth centuries – no mention of any King Arthur, for example – and as a result we know almost nothing about events in Britain during this period: the 'lost centuries' as they have been aptly named. With the seventh century we are nearer Bede's lifetime and on firmer ground, but even for this period the apparently simple – as we might think – task of putting things in the correct chronological order was to present enormous technical problems and drive Bede to find solutions which we now take for granted. In order to write an accurate comparative history, it is necessary to adopt an era – one important event from which to date all other events. Bede chose the era of the Incarnation, or Christ's birth, and he used it consistently, the first European historian to do so. One near-contemporary, Nennius, used no less than twenty-eight different eras – rather confusing. But having decided on the method it still remained to apply it to the vague traditions and inadequately dated documents from which Bede was to write his history. In each kingdom events were dated by the appropriate regnal year, for example 'in the 7th year of King Osric'. So where did an event in one kingdom stand in relation to events in another? Only by a painstaking series of inquiries and sometimes by brilliant detective work was Bede able to answer this question and then fix that event by giving it a date AD. So successfully did he employ the method that the system of dating BC and AD has remained in use ever since.

It is hard not to succumb to the power of Bede's creative imagination, not to see the seventh century in any other light than that in which he, with great artistry and style, presents it to us in his masterpiece, *Historia ecclesiastica gentis Anglorum* ('Ecclesiastical History of the English People'). It is significant that he called it an 'Ecclesiastical History'. Not that it is solely concerned with churchmen and synods. On the contrary, kings and armies aplenty march across its pages. But his main theme, the connecting thread of his narrative, was a religious one: the growth and expansion of the Christian faith in Britain since Roman times with, at its heart, the conversion of the Germanic newcomers. Different from each other in many ways though the various new arrivals may have been, that which they had in common was, in Bede's eyes, crucial: their paganism. Despite their internal divisions they were being guided towards the one true God in the land

which they had parcelled out among them – like the Israelites in the land of Canaan (and Bede, of course, knew his Old Testament history inside out). This was their shared destiny. In this sense West, East and South Saxons, Kentishmen, East Anglians, Mercians, Northumbrians, all of them were one people, God's chosen people.

Bede's story of God's dealings with his chosen people began at Rome, with Pope Gregory I's decision to send Augustine to Britain. In AD 597 Augustine landed in the territory of Aethelberht, King of Kent. He established an episcopal see at Canterbury and he became, in effect, the King of Kent's bishop. Subsequently, when other kings became Christians, they too wanted – and got – their own bishops. Thus diocesan boundaries followed the frontiers of kingdoms, and episcopal sees were shaped by the ebb and flow of secular politics. But this was not how Gregory had envisaged things. As a Roman he thought in terms of a reconstituted Roman province of Britannia and he gave Augustine authority over all the bishops of Britain. Here lie the origins of the primacy of Canterbury. Not unnaturally the church of Canterbury was to take the rights and responsibilities which Gregory granted it very seriously indeed. By the time Bede was a boy the Bishop of Canterbury was claiming to be 'Archbishop of Britain'. No matter how many different kingdoms there were, for all who accepted the pastoral framework of the Roman Church there was only one flock. But Gregory not only created, at least in theory, a single ecclesiastical organization for Britain, he also gave a name to those pagan peoples whose conversion had lain at the heart of his endeavour. In the slave market at Rome, or so Bede tells us, he saw

King Athelstan (d.939) presenting St Cuthbert with a copy of Bede's works. St Cuthbert was the seventh-century Bishop of Lindisfarne who became one of the most venerated English saints.

some boys from Britain for sale and, on inquiry, found out that they were Angles, members of the *gens Anglorum*. From then on he thought of his mission to Britain as a mission to convert the *gens Anglorum*, the English people.

Bede's 'research assistant' Nothelm (himself a later Archbishop of Canterbury) went through the papal archives at Rome and brought back copies of Gregory's letters. For Bede then, thoroughly immersed as he was in Gregory's theological and pastoral writings, it made sense to write his history in Gregorian terms, transmitted to him via the church of Canterbury: the Ecclesiastical History of the English people. Bede was, it is true, himself an Angle but this view of history was anything but the parochial prejudice of an isolated northerner. From the deceptively narrow confines of his monastic cell Bede was able to set his history within the widest possible Roman and biblical perspective and from this it derives its idealistic power.

During the seventh and eight centuries continental writers always referred to the Germanic inhabitants of Britain as Saxons – as, of course, Celts still do today. But as Bede's reputation and writings spread throughout the Christian world so also did his terminology and interpretation. In Britain the old political divisions remained and Canterbury's claims to an over-arching authority were sometimes disputed. But Bede's history had little to do with the 'real' world of conflicting material and political interests, and its authority remained undisputed. He had sent his book to be read by King Ceolwulf of Northumbria, but it was also read at the courts of Mercia and Wessex. Indeed it was one of the books which King Alfred had translated into English. Thus it became, for all Anglo-Saxons, the accepted view of their past. If, in time, they began to think of themselves not as Northumbrians, Mercians or Saxons but as English, this was due in part to the extraordinary coincidence that the first historian of the English people was also the greatest English historian of all time.

KING ALFRED

849–899

IN JANUARY 878, when the Twelfth Night festivities were scarcely over, a Viking army under Guthrum's leadership launched a surprise attack on King Alfred's palace at Chippenham. The King and his family fled to the Isle of Athelney in Somerset and here, in a desolate fenland countryside, they found a safe refuge. If, as has been plausibly conjectured, Guthrum's sudden swoop at a time when the army of Wessex was disbanded had been intended to capture the King himself, then Alfred was lucky to be alive. In these early centuries there were no ransoms for kings who fell into the hands of their enemies. The Vikings had already killed Kings Aella of Northumbria and Edmund of East Anglia, possibly sacrificed to Odin in the ritual of the blood-eagle, their ribs and lungs ripped out to mark their corpses with the shape of the spread-eagle. Up to a point then, Guthrum's strike had failed. Nonetheless, Alfred's precipitate flight could well have confirmed contemporary pessimists in their conviction that the outlook was a gloomy one.

Ever since the reign of Beorhtric of Wessex (786–802), Anglo-Saxon kings had had to take account of the Vikings, although for the first two-thirds of the ninth century these sea-borne raiders had been no more than an occasional nuisance. The age-old rivalries between the four major Anglo-Saxon kingdoms, Northum-

bria, Mercia, East Anglia and Wessex, were of much greater moment. But all this changed in 865, when Alfred was sixteen years old, with the arrival of the Danish 'Great Army' led by Halfdan and Ivar the Boneless. By 869 the once great kingdoms of Northumbria and East Anglia were no more. Then, reinforced by the arrival of another large force in 871 (the year in which Alfred came to the throne), the Danes proceeded to conquer and occupy most of Mercia (874–7). It was at this point, with only Wessex still surviving, that Guthrum launched his surprise attack.

In the words of the Anglo-Saxon Chronicle's entry for 878, 'the enemy occupied the land of the West Saxons and settled there, and drove a great part of the people across the sea and conquered most of the others; and the people submitted to them, except King Alfred. He journeyed in difficulties through the woods and fen-fastnesses with a small force.' It conjures up a vivid picture of an heroic king standing alone in his resistance to the invader and it is, of course, this picture of the King at Athelney which has entered legend. Here it was that he burned the cakes; here that he saw a vision of St Cuthbert or St Neot (or both) prophesying victory when all seemed lost; and from here that, disguised as a minstrel, he went into the enemy camp to discover their plans. A few months later he won a decisive battle at

Edington and forced the defeated Guthrum to accept baptism. Slowly Alfred himself went over to the offensive. In 886 he captured London (formerly a Mercian town) and was then recognized as ruler of the Mercians who lived west of a line (Watling Street) between London and Chester. Alfred's heirs, Edward, Athelstan and Edgar, building on his foundations, conquered and annexed the midlands and the north. By the end of the Golden Century of Wessex's history (878–978) the kingdom of England had taken shape.

Thus 878 is the Dunkirk at the beginning of English history; a glorious national victory snatched from the jaws of shattering national defeat, and King Alfred, at bay in Athelney, stands as the founding father of the English nation. From that day on Alfred was revered as a model king, each generation re-shaping the

Detail from a twelfth-century copy of Alfred's treaty with Guthrum in 886, with a miniature showing Alfred.

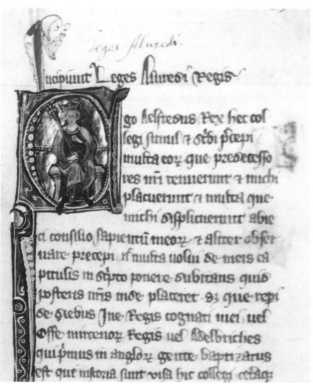

image to conform to its own expectations. In the early fourteenth century Andrew Horn described an Alfred who summoned Parliament every two years, took the advice of his lords and hanged many judges – a good king indeed! For the Victorians he was the founder of the Royal Navy and the initiator of a nationwide programme of Christian education for the youth of England. In one Alfredian anniversary after another – in 1849 his birth, in 1871 his accession, in 1878 Athelney and Edington, in 1899 his death – the Victorians celebrated a thousand years of English nationhood. No wonder that Victoria decided that in the mausoleum at Frogmore she and Albert should be immortalized in the guise of an Anglo-Saxon king and queen.

That the later legends are largely fiction no one doubts. The real problem comes with the supposedly factual account that is the basis of it all, the Anglo-Saxon Chronicle. Just how reliable is it? In 878, for example, did all the people of Wessex except for Alfred and his small force really submit to the Danes? Clearly not, since the Chronicle itself goes on to say that another Danish army was defeated in Devon – and not by Alfred's small force but by local levies. Moreover the victory at Edington was won with the aid of levies from Wiltshire and Hampshire as well as Somerset. In other words the Chronicle exaggerated the extent to which Wessex fell under Danish domination in 878 and did so in a manner designed to emphasize the significance of Alfred's stand. This is indeed characteristic of the Anglo-Saxon Chronicle. Time and again it presents a version of events which suited the King. There can be little doubt that it is a work of propaganda conceived and executed at Alfred's court. It was then copied out and circulated to various centres of learning throughout the kingdom. It was intended to cultivate the image of a great king who upheld the traditions of his ancestors. A similar concern can be detected in the biography of Alfred written by his Welsh friend and adviser, Bishop Asser. As propaganda these works were supremely successful. The image they projected has remained to this day the conventional picture of Alfred – the only king in English history to be called 'the Great'. But if we think of him as Alfred the Great it is largely because he tells us that that is what he was.

Yet to say this is not to debunk Alfred, nor to belittle his achievement. Propaganda can be recognized for what it is on those occasions when it distorts the truth. Nonetheless, we should remember that the more closely it resembles the truth the more likely it is to be effective. It is possible that by 878 the Danish assault was running out of steam as more and more Viking warriors settled down in the conquered territories to become yeomen farmers or country gentlemen. Guthrum's midwinter attack may have been a gambler's throw, a last desperate attempt to conquer Wessex before his army finally dissolved. But 878 did not mean the end of the struggle. A crisis had been surmounted but there was still much fighting to be done. Even those years free of war were filled with the bustle of preparation for war: towns planned and fortified, ships designed and built, the militia reorganized. Thanks to these measures, when another large Viking army landed in Kent in 892, Alfred was able to contain it. If his defence measures worked it was largely because men were persuaded that it was worth their while to carry out his instructions. And how were they persuaded if not by Alfred's intelligent use of

A contemporary scene showing a king and his court, from a tenth-century document, the Junius manuscript, illustrating the Book of Genesis.

the media of the day? If Alfred was going to extend his authority beyond the traditional borders of Wessex, then he had to persuade people, above all Mercians, that they had reason to prefer his rule to rule by fellow Mercians or, indeed, to rule by Danes. So he tried to present himself as the head of a wider community and he exploited Bede's Gregorian terminology, the language of Englishness, speaking not of Mercian or Saxon but of 'English' and of 'the land of the English folk'. As much as any twentieth-century political leader Alfred was aware of the need to influence public opinion, of the value of propaganda. This was certainly not an insight unique to Alfred. Like all early medieval kings in a largely illiterate society, he and his ancestors found plenty of song-writers to sing their praises. What was special about Alfred was not his use of propaganda but the fact that he chose to set some of his propaganda in a medium which turned out to have a relatively high survival rate: written English prose.

Here we touch upon another aspect of Alfred's many-sided genius. When he was about forty years old he made himself learn to read Latin and then set about implementing a remarkable plan which can best be described in his own words:

> I remembered how it was here before everything was ransacked and burned. The churches were full of treasures and books, but few men could understand what was in those books because they were not in their own language. I remembered too how the Greeks had translated the Old Testament out of the Hebrew into Greek; then the Romans had translated it into Latin. Therefore it seemed right to me that we should turn some books – those from which we can gain most – into English. So, busy though I was with the manifold cares of the kingdom, I began to translate the *Cura Pastoralis* [a manual of instruction for churchmen written by Pope Gregory I]. And I shall send a copy of my work to each diocese in England.

He found the time, indeed, to translate three more books and encourage the translation of others. Just how extraordinary an achievement this was we can estimate if we remember that he is the only king in more than 300 years of English history, including the whole of the ninth, tenth, and eleventh centuries, who is known to have been able to read and write, and the only English king before Henry VIII who wrote books. Like Charlemagne, Alfred had a programme of education based on a circle of intellectuals under his patronage. He insisted that his own youngest child, and the boy's companions, should be brought up in the scholarly atmosphere of a bookish court. To what extent this educational programme caught on it is impossible to know – though Asser gives an engaging picture of judges groaning but nonetheless 'in an amazing way applying themselves to learning how to read'. (At least it was better than being hanged.) What is beyond doubt, however, is that the King's own writings helped to lay the foundations of English prose.

Asser also tells us something of the King's inner life. He presents him as an intensely religious man who had gone through a troubled adolescence, tormented to the point of illness by sexual desires which he was afraid to indulge lest he should thereby incur God's displeasure. His marriage feast was spoiled when 'he was struck without warning in the presence of the entire gathering by a sudden severe pain that was quite unknown to all physicians. And worst of all, alas, it plagued him remorselessly from his twentieth year to his forty-fifth. If at any time by God's mercy that illness abated for a day or even an hour, his fear and horror of that accursed pain would never desert him, but rendered him virtually useless – as it seemed to him – for religious and secular duties.' To have ensured the political and military survival of Wessex while other kingdoms tumbled; to have extended West Saxon power northwards and so prepared the ground for the 'unification of England' carried through by his descendants in the next century; to have sponsored a revival of learning and laid the foundations of English prose: not a bad achievement for a man who was virtually useless.

WILLIAM I

1028–1087

WILLIAM THE CONQUEROR, or the Bastard as he was known to contemporaries, was Duke Robert of Normandy's only son (born probably in 1028) and so, despite his illegitimacy, he succeeded to the Duchy when his father died. But at this date (1035) William was just a boy. He was lucky to survive the perils of his minority. A boyhood spent among scenes of violence and intrigue left its mark. He learned that few men could be trusted and those few in whom he did place his trust were mostly the friends he made in childhood. In the mid-1040s William began to govern for himself. He was almost continuously at war, either against neighbouring princes or Norman rebels, or both. He became a hard and ruthless campaigner – though flatterers said he was the best knight in the world. In 1060 his two main enemies, King Henry I of France and Count Geoffrey of Anjou, both died, thus opening the way for William to embark on a career of conquest. In 1063 he conquered Maine. Then he turned his eyes upon England.

By 1066 the Kingdom of England had been in existence for a century or so. Hammered together by Alfred's descendants, the warrior kings of Wessex – Edward the Elder, Athelstan, Edmund and Eadred – it had been moulded into the most sophisticated political structure in Western Christendom. It was in the tenth century that the English system of

shires was stabilized in the shape which was to last a thousand years, until the boundary changes of 1974. Further administrative subdivisions – hundreds, wapentakes and tithings – ensured that at times every locality felt the weight of national government, above all its capacity to collect rents and taxes. Economic expansion meant that crown revenues increased and led to the establishment of a permanent royal treasury at Winchester. A highly organized system of mints put millions of silver pennies into circulation. The sensational work of English silver- and goldsmiths only served to heighten the impression of a fabulously wealthy land: the eldorado of northern Europe.

Although William was only a distant cousin of Edward the Confessor, in 1051 Edward had dangled before William the prospect of succeeding to the English throne, perhaps to win Norman support in a quarrel with his powerful father-in-law, Earl Godwin. Edward himself was childless and since kings were not yet chosen according to a strict order of heredity, there were several candidates for the succession. Among them was Harold, son of Earl Godwin and brother of Edward's wife Edith. By 1066 Edward was reconciled with the Godwin family, and on his deathbed he nominated Harold, the most powerful magnate in the kingdom, as his heir.

William felt cheated of his prize and prepared at once for an invasion of England. He claimed that on a visit to Normandy in 1064, Harold had recognized William as Edward's heir; on this basis he won papal approval for an expedition against a usurper and perjurer. In his careful preparation for invasion William showed himself at his formidable best. It was an enterprise far beyond the resources of his Duchy and so he recruited soldiers from all over northern France and Flanders. The prospect of laying hands on the wealth of England, its land and its silver, attracted thousands to his banner. Throughout the spring and summer of 1066 ships were built and military supplies assembled. But however meticulous his preparations, William cannot have expected the rapid and overwhelming success he in fact achieved – success which, as his contemporary biographer pointed out, far outstripped anything Julius Caesar was able to achieve in Britain. It must have seemed likely that he was facing many years of hard campaigning against an enemy whose wealth and military resources were greater than his own. But an extraordinary series of lucky chances brought things to a swift and dramatic conclusion.

By August 1066 William's expeditionary force was ready. The longer he postponed embarkation the more likely it was that his soldiers would have to face the grim prospect of a winter campaign. Yet if he had sailed in August he would have found Harold and an English fleet waiting to receive him. If he had managed to defeat the English he would then have had to face another contender for the throne, that great Viking warrior, Harold

William, with Bishop Odo of Bayeux, gives orders for the building of an invasion fleet (Bayeux tapestry).

Hardrada, King of Norway. As it happened, for long periods the wind was against William. Whether he wanted to wait or not, merely to hold his impatient army together was a considerable achievement. Meanwhile, however, some of William's greatest problems were being solved for him. In September Harold Hardrada, accompanied by one of his wives and several of his children, reached the Tyne and then defeated the northen levies in a pitched battle near York. As soon as he heard of the Viking landing, Harold Godwinsson marched north and routed the Norwegians and their allies at Stamford Bridge on 25 September. Two days later the wind in the Channel changed direction. William set sail and was able

to make an unopposed landing at Pevensey. During the next two weeks his soldiers fortified their beachhead and pillaged the area. But what then? Would William dare march inland, losing contact with his fleet and the line of communication with Normandy? Fortunately the problem was solved by Harold who came rushing back from the north and allowed William to bring him to battle. On 14 October 1066 the two armies met in the most famous confrontation in English history. After a long struggle William's skilful handling of a combined force of infantry and cavalry enabled him to break down the English shield wall. The fact that Harold and his brothers died fighting meant that after Hastings there was no leader capable of organizing further resistance. The

English earls and bishops hesitated, took a few indecisive steps and then decided to submit.

On Christmas Day 1066 William was acclaimed King in Westminster Abbey. The shouts of acclamation – in English as well as in French – alarmed the Norman soldiers nervously standing guard outside the abbey. Afraid that inside the church something had gone horribly wrong, they set fire to the surrounding houses. A Norman monk recalled the chaos of that day. 'As the fire spread rapidly, the people inside the church were thrown into utter confusion. Some rushed out to fight the flames; others to join in the looting. Soon only the King, who was trembling violently', – had God deserted him in his hour of triumph? – 'the monks, the bishops and a

few clergy remained. Though they were all terrified, they managed to carry on and complete the consecration of the King.'

William had good reason to tremble. It was to take another five years before he could feel fairly confident that the conquest had been completed. There were risings against Norman rule in every year from 1067 to 1070: in Kent, in the south-west, in the Welsh marches, in the Fenland and in the north. There may well have been no more than 10,000 Normans living in the midst of a hostile population of one or two million. They had to live like the army of occupation they were, living, eating and sleeping together in operational units. They had to build castles – strongpoints from which a few armed men could dominate an oppressed majority. At first many Englishmen had been able to retain their lands. But revolts were punished by devastation – above all the atrocious harrying of the north during the winter of 1069–70 – and by confiscations on a massive scale. By 1086 there were only two surviving English lords of any account. More than 4000 thegns had either lost their lands altogether or now held them only as tenants of a group of less than 200 French barons, most of them Normans. The English church suffered the same fate as the English nobility. By 1096 there was not a single bishopric or important abbey in English hands and the new prelates treated the traditional learning and liturgy of the English church with contempt. As a result of the years of insecurity after 1066, England received not just a new royal family but also a new ruling class, a new culture and a new language. Probably no other conquest in European history has had such disastrous consequences for the defeated.

The new Norman élite naturally retained its old lands on the continent. Thus Normandy and England, once two separate states, now became a single cross-Channel political community, sharing a single Anglo-Norman aristocracy as well as ruling dynasty. The survival of this Anglo-Norman (and later Angevin) realm depended upon a system of cross-Channel ferries, with horses being transported as readily as cars today, but, given the economic ad-

BELOW *Norman soldiers on board a ship, from a contemporary manuscript.*

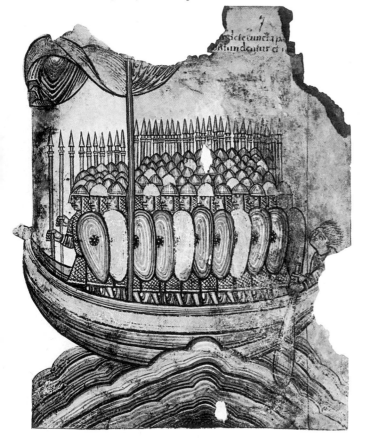

RIGHT *A fourteenth-century representation of the Battle of Hastings, suggesting William killed Harold.*

Apres seynt Edward rey
na Harald le fiz Gode
wyn. eount de kent. a forz
ea tort. ix. moys. Dunke ve
entre will bastard. e ly tol
yst la vye e le regne e qquist
la tere. harald gist a walthm.

Pur regna will vai
ned xxi. an. puis mo
rust. e gist a kame en
Smundye.

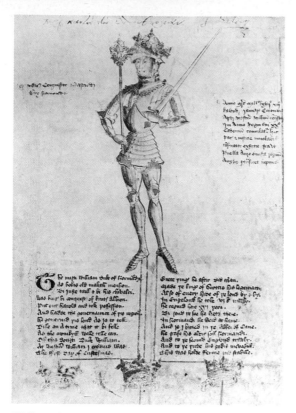

William the Conqueror, as portrayed in a fourteenth-century manuscript.

vantages of water transport, this was no great problem. While they were under a single ruler the Channel no more divided England from Normandy than the Thames divided Middlesex from Surrey. From now on the French connection, reinforced in 1154 by the accession of Henry of Anjou and Eleanor of Aquitaine, was to be of paramount importance. In the twelfth, thirteenth and fourteenth centuries anyone who was ambitious or wished to be thought civilized would have to speak French. It was the language of the law and estate management as well as the language of chanson and romance. Inevitably this had a tremendous impact upon the development of the native language. For centuries now we have been speaking 'Frenglish'. From 1066 until the fifteenth century the King of England was also a French prince; indeed, from 1340 the Kings of England claimed to be Kings of France, a title that was not relinquished until the seventeenth century.

But not everything changed as a result of the Norman Conquest. When they were in England, William and his royal successors continued to rule in the West Saxon manner. Like their predecessors they stayed mostly in the palaces and hunting lodges of the Thames Valley and central Wessex. They retained English institutions. They expected their Norman baronage to perform exactly the same functions as the old Anglo-Saxon nobility: to give them aid and counsel both in peace and war in return for the estates which they held from them. After all, if William wanted to exploit the wealth of England, it was not in his interest to tamper with a judicial and governmental system more advanced than anything in Normandy. Domesday Book still stands as a monument to the comprehensive efficiency of which this ancient system was capable.

After 1071 William's hold on England was fairly secure. Scandinavian rulers continued to look upon England with acquisitive eyes but the ever-present threat of another Viking invasion never quite materialized. From 1071 to the end of his reign most of William's attention was taken up by war and diplomacy on the continent. In July 1087 he was injured while campaigning against the King of France and on 9 September he died. His body was carried to his great church of St Stephen at Caen. Towards the end of his life he had grown very fat and when the attendants tried to force the body into the stone sarcophagus, it burst, filling the church with a foul smell. It was an unfortunate ending to the career of an unusually fortunate and competent king.

GEOFFREY OF MONMOUTH

d. 1154

STRICTLY SPEAKING, Geoffrey was not a maker of English history. But, ever since the fifth and sixth centuries when the Anglo-Saxons drove the Britons into Wales, and some of them across the Channel to Armorica (giving it a new name, Brittany), the relationship between English and British history has been a close, if often uneasy one and there is certainly no one who did more to create British history than Geoffrey. He can, indeed, be said to have invented it. In his *Historia Regum Britanniae* ('History of the Kings of Britain') he records the reigns of no fewer than ninety-nine kings from Brutus, the great-grandson of the Trojan Aeneas, down to Cadwallader, who died in 689 AD. To present almost 2,000 years of British history in one majestic sweep was a stunning achievement. It certainly stunned its earliest known reader, Henry of Huntingdon, who records his astonishment at coming across Geoffrey's work in 1139. Henry went on to summarize its contents and to incorporate some of them in a revision of his own *Historia Anglorum* ('History of the English'). Other readers were equally impressed and the work rapidly became a medieval best-seller. Not only does it survive in more manuscripts than Bede's History, but, thanks to its central creation – the figure of King Arthur – it had an immediate and immense impact on literature and art. What makes Geoffrey's achievement all the more remarkable is the fact that he had no predecessors. Until he set to work in the 1130s a British history did not exist. There was an account of fifth-century Britain written by Gildas in the mid-sixth; there was also an early ninth-century compilation known as the *Historia Brittonum*, but the author of this had only the most fragmentary source materials at his disposal and his compilation is, in consequence, itself fragmentary and disjointed. Geoffrey of Monmouth faced precisely the same problem as this anonymous ninth-century compiler (usually known as Nennius), but he solved it in an entirely different manner, creating a coherent and forceful artistic whole. Unquestionably Geoffrey's History is one of the supreme achievements of the historical imagination.

It is also, of course, almost entirely a work of fiction – the most influential historical novel of all time. Many people in the twelfth century had reservations about some of it, and some simply dismissed it as a tissue of lies. Writing in the 1190s, for example, Gerald of Wales remembers a man who saw demons dancing on a liar's tongue every time he told a lie; if Geoffrey's History was placed on his lap, the demons would rampage all over him. There were always sceptics, men like those who, as Caxton reported, 'hold opinion that there was no such Arthur'. But the sceptics were generally outnumbered by the believers, and even severe critics, like Polydore Vergil in the early sixteenth century, were prepared to accept some of Geoffrey's inventions. And as late as 1833 the Society for the Diffusion of Useful Knowledge, in a work confidently entitled *A Million of Facts*, was prepared to include much of Geoffrey's History in that million. Even today there are still people who cannot bring themselves to renounce their belief in the towering figure of Arthur, and so they write books with titles like *Arthur's Britain* or *The Age of Arthur*.

Who was Geoffrey and what moved him to write his stupendous masterpiece? Since he called himself Geoffrey of Monmouth it is probable that he came from Monmouth. Moreover he shows a remarkable interest in the nearby Caerleon-on-Usk, making it into the seat both of Arthur's court and of the equally fictitious primate of Britain. The lord of Monmouth was a Breton and since Geoffrey himself evinces a special sympathy for Bretons it may be that he was the son of one of the many Bretons who came over after 1066. Since he was known by the name Geoffrey Arthur even before he published his History it is possible that his father's name was Arthur. In the 1130s and 1140s he was a canon of the church of St George at Oxford. He wrote his History in the 1130s, completing it about 1136–8. In the late 1140s he published *Vita Merlini* ('Life of Merlin'). He became Bishop of St Asaph in 1152 and died soon after, probably in 1154.

In the preface to his History he explains that he had been 'unable to discover anything at all on the kings who lived here before the Incarnation, or indeed about Arthur and all subsequent British kings'. But then a fellow-canon of St George's gave him 'a certain very ancient

Geoffrey created the legendary figure of King Arthur, here shown in a fourteenth-century manuscript at a tournament with Sir Lancelot and Queen Guinevere.

book written in the British language' and all he had to do was translate it into Latin. It is never easy to prove beyond doubt that something did not exist. A war-leader called Arthur may, for example, have existed – since there must have been many British war-leaders in the fifth, sixth, seventh and eighth centuries, there would be nothing remarkable about that – but to believe that the legends of Arthur can throw any light on the history of this hypothetical figure is like believing that the stories about Santa Claus can tell us something about a historical St Nicholas. Similarly, despite frantic searches, no one has ever found evidence to confirm the existence of some such 'ancient book'. On the other hand it was common practice for authors wishing to lend a spurious air of authority to their own work, to claim that they were merely following an ancient text. Moreover the whole structure of the History is well calculated to give an appearance of authority. It is only in the second half of the book that the figures of Merlin and Arthur appear and, with them, that combination of magic and romance which gave the History so wide an appeal. In the first half the reader is offered a chronicle of events, some of them, like the British campaigns of Caesar and Claudius familiar to him, others, like the capture of Rome by the British king Belinus – who gave his name to Billingsgate – doubtlessly unfamiliar, but all narrated in a lucid and comparatively sober style. Geoffrey, in other words, has delayed Merlin's entry until the reader is predisposed to believe what he says.

Geoffrey's epilogue is more revealing than his preface. In it he addresses William of Malmesbury and Henry of Huntingdon, the two scholars who, in recently published works, had made a greater contribution to the understanding of Anglo-Saxon history than anyone after Bede and before the nineteenth century. It was natural that someone should want to do for the Welsh what they had done for the English. William indeed had suggested that it was high time Arthur was rescued from the mendacious hands of the story-tellers and made the subject of a proper history. This, of course, is what Geoffrey claims to have done, and he advises the English historians to stick to English history. Since they don't have access to the essential sources they should steer clear of the kings of the Britons. Similarly, it is hard not to see Geoffrey's story of how Merlin built Stonehenge as anything other than a response to Henry of Huntingdon's observation that Stonehenge was one of the wonders of England, but that no one had ever been able to discover how it was built or for what purpose. Indeed, throughout his work Geoffrey seems to be telling people what they wanted to know. Who built the roads? Why was there a dragon standard deposited at Winchester? Above all,

why do the rivers and places bear the names they do? To all of these questions and many others, Geoffrey's History offered satisfying explanations and this doubtless is one reason why so many people wanted to believe him.

But having taken the work of William and Henry as a challenge, why did Geoffrey choose to respond in this inventive fashion? In part, just for fun. He wanted to tease two such distinguished and serious-minded historians. William, for example, had attributed the building of the baths at Bath to Julius Caesar. Geoffrey, having his 'ancient book', is able to correct this. Actually they were built by King Lear's father, Bladud, an intriguing character who was an early aviation pioneer. (Significantly, William of Malmesbury had credited similar experiments to a monk of Malmesbury.)

But underlying the jokes and tongue-in-

Page from Geoffrey's History of the Kings of Britain.

cheek approach there may also have been a more serious intent. That Geoffrey was glorifying the British past is obvious. His method was to show how in every sphere of life, law-giving, road-building, warfare, empire-building, the achievement of the British was at least as great as that of the acknowledged masters in these fields, the Romans. (Thus his account of Bath is characteristic.) The effect of this was to give modern Britons, the Welsh and Bretons, a Golden Age to which they could look back with pride and which they could hope to re-create. By the early twelfth century the Welsh need for some such vision was greater than ever. No previous English king had ever achieved anything remotely approaching Henry I's domination over the Welsh. To an English author it seemed as though he had turned Wales into a 'second England'. To the Welsh, however, it seemed as though he was determined 'to exterminate all the Britons' and one response was to dream of 'restoring the kingdom of the Britons'. This is the context in which Arthur, already a legendary figure in the ninth century – if not an altogether admirable one – came to be seen as the warrior who had never really died and who, one day, would return to save his people.

But Geoffrey went much further than this. He turned Arthur into the great ruler who restored peace and civilization at home, then conquered Gaul and even defeated the combined forces of the Roman Empire. By portraying his hero not primarily as the hammer of the English, but as a civilized and chivalrous king, Geoffrey demonstrated that the British, and by implication the Welsh and Bretons, were far removed from being a necessarily primitive people. The precise form of words chosen by Geoffrey's fiercest twelfth-century critic, the

English historian William of Newburgh, is worth noting. He says that when Geoffrey used British legends to concoct the most ridiculous lies, he did so 'in order to atone for the sins of the British'. The trouble was that in the twelfth century closer acquaintance with Welsh society – the result of Henry I's expansionist policy – was beginning to give a much sharper, contemporary edge to the belief (for which they could find support in Gildas and Bede) that the Britons were a vicious and barbarous people. Above all, it seemed to enthusiastic churchmen – and in Henry I's reign the newcomers founded no fewer than eighteen monasteries and priories in South Wales – that Welsh society was different from, and significantly worse than, their own, less moral and less cultivated. By the mid-twelfth century, references to the 'bestial' life-style of the Welsh were a commonplace. This attitude, an assumption of English moral and cultural superiority, was to remain a characteristic feature of the relationship between the English and Celtic peoples for many centuries to come. Geoffrey composed his History, in other words, at a crucial moment in the history of English expansion within the British isles. Fiction it may be, but against a rising tide of contempt for Welsh law and custom, it asserts that there will come a day – the day which, in Geoffrey's words, 'Merlin prophesied to Arthur' – when the British will recover not only their political independence but also their ancient civilization. A forlorn hope. By incorporating Arthur into their own culture as a kind of honorary Englishman, a process which, ironically, was inspired by Geoffrey's masterpiece, the English effectively emasculated him. And in the 1180s they found his grave at Glastonbury, thus proving that he was well and truly dead.

WILLIAM DE LA POLE

d. 1366

THE WEALTH of medieval England was its land. Over 90 per cent of the people lived in the country and earned their daily bread and ale from the resources of the land – arable, pasture, woodland and fen. Most men were farmers and fishers. Society was dominated by landowners – lords and gentry – who lived in style on the revenues generated from their landed estates. At the apex of society was the king, the richest landowner of them all. Yet while in the broadest economic terms this always remained true, it would be a mistake to conclude that we are dealing with a static 'feudal' society in which nothing changed. Commerce came to play an increasingly large part in the economic and political life of the nation. By the fourteenth century there were far more opportunities for the enterprising businessman than ever before. And among the new class of English entrepreneurs none grasped his opportunities more dramatically than William de la Pole. Beginning life as the son of a Hull merchant, he became a financier, which took him, in 1339, into the ranks of the aristocracy. His son, Michael de la Pole, became Earl of Suffolk. In the next century the de la Poles became dukes and one of them was recognized as heir to Richard III's throne. Had the outcome of the battles of Bosworth or Stoke been different there might have been a Pole king of England.

The critical development which made poss-ible the career of William de la Pole was the rise of the market economy in the twelfth and thirteenth centuries. Between the time of Domesday Book (1086) and the Black Death (1347–8) the population of England trebled in size, very roughly from 2 to 6 million. In this same period the crown made nearly 2,000 grants of the right to hold a market. Since the main economic function of towns was to act as local markets, the increasing density of rural population naturally meant that towns in-creased both in size and number. Between 1100 and 1300 no less than 140 new towns were founded, among them Leeds, Portsmouth and Salisbury. Mostly they were founded by local lords who expected to make a profit out of the money rents and tolls they planned to collect. By the end of the thirteenth century there were over 200 million coins in circulation compared with under 10 million in 1086. An expanding internal market went hand in hand with a growth in foreign trade, notably the import of wine from Bordeaux and the export of wool to supply the cloth manufacturing towns of Flan-ders and Northern Italy. The finest wool in Europe came from the backs of England's 15–18 million sheep, and by the early four-teenth century some 40,000 sacks (each sack containing at least 250 fleeces) were exported each year. To cope with the expanding volume of trade a new type of ship had been designed –

the tubby bulk-carrier known as the cog – and new coastal ports like Hull, Liverpool, Boston and King's Lynn were founded in order to accommodate it. The sea route between the Mediterranean and northern waters was opened up; in the 1270s and 1280s Italian galleys began to come to Sandwich and London.

The arrival of the Italians was to be crucial. The big banking and international finance houses, firms like the Ricciardi of Lucca and the Frescobaldi of Florence, possessed the reserves of liquid capital which enabled them to outbid all other competitors. By 1300 two-thirds of England's wool export trade was in the hands of foreigners, especially Italians. They were unpopular but by lending large sums to the King they could obtain royal patronage and protection. The question was, how were their loans to be secured? In 1275 on the advice of the Ricciardi, Edward imposed an export duty on wool, thus enabling him to repay them out of the proceeds of the duty, initially at the rate of 6s 8d a sack. The wool custom of 1275 marked the beginning of the first permanent national customs system in English history, and in consequence the beginning of a radical transformation of government finance. Whereas in the mid-thirteenth century taxation of foreign trade contributed almost nothing to the regular revenues of the crown, by the mid-fourteenth century the export duty on wool had come to provide no less than two-thirds of the King's normal annual income. From now on the Crown's cash flow problems were eased by the ready availability of massive loans. In the years 1272 to 1294, with an average annual income of £40,000, Edward I's debt to the Ricciardi totalled £400,000, almost half of which was repaid out of customs revenue. This was the Golden Fleece of the English crown. No wonder that huge fortunes were made by financiers, like William de la Pole, who advised the king how his subjects' sheep could most profitably be shorn.

William de la Pole, like his father and elder brother, belonged to that group of northern businessmen who took full advantage of the English attempt to conquer Scotland in the late thirteenth and early fourteenth centuries. For several years the royal administration was based at York and this meant profitable government contracts. In 1328 William and his brother Richard were granted assignments on the customs of Hull and elsewhere in return for meeting the expenses of the royal household at the rate of £20 a day (£7,300 a year). In 1329 William exported no less than 2,377 sacks of wool, mostly from Hull. Ports like Hull became important army supply points. In 1335 William was paid over £6,000 for the purchase of provisions. In 1332 he became Hull's first mayor, an office he held for four years.

But the entrepreneurial opportunities provided by the Scottish war were dwarfed by the prospects which opened up when Edward III declared war on France in 1337, the start of the Hundred Years War. By the end of 1340 Edward had borrowed and spent about £400,000 and government expenditure was running at about 30 per cent of total money supply in England. In order to meet his debts Edward came up with an unprecedented array of taxes and financial schemes. He made wool export a royal monopoly and required groups of financiers, Italian and English, to handle the trade on his behalf. William de la Pole took a prominent role in organizing the English Wool Company which sent 10,000 sacks (supplied by 300 merchants) to the Netherlands in November 1337. But a sudden excess of supply over demand contributed to the collapse of the scheme. Edward issued the merchants with bonds for the repayment of the assessed value of their wool but as his debts mounted he persistently refused to honour the bonds, forcing many of the poorer merchants to sell them at a discount to the wealthier members of the Company, the English merchant capitalists who were now beginning to follow where the Italians had led. In 1338–9 Edward borrowed £125,000 from the big two Florentine banks, the Bardi and the Peruzzi, but in the same period an English consortium headed by Pole lent at least £111,000.

Unfortunately all that was happening in the short run was that Edward III was plunging ever deeper into debt. Late in 1340, when his affairs were at their lowest ebb, he suddenly turned against his ministers and most prominent advisers. William de la Pole, like many others, suffered arrest and imprisonment. He was found guilty of smuggling, though his real offence was probably that he was no longer willing or able to lend any more money. But in the crisis of 1340–41, by far the biggest losers were the two greatest banking houses of the entire Middle Ages – bigger than the more famous Medici bank – the Bardi and Peruzzi.

Two contemporary illustrations of aspects of the wool trade, the major source of William's wealth.

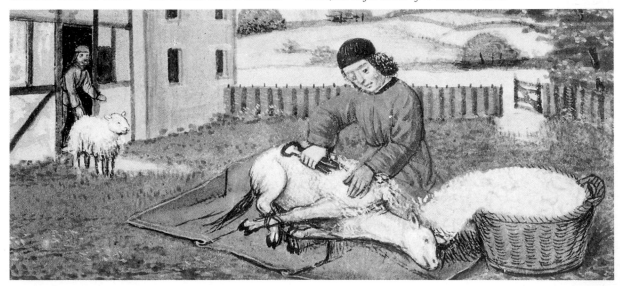

Edward's repudiation of his debts led directly to their collapse. After this the Italian banks were naturally reluctant to lend him any more money and he had to rely on the domestic money market. This meant that William de la Pole's financial expertise was once again indispensable. He was formally rehabilitated in the Parliament of 1344. In fact behind the scenes William had already organized a new English company, the Company of the Staple. The King granted them a monopoly of wool export in return for a high customs duty – at 40s a sack, no less than six times the old rate. Collection of these customs duties was put in the hands of the richest men in the Company, the merchant capitalists who could afford to lend money to the crown, among them William de la Pole. Between 1337 and 1343 Edward had first of all taken over the wool trade and then decided to 'privatise' what had looked like becoming a state monopoly. After the excitements and doubtless the sleepless nights of the speculative years in the late 1330s and early 1340s it is hardly surprising that William withdrew somewhat from the limelight. But he continued to enjoy the King's favour and another twenty years of prosperity. He died in 1366 and was buried in Hull.

Such tremendous changes affecting landowners (as sheep farmers) as well as merchants were inevitably immensely controversial. Not surprisingly Parliament, representing landowners who believed that a high duty tended to force down the price which merchants paid for their wool, resented this cosy arrangement between government and city financiers. Eventually Edward conceded the principle of parliamentary control of the wool custom, but military success in France and good political management at home ensured that a mollified Parliament now gave him what he wanted. With the wool custom firmly established as the backbone of the parliamentary tax system, it is no surprise to find the Lord Chancellor sitting on a woolsack.

Doubtless these fundamental developments in the English political and financial system were of no concern to Pole. Presumably he was a businessman seeking his profit wherever he could find it, as shipowner, property speculator, money lender, commodity dealer – trading in salt, wine, corn, and metals as well as wool. Some of his accounts survive and from them it is possible to see something, not of the man's personality, which largely escapes us, but of his quality as a businessman. He was significantly more systematic than his fellow merchants in his method of costing. He paid his agents more than they did and yet he frequently made higher profits. This suggests that he chose his agents well and they repaid him by giving him a better service than his rivals were able to obtain. The efficiency and intelligence revealed by these accounts help to explain why Pole's services to the crown were so richly rewarded. He was granted possession of the Lordship of Holderness, twelve royal manors in Nottinghamshire and Yorkshire and the houses in Lombard Street which had once belonged to the Bardi; he was appointed a baron of the exchequer; and in 1339 he was created a banneret, the first time in history that this military rank was awarded for financial services. Edward even promised to find wealthy husbands for William's daughters. Never before, and rarely since, has an English businessman been accorded such public recognition. But then it is not often that a businessman has played so central a role in re-shaping the nation's finances.

JOHN WYCLIF

c.1330–1384

FOR CENTURIES John Wyclif has been regarded as one of the makers of Protestant England. In J.R.Green's influential *Short History of the English People* (1874), he appears as 'the first Protestant ... the first Reformer who dared, when deserted and alone, to break through the tradition of the past, and with his last breath to assert the freedom of religious thought against the dogmas of the Papacy'. By then this was Protestant dogma, set firmly within the tradition of John Foxe's *Acts and Monuments* (1563). 'When all the world', wrote Foxe, 'was in most desperate and vile estate this man stepped forth like a valiant champion even as the morning-star in the midst of a cloud.' And it was as 'the morning-star of the Reformation' that John Wyclif passed into popular Protestant history.

Nowadays Wyclif tends to cut a less heroic figure. As a pluralist and an absentee clergyman he was an exponent of two of those 'Romish' abuses which reformers liked to criticize. It has even been suggested that he was a careerist who turned to heresy only when his ambitions were disappointed and that his more radical doctrines were symptoms of high blood pressure. Yet however much we may try to cut him down to size, the fact remains that he was the undisputed founder of the first 'nonconformist' movement in English history, the Lollards, a heretical sect which believed itself

capable of overthrowing Henry V and which defied all attempts to stamp it out.

He must have been born *c.*1330 but we know nothing about his family or his background. The fact that he was later patronized by John of Gaunt lends some support to the tradition that he came from Wycliffe, a Yorkshire village near Richmond, a lordship belonging to Gaunt. (But his enemies were to say that the true meaning of his name was as a sign that he led a wicked life.) He first emerges from obscurity in 1356 as a clerk at Oxford. After completing the arts course – a general degree with logic as its core subject – he stayed on to study theology. A careerist would have chosen law. In 1372 he obtained his D.D. (Doctor of Divinity). Anyone who progressed this far in a system of education which relied principally on lectures and disputations must have possessed a superb memory and a razor-sharp talent for argument. These were qualities which were bound to attract the attention of any government which had an ideological controversy on its hands.

In fourteenth-century England the Crown was generally successful in its attempts to exclude papal influence and bolster its own authority over the nation's Church. Nonetheless, while men paid lip-service to the traditional clerical argument that the Church's authority, being spiritual, outranked the worldly authority of the state, the Pope's theoretical position was obviously a strong one. According to Wyclif, however, all power and dominion derived from God and ought to belong only to the elect, those who were in a state of grace. On these grounds there could be no special authority for popes since there could be no certainty that popes were among the elect; indeed, to all appearances some were in a state of mortal sin. Clearly an Oxford philosopher had his uses, and in the summer of 1374

BELOW *John Wyclif, a forerunner of Protestantism in England and inspirer of revolution in Bohemia.*

IOANNES WICLEFVS ANGLVS.
Quanta fuit rabies odijque potentia vestri,
Pontifices olim, carnificesque truces?
Ossa inhumata diu vobis muisa virorum
Sanctorum, requie non potuere frui?

Cum priuillegio.

Wyclif was attached to the English delegation sent to confer with Pope Gregory XI's envoys over such issues as the pope's right to tax the English Church or to make appointments to English benefices.

But Wyclif's theory of the relationship between 'dominion' and 'grace' was capable of still wider application. If the true Church was not a hierarchy in which laymen were subordinate to churchmen, then churchmen should leave secular affairs to secular men; for them to become involved in the material world would be a perversion of their spiritual office. Here was an argument which could be used to justify a programme of clerical disendowment, a useful threat to hang over the head of obstinate churchmen. In the internal political disputes of the 1370s – disputes in which William of Wykeham, Bishop of Winchester and long-serving minister of the crown, played a central role – it was an argument which appealed to the Bishop's opponents, at their head John of Gaunt.

In 1376 Wyclif was brought to London to preach against the 'Caesarean clergy' – his term for those churchmen who rendered Caesar all too much service. Early in 1377 the Bishop of London, William Courtenay, tried to discipline Wyclif but the judicial hearing broke up in chaos, largely as a result of Gaunt's intervention on his protégé's behalf. Then Pope Gregory took a hand, condemning as erroneous eighteen propositions taken from Wyclif's writings on lordship. Oxford leapt to Wyclif's defence. The chancellor of the university, after consultation with other theologians, declared that Wyclif was in the right and that to suppress the truth simply 'because it sounded

RIGHT *Page from a fifteenth-century Wycliffite Bible.*

Forsoþe you þe
opistle first I maad
a sermoun or word
of alle þe þingis
þat iesus bigan
for to do & teche;
til in to þe day
in þe whiche he comaundede to þe
apostlis bi þe hooly goost; whiche
he chele was taken up. To whom
& he ȝaue hym self alyue or quyc
after his passioun in many ar
gumentis or preuyngis by fourty
days; apperynge to hem & spekynge
of þe reume of god. And he etynge
to gydere comaundide to hem þat
þei schulen not depte fro ierusalem
but þei schulen þe abide þe biheeste
of þe fadir þe ȝe herden he seiþ by
my mouþ. Sopely ioon baptizide in
water: but ȝee schuln be baptizid
in þe hooly goost: not after þes ma
ny days. Þerfore þei camen to gi
dre: axeden hym seyinge. Lord ȝif
in þis tyme: schalt þou restore þe
kyngdome of irael. forsope he sei
de to hem. It is not ȝoure for to
haue knowe þe tymes or mouen
tis: þe whiche þe fadir haþ putte
in his power. But ȝee schuln take
þe vertu of þe hooly goost comynge
fro aboue in to ȝou & ȝee schulbe
witnessis to me in ierln in al iu
dee and samarie: & vnto þe vtmeste
of þe erþe. And whenne he hadde
seide þese þingis hem seeynge: he
was lifup and a cloude receyuede
hym fro þe eȝen of hem. whanne
þei biheelden hym goynge in to
heuene. loo two men stooden niȝ
besides hem in whiit cloþis þe
whiche and seiden. men of galilee.
what stonden ȝee byholdinge in
to heuene. þis iesus þat is take
up fro ȝou in to heuene: so schal
come as ȝee sawe hy goynge in to

heuen. Þan þei turneden aȝein
to ierln fro þe hill þat is clepid
of olyuete þe whiche is bisidis
ierusalem: hauynge þe iourneye
of a saboth. And whane þei had
den entrid in to þe soupinge place
þei wenten up in þe inzer þingis
Wher þei diwetten petir & ioon ia
mes & andrew philip & thomas.
bartholomewe & mathu iames of
alphey and symozelotes: & iudas
of iamys: alle þes weren diwellinge
or lastynge to gidre in preyer wt
wymmen and marie þe moder ofie
su and wt his breþeren. In þo
dayes petir risynge up in þe my
dil of breþeren: seide. forsope þer
was a cumpanye of men to gidre: al
meest an hundriþ and twenty men
breþeren it byhoueþ þe scripture to
be fulfillid. whiche þe hooly goost
before seide by þe mouþ of dauiþ. of
iudas þat was leder of hem: þat
token iesu þe whiche was noun
brid in vs: & gat þe sort of þis my
nystre. And forsope þis weldide a
feeld of þe hiur of wickidnesse and
he hangid to brast þe myddil: and
alle his entrails ben sched abrod
& it was maad knowen to alle men
diwellinge in ierusalem. so þat þe
ilk feeld was clepid acheldemac in
þe laugage of hem: þat is þe feld
of bloode. forsoþe it is write in
þe booke of psalmis. The habita
cioun of hym be maad desert and
be þer not þat diwelle in it: and
an oþer take þe bischophiche of
hym: þerfore it bihoueþ of þis men
þat maad ben gadrid to gidre in
vs in alle tyme: in whiche þe lord
iesu entride in & wente out amoug
us bygynnynge fro þe baptime
of ioon vnto þe day in whiche
he was taken up fro vs: oon of
þese for to be maad a witnesse

ill to sinners and ignoramuses would render all Holy Writ liable to condemnation'. Not surprisingly this was exactly the line which Wyclif took. In 1378 he wrote his treatise 'On the Truth of Holy Writ', arguing that the only certain source of authority was the word of God as revealed in the Bible. The Bible's meaning might not always be crystal clear but each one of the elect should read and interpret it for himself. Doubtless the early Christian fathers had been among the elect, but no one should rely upon the interpretation pronounced by an increasingly wealthy and corrupt Church. In this notion lay the inspiration for the Wycliffite translations of the Bible into English. Here there were obvious dangers for the established Church since nowhere in the Bible was there any mention of popes, monks or friars.

Wyclif's call for a restructuring of Christian society, for a purification of the Church and for its forcible return to a condition of apostolic poverty was a radical programme but also one for which the soil had been well prepared by centuries of criticism of the corruption and worldliness of the clergy. Anti-clericalism and its corollary anti-papalism fed on the gap between clerical ideals and reality, and as the Church became more powerful and more bureaucratic in the twelfth, thirteenth and fourteenth centuries so the gap become more obvious. Moreover it was a programme well suited to the interests of secular government and influential laymen – to precisely those groups who stood to gain most if ecclesiastical property were to be returned to the descendants of the original donors. Thus the political theology which led to Wyclif being recognized as the outstanding English philosopher of his generation was one which assured him of

powerful patrons as well as a receptive audience.

But in 1379 he published his *De Eucharistia*, his denial of transubstantiation, arguing that the substance of bread remained after consecration. This was an undeniably heretical doctrine and one which suited no one's vested interests. Given the fact that the Pope had already condemned him for his views on dominion and grace, this was jumping out of the frying pan into the fire: an act of intellectual defiance if ever there was one. Even after this John of Gaunt continued to protect him; Wyclif was neither excommunicated nor imprisoned. But after this, unless he recanted, there could be no hope of promotion to high ecclesiastical office. If Wyclif had ever harboured dreams of becoming a bishop – as his enemies were to assert – this was not the way of going about it. Early in 1381 a university commission condemned his eucharistic views and soon afterwards he withdrew to the relative isolation of his rectory at Lutterworth. But he did not recant. On the contrary he plied his pen busily, developing and popularizing his views until he suffered a stroke – while hearing Mass on Holy Innocents' Day – and died on 31 December 1384. Although condemned, he had not been excommunicated and so he was buried in consecrated ground. Not until 1428 did a hostile Church have his bones dug up and burnt, and the ashes thrown into a stream. It is possible that for a few years in the mid-1370s he was attracted by the world of 'great affairs', but careerism is the one charge which cannot be levelled at a man who chose to become first a theologian and then a heretic.

He had not been at Lutterworth long when his public reputation suffered an even greater blow as the result of events over which he had no control: the Peasants' Revolt of June 1381. He sympathized with the sufferings of the poor and believed that a remedy should be found, but he did not believe in violence and he condemned the revolt. Nonetheless, it was natural that he should be held responsible for what appeared to the establishment to be an unprecedented act of sedition. Rebels and Wyclif did, after all, have some views in common. Simon Sudbury, executed by the rebels on 14 June, was put to death not because as Archbishop of Canterbury he was God's servant but because as Chancellor he was the King's: a Caesarean clergyman had been duly punished. Moreover some of the rebels demanded the disendowment of the clergy, though their idea that the forfeited property should be used to the benefit of all parishioners was not what Wyclif had in mind. In 1377 Pope Gregory had suggested that Wyclif's teaching was subversive of all authority, of the state as well as of the Church, and now the events of 1381 had seemed to prove him right.

In 1382 William Courtenay, now Archbishop of Canterbury, seized the opportunity to move in on Oxford. In a determined campaign he ensured that the university would never again be the safe stronghold of Wycliffitism. In consequence, committed supporters of Wyclif, driven out of Oxford, took to the road and began to preach to the people. In this way the Lollard movement was born – 'lollard' being a continental term of abuse for a zealot of suspect religious opinions. The early Lollard preachers achieved an uncomfortable degree of success, largely because they succeeded in bridging the gap between ideal and reality – as their enemies conceded when claiming that they hid the perversity of their doctrine under a veil of sanctity. As itinerant preachers hounded by the authorities, they were inevitably poor. In an age when clerical sexuality was a favourite subject for humour they were remarkably chaste. Indeed their opponents were inclined to sneer at their chastity. It was said of one early convert that because he was ugly and unable to find a wife he became a Lollard, making a heresy out of necessity. And whereas the Church had claimed that priests were different from and superior to laymen – though few of them behaved as though they were – the Lollard preachers emphasized the priesthood of all the elect, whether clerk or layman.

The Church authorities turned to the government for help. Sheriffs were ordered to seek and destroy heretical books. Eventually in 1401 the statute *De heretico comburendo* brought in the death penalty for obstinate heretics and in the next twelve years two Lollards were put to death by burning. The accession of the rigidly orthodox Henry V was a further blow. The result, in 1414, was a desperate throw: the Lollard rising led by Sir John Oldcastle. This was easily suppressed and it meant the end of upper-class support. From now on Lollardy was an underground movement of Bible-reading craftsmen, but as such it survived, and thrived. The Lollards had their own priests, schoolmasters and schools, and an extensive vernacular literature. Although the movement became less academic, it always remained conscious of its intellectual and spiritual debt to its founding father. Yet as a prophet Wyclif won greater honour in another country: Bohemia. His ideas were to provide the original inspiration for the Hussite Revolution, and perhaps his best epitaph was written by none other than John Hus, the great Czech reformer who was burnt at the stake in 1415: 'Wyclif, Wyclif, you will unsettle many a man's mind.'

GEOFFREY CHAUCER

c.1340–1400(?)

CHAUCER was undoubtedly one of the 'makers' of English history. Indeed, in the view of one who knew him, Thomas Usk, author of *The Testament of Love*, written *c.*1387, Chaucer '(sur) passeth all other makers'. Usk, it must be admitted, was using the word 'maker' in the sense of 'poet' or 'writer', one of its normal fourteenth-century meanings. And as every unwilling schoolboy reader of the Prologue to *The Canterbury Tales* knows, in this sense of the word Chaucer's name would be on everyone's list of makers. In the opinion of all subsequent poets, Chaucer was one of the greatest of English poets. Some writers have gone further still. Drawing on views like those of Hoccleve (*c.*1370–1450), who described Chaucer as 'the first finder of our fair language', and Dryden, who in 1700 wrote that 'from Chaucer the purity of the English tongue began', they have seen in Chaucer the 'great genius' (Chesterton's phrase), who took hold of various Middle English dialects, mixed them up with a bit of French, and so created 'our glorious English language'. In fact, as Dr Johnson long ago recognized, Chaucer wrote in the ordinary English of cultivated Londoners of his day and, even if he had never existed, owing to London's central place in the

A miniature showing Chaucer, from the Ellesmere edition of The Canterbury Tales, *1400–1410.*

business and administrative life of the nation, this 'chancery English' would still have become our standard English.

Since Chaucer was a Londoner deeply involved in the business and administrative life of the nation, we know a great deal about his life, much more than about most early English authors – including Shakespeare. We first hear of him in 1357 when he was in the service of Elizabeth, Countess of Ulster, wife of Edward III's son, Lionel. And for the rest of his life Chaucer remained in the service of the royal family, sometimes in the household of the King himself, at other times attached to the staff of the Black Prince or John of Gaunt. He saw military service in France in 1359 and 1369. Between 1365 and 1378 he was frequently employed on diplomatic missions: to France, Flanders, Navarre and Italy. From 1374 to 1386 he was Controller of the Custom and Subsidy of Wool in the Port of London. From 1389 to 1391 he was Richard II's Clerk of Works, responsible for the building and maintenance of various royal lodges and palaces, including the Palace of Westminster. After 1391 he was no longer actively engaged on government business but he continued to enjoy royal favour, receiving in 1395, for instance, the annual grant of a tun of wine (a useful 210 imperial gallons).

But though we know so much about his

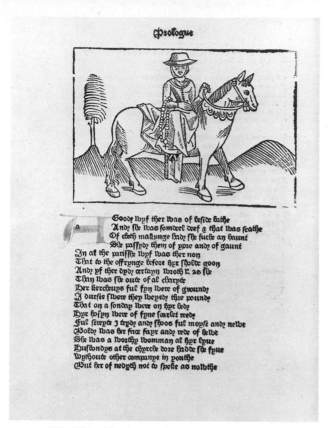

Good wyf ther was of beside Bathe
And she was somdel deef & that was scathe
Of cloth makynge she hadde suche an haunt
She passed them of ypre and of gaunt
In al the parisshe wyf was ther non
That to the offrynge before hyr sholde goon
And yf ther dyd certayn wroth R as she
Than was she out of al charyte
Her kerchyefs ful fyn were of grounde
I durste swere they weyed ten pounde
That on a sondap were on hyr hede
Hyr hosyn were of fyne scarlet rede
Ful streyte J tyed and shoos ful moyst and newe
Bolde was her face fayr and rede of hewe
She was a worthy woman al hyr lyue
Husbondes at the chyrche dore hadde she fyue
Wythoute other companye in youthe
But ther of nedyth not to speke as nowthe

The Wife of Bath from Caxton's 1492 edition of The
Canterbury Tales.

official career, what we know tells us practically nothing about Chaucer the poet. His name crops up in numerous contemporary records, but not one of them refers to his literary achievement. He was the first poet to be buried in Westminster Abbey, but he was buried there not because he was a poet but because he leased a house in the abbey precincts. Of his personal life we know very little. We do not know when he was born, though it was probably in the early 1340s. We do not know when he died, though according to sixteenth-century tradition – inscribed on his tomb – it was on 25 October 1400. We do not know whether he was educated at university, or at the Inns of Court, or at both, or at neither. We know he was married to Philippa Roet for about twenty years (roughly 1366 to 1387), but for all his brilliant exploration of the married state in *The Canterbury Tales*, we know nothing of the personal relationship between him and Philippa.

Yet even so, the bald, impersonal record of missions accomplished, offices held and annuities received, can be made to tell us something. We see that he was following in his father's footsteps; John Chaucer had also served the King, both on campaign and in the customs service. Born into a family of wealthy London wine merchants, all the signs are that Geoffrey became wealthier still. He bought property at Greenwich, became a JP and an MP for Kent. Like the franklin in *The Canterbury Tales*:

As Justice at the Sessions none stood higher;
He often had been Member for the Shire.

And the Chaucer family continued to rise. From 1389 his son Thomas was one of John of Gaunt's most trusted retainers and after 1399 he became an unusually influential member of the King's council, acting as Commons Speaker in no less than five Parliaments during the reigns of Henry IV and Henry V. Thomas Chaucer's standing as a cousin of the Beauforts, the most powerful family in early fifteenth-century England, reminds us not only that Geoffrey's wife was lady-in-waiting to the Duchess of Lancaster but also that her sister was Katherine Swynford, the mother of the Beauforts, John of Gaunt's mistress from 1372 and third wife from 1396. Chaucer's own missions abroad on 'the King's secret business', including matters as vital as the King's marriage, suggest that he was discreet and reliable, but not that he was the kind of civil servant who buries his nose in his official papers and steers clear of politics. As London

Controller, Chaucer was responsible for supervising and checking the collection of some £20,000 a year in customs duties, about a quarter of the total annual revenue of the Crown – no small task. Moreover, during his long tenure of office the Collectors of Customs were the richest and most influential businessmen in the realm, men like Nicholas Bramber, mayor of London for over five years, knighted by Richard II in Clerkenwell Field on 15 June 1381, within hours of the killing of Wat Tyler. It was the huge loans made by merchant capitalists like Bramber and his fellow London Collector, Sir John Philpot, that kept the machinery of government ticking over in the 1370s and 1380s. In these circumstances to be Controller of the London Customs was to hold a politically sensitive office. Doubtless, Chaucer was not as immersed in party politics as Thomas Usk – executed in 1388 along with his master, Nicholas Bramber. Nonetheless, the fact that Chaucer lost office in 1386 during a purge of Richard II's favourites while John of Gaunt was in Spain; and that he remained out of office until 1389, when the King once again resumed personal control of the reins of power and when Gaunt was on the way back home, does suggest that he was a political appointee.

This also suggests that Chaucer was, as usual in his references to himself, presenting only a mocking half-truth in the famous self-portrait in the *House of Fame*. Here, in a dream, one of his characters upbraids him for going straight home from the office and opening a book instead of seeking a different form of relaxation or amusement:

> And also dumb as any stone
> Thou sittest at another book
> Till fully dazed is thy look

so that, in this condition, not only was he unaware of what was happening in the great world

> But of thy very neighbours
> That dwell almost at thy doors
> Thou hearest neither that nor this.

Chaucer was certainly a very learned and bookish poet but no man who wrote *The Canterbury Tales* can have been oblivious to goings on around the corner. He may, as he often implies, have read himself to sleep night after night but such are his powers of observation that he gives the impression of having slept, like the song-birds of the Prologue, 'with open eye'.

What all this means is that when he takes us into the world of court intrigue and international politics, as in *Troilus and Cressida*, set against the background of the Trojan War, he knows what he is talking about; similarly with the world of big business, banks and exchange rates that is the background to 'The Shipman's Tale'. Chaucer's own diplomatic missions may also help to explain his knowledge of contemporary French literature, of poets like Machaut and Deschamps. But as Froissart's career indicates, there were already – and had long been – close cultural links between France and the English court. At least one of his trips abroad, however, is likely to have had a far greater impact: his trip to Genoa and Florence in 1372–3, with his impressions reinforced by a second trip to Italy in 1378. In London he would have met Italian merchants and perhaps have learned to speak some Italian. To judge from the prologue to the 'Clerk's Tale' it is possible that some of Petrarch's writings were known at Oxford. But no other fourteenth-century Englishman even begins to approach

Chaucer's familiarity with the work of Dante, Petrarch and Boccaccio, and it is impossible not to associate this with his visit to Boccaccio's Florence where Dante was a cult figure – a heady atmosphere for an ambitious young man who, like Dante, was both a learned layman and a vernacular poet. Chaucer's awareness of the great Italians makes him unique among medieval English poets. But he was in no sense a revolutionary poet, not in form, not in content, not in self-awareness – in his own words:

For out of old fields, as men seyth
Cometh all this new corn, from year to year.

Even *The Canterbury Tales* is firmly based on traditional satire. Chaucer's genius lay in the way in which he reworked familiar material and stories. As the Man of Law put it:

I can't recall a pithy tale just now;
But Chaucer, clumsy as he is at times
In metre and the cunning use of rhymes,
Has told them in such English, I suppose,
As he commands; for everybody knows
That if he has not told them, my dear brother,
In one book, he has told them in another.

Nor does his work stand alone. The second half of the fourteenth century was a great age of English literature, its first great age. Among his contemporaries are at least two other 'giants', William Langland, the author of *Piers Plowman*, and the unknown author of *Sir Gawain and the Green Knight*. Then there are Gower, Hoccleve, Usk, Clanvowe as well as other poets who, like the author of *Winner and Waster*, unfortunately remain anonymous. It is also, of course, the period when English was established as the main language of literature after centuries of coming third, after French

and Latin. The court remained bi-lingual but even courtiers – not just Chaucer's prioress – had problems with the French of Paris. Froissart tells how, during the course of negotiations with France in 1393, the English envoys, led by the Dukes of Lancaster and Gloucester, observed that the French proposals were not drafted in 'the French they learnt at home during their childhood'. Even so French remained the international language of chivalry and books of French romances were among the most treasured possessions of kings and nobles. As before, the essential accomplishment of the well-educated man was that he could read and write Latin. In this society, as in twelfth- and thirteenth-century England, there were many who were tri-lingual – and took it for granted. Of John Gower's three major works, totalling some 80,000 lines of verse, one is in Latin, one French and one English. But as more and more people, both in town and country, learned to read so there was a growing demand for literature in the language which all could understand. For, as a fourteenth-century Yorkshire lawyer phrased it:

Both learned and simple, old and young
All understand the English tongue.

It had to be a literature, moreover, which met their need for both edification and entertainment. This Chaucer's work did superbly, unsurpassed in its fluency, grace and wit. In terms of numbers of surviving manuscripts *The Canterbury Tales* was the second most popular work of the period. And the most popular? An anonymous didactic verse treatise known as *The Pricke of Conscience*.

A miniature showing Chaucer reading his poem Troilus and Cressida *at the court of Richard II, c. 1420–30.*

WILLIAM CAXTON

c.1422–1491

IN THE summer of 1471 William Caxton, a successful English businessman, went to Cologne on a trade mission and while there he took the momentous decision to learn the new craft of printing. Printing with movable type, a revolutionary method of reproducing script, had been perfected by Johann Gutenberg of Mainz in the 1450s. So complete was Gutenberg's technological breakthrough that there was to be no significant further advance for another 300 years.

But at first printing spread slowly. It took time for men to master the new combination of technical and managerial skills which was needed. In 1471 printers were still confined to the Rhineland and to Italy – the two most advanced regions in fifteenth-century Europe. In Cologne alone, however, there were no fewer than three active printers and with one of these Caxton studied for about a year. Then he moved to Bruges, the commercial capital of northern Europe, and set up his own press. In the early months of 1475 he at last completed the production of the first book printed in English, the *Recuyell of the Histories of Troy*. In the same year he also published the first books ever printed in French. The following year he moved his business to Westminster. In the late 1470s other printers set up presses in St Albans, Oxford and London, but in 1486 they all went out of business and for the last five years of his

life (he died in 1491) his was once again the guiding hand behind the take-off of the printing industry in England.

Caxton had probably been born in the early 1420s, so he was about fifty years old when he decided to learn – at his own expense – a new trade. What was it that persuaded a middle-aged businessman to take so remarkable a step? Fortunately for us Caxton liked to add semi-autobiographical prologues and epilogues to the works he printed – most early European printers did not do this – and so by combining his own words with the evidence of commercial and government records it is possible to reconstruct the crucial stages of his life in some detail. Up until 1471 Caxton's career, first as a London apprentice and then as a fully-fledged member of the Mercers Company, had been in the import-export business, concentrating on the flourishing connection between England and the Low Countries. He sold English cloth in the great Netherlands markets, notably Bruges and Antwerp; there he bought manufactured goods and luxury articles to sell in England. He became the leading representative of the English business community in Bruges and since it was the wealth of Flemish towns like Bruges which sustained the

Caxton presents his translation of the Recuyell of the Histories of Troy *to Margaret of York in 1475.*

ABOVE *Woodcut of St Jerome from* Golden Legend.
BELOW *Woodcut of a blacksmith from* The Game and
Playe of the Chesse, *c. 1483.*

flamboyant court culture of the Dukes of
Burgundy, this brought him into close contact
with the Burgundian court, particularly after
1468 when Duke Charles of Burgundy married
Edward IV's sister Margaret.

Caxton's own love of reading and writing
was vital. He was to translate many of his
books himself – more than a million words in
all – mostly from French, but also from Dutch
and Latin. He wanted to make the latest
Burgundian best-sellers available to the English reading public. In 1469 he started work on
the *Recueil des histoires de Troie* written by Raoul
Lefèvre, a chaplain at the Burgundian court.
Caxton was encouraged and rewarded by
Duchess Margaret. But it was a huge task – no
less than 210,000 words – and not surprisingly
by the time he finished it, at Cologne, he was
feeling a bit tired. 'My pen is worn, mine hand
weary and not steadfast, mine eyes dimmed
with over-much looking on the white paper.'
But he had promised copies of his work to
several friends, so how was his promise to be
kept? Doubtless, he had seen printed books for
sale in Bruges but not until he went to Cologne
did he actually see a printing press in operation.
'My courage not so prone and ready to labour
as it hath been and age creepeth on me daily and
feebleth all the body. ... therefore I have
practised and learned at my great charge and
dispense to ordain this said book in print.' So,
if we are to believe Caxton, he took this step
into a new world because he was getting old
and tired, ready to opt for the easy way out.
Considering that one early printer could claim,
in 1469, to be able to 'print more in a day than
could be written in a year', we can see how
Caxton might describe it in these terms. But
rueful humour is a Caxton speciality and an
easy way out it certainly wasn't. Setting up a

press was a time-consuming and expensive business. There was equipment to be constructed and the specialized staff to be hired and trained. Moreover printing was a high-risk operation. Many early master printers went bankrupt (including both Caxton's earliest partners, Johann Veldener and Colard Mansion). It was not because there was no demand for their products. On the contrary they went bankrupt for the same reason as computer manufacturers today; in a time of rapidly expanding demand it was easy to get carried away and believe that you could sell huge quantities of everything.

Caxton, however, had identified a clearly defined market and his earliest books were produced with this in mind. His market was the royal court, those who ministered to its needs and those who followed its fashions. His second book, *The Game and Playe of the Chesse*, also printed in 1475, was dedicated to the Duke of Clarence. When he moved to Westminster he set up shop adjoining the Abbey's Chapter House (where the Commons met in Parliament) and on the path which led from the Abbey across the Palace Yard to the Palace itself. His first major work in England was the *History of Jason*, also by Lefèvre, and dedicated to the Prince of Wales; his second, another Burgundian favourite, the *Dictes and Sayenges of the Phylosophers*, was translated into English by none other than the Queen's brother, Earl Rivers. (Caxton noticed that Rivers had omitted some misogynous remarks attributed to Socrates and so he added them at the end, remarking that they weren't really applicable to England anyway since no matter what women were like in Greece 'the women of this country be right good, wise, pleasant, humble, discreet, sober, chaste, obedient to their husbands, true,

secret, steadfast, ever busy and never idle, temperate in speaking, and virtuous in all their works, or at least should be so'.) In these early works Caxton's choice of type and layout was designed to re-create in print the lavish style of Burgundian luxury manuscripts. Everything suggests that court patronage was crucial to Caxton's start as a printer and that he had expected this to be so. Presumably a patron commissioned a work, took a large number of copies himself and then distributed them as gifts to his friends and clients.

But he did not depend entirely upon prestigious commissions for major works such as *The Canterbury Tales* (1478) and the *Chronicles of England* (1480). Indeed it looks as though loss of court patronage in the early years of Henry VII's reign forced him to look for new customers. So he widened his range of titles, publishing school books, phrase books, editions of parliamentary statutes and religious books, above all devotional works and service-books – the Sarum Missal for example, of which every church or chapel in the country was supposed to own or share a copy. There was also money to be made from publishing pamphlets, news sheets and indulgences. Since only a tiny proportion of these ephemera, often printed on single sheets, would have survived the ravages of time, it is likely that this kind of jobbing work was always more important than the evidence suggests.

No matter how small early editions may have been – averaging perhaps only 250 copies – when compared with the slow progress of scribes, this was an immediate and revolutionary increase in productivity. It could be sustained only because a sufficiently large reading public already existed. But printing certainly helped to raise the level of literacy further still.

Here it is so that euery humayn Creature by the
suffrance of our lord god is born & ordeigned to
be subgette and thral vnto the stormes of fortune
And so in diuerse & many sondry wyses man is perplex-
id with worldly aduersitees/Of the whiche I Antoine
Wydeuille Erle Ryueres, lord Scales &c haue largely &
in many diffirent maners haue had my parte And of hem
releued by thynfynyte grace & goodnes of our said lord
thurgh the meane of the Mediatrice of Mercy/whiche hee
euidently to me knowen & vnderstonde hath compelled me
to sette a parte alle ingratitude/And droof me by reson &
conscience as fer as my wreckednes wold suffyse to gyue
therfore synguler louynges & thankes/And exorted me to
dispose my recouerd lyf to his seruyce/in folowing his lawes
and comandementes/And in satisfaccon & recompence of myn
Inyquytees & fautes before don/to seke & execute þ werkes
that myght be most acceptable to hym/And as fer as myn
fraylnes wold suffre me I rested in that wyll & purpose
Durynge that season I vnderstode the Jubylee & pardon to
be at the holy Apostle Seynt James in Spayne whiche
was the yere of grace a thousand. CCCC. lxxiij. Thenne
I determyned me to take that voyage & shipped from southampton in the moneth of Juyll the said yere/And so
sayled from thens til I come in to the Spaynyssh see there
lackyng syght of alle londes/the wynde beyng good and
the weder fayr/Thenne for a recreacon & a passyng of tyme
I had delyte & axed to rede some good historye And amõg
other ther was that season in my companye a worshipful gen-
tylman callid lowys de Bretaylles/whiche gretly delited

Caxton's assistant and successor, Wynkyn de Worde, published about 800 titles between 1491 and 1535; of these more than 300 were intended for the use of grammar school boys. Naturally all this was of immense importance for the dissemination of ideas. While works circulated in manuscript only, they were all too likely to get lost and the ideas they contained to fall into oblivion. Earl Rivers produced his translation of the *Dits des philosophes* not knowing that there were two English translations in existence already. Caxton's own longest work of translation, the 600,000-word *Golden Legend*, was produced in ignorance of one made *c.*1430. After the advent of printing this kind of mistake was much less likely to occur. There was very little that was original about the ideas of the Renaissance; the important thing about them was that printing preserved them for posterity. From now on what was known once was likely to remain known. If the Viking discovery of America had been made in the press age, there would have been nothing for Columbus to re-discover.

The authorities of Church and state were quick to see the tremendous potentialities of the new craft. It made possible the mass production of indulgences and royal proclamations. But there were obvious dangers. While there was nothing new, for example, about criticism of the abuse of indulgences, printing undoubtedly fuelled the controversy since it had the effect of simultaneously making both indulgences and the views of their critics much more readily available than ever before. In the 1520s, as a response to the spread of Lutheran-ism, governments began to make serious attempts to control the press. In 1534 Henry VIII prohibited the import of books published abroad. A royal proclamation of 1538 insisted that all books printed in England had to be licensed by the Privy Council. Controlled uniformity of thought was what was wanted. A proclamation of 1543 even required all schoolmasters to use the same Latin textbook. And the fact that in the late fifteenth and sixteenth centuries there were very few presses outside London and Westminster meant that, compared with other European countries, the English government found the printing and publishing industry fairly easy to control. Where men were deeply and passionately involved, in other words in religious matters, there were some attempts to challenge the government monopoly of opinion, but not in less vital areas. In this way, for example, a Tudor view of English history became universally accepted as truth about the past.

In other ways too uniformity became increasingly the order of the day. One of Caxton's most famous stories tells how a London mercer asked a Kentish housewife for eggs. 'And the good wife answered that she could speak no French, and the merchant was angry for he also could speak no French.' Not until another traveller used the Kentish word for eggs, i.e. *eyren*, was the misunderstanding cleared up. For obvious reasons printing was to be a major factor in the gradual standardization of the language. For good or ill Caxton set in train a massive cultural transformation of English society.

LEFT *A page from Caxton's* Dictes and Sayenges of the Phylosophers, *1477, the first book printed in England.*

LEFT *William Caxton's bold initials identified the first books he printed in England.*

MARGARET BEAUFORT

1443–1509

IN 1483, when she was forty years old, Margaret Beaufort was unexpectedly catapulted to the centre of the stage of English history. In that year the Princes in the Tower disappeared from public view. It was widely, and probably correctly, believed that they had been murdered by their uncle, Richard III, and it was the revulsion caused by this belief that gave Margaret Beaufort an unlooked-for opportunity. She began at once to conspire to win the throne for her only son, Henry Tudor. Two years later her schemes came to a triumphant conclusion on the battlefield of Bosworth, when her husband, Thomas Stanley, placed the crown on her son's head. For the last twenty-four years of her life, from 1485 to 1509, Margaret Beaufort was deservedly the most powerful woman in England, a force in the realm of education and culture as well as in politics.

She was born on 31 May 1443, the only daughter and heiress of John Beaufort, Duke of Somerset, and his wife Margaret Beauchamp. Since the Duke, her father, was great-grandson of Edward III, she had royal blood in her veins, but not much and that of doubtful quality. As the bastard children of John of Gaunt and Katherine Swynford, the Beauforts had been legitimized in 1397, but in 1407 this legitimization was modified by royal letters patent which allowed them to inherit anything except the Crown.

ABOVE *Propagandist Tudor portrait of Richard III.*

The experience of death, marriage and birth was to come early to Margaret. Her father died a few days before her first birthday, possibly by his own hand when he returned home in

RIGHT *Execution of Margaret's cousin Edmund in 1471 – an illustration which exemplifies those troubled times.*

Et doncques ceste battaille
 amsy acheuee le roy se tray
en la ville de tewkasburi
en laquelle lui sa venue
le vi. iour dudit mois de may fist decoller

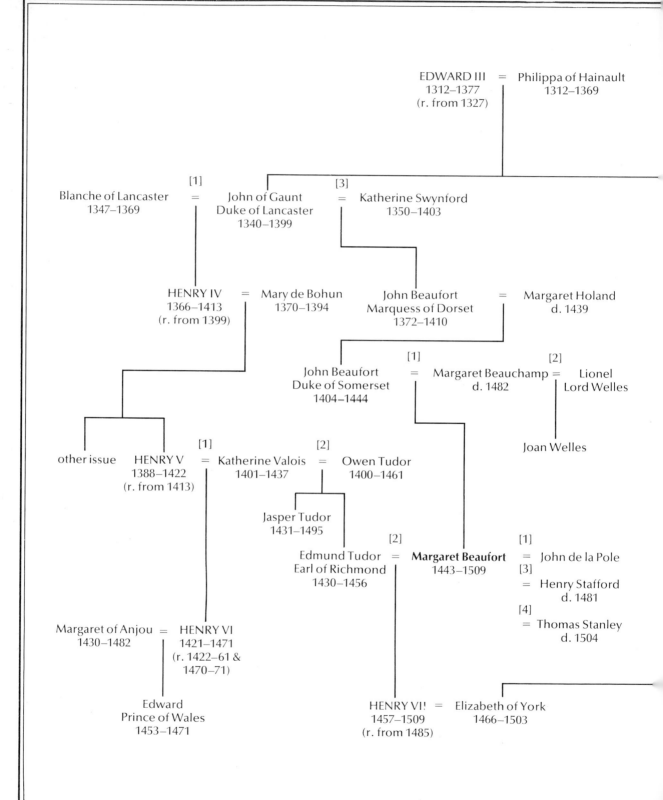

EDWARD III = Philippa of Hainault
1312–1377   1312–1369
(r. from 1327)

Blanche of Lancaster [1] = John of Gaunt [3] = Katherine Swynford
1347–1369   Duke of Lancaster   1350–1403
                       1340–1399

HENRY IV = Mary de Bohun   John Beaufort = Margaret Holand
1366–1413   1370–1394   Marquess of Dorset   d. 1439
(r. from 1399)   1372–1410

                    John Beaufort [1] = Margaret Beauchamp [2] = Lionel
                    Duke of Somerset   d. 1482   Lord Welles
                    1404–1444

                                                    Joan Welles

other issue HENRY V [1] = Katherine Valois [2] = Owen Tudor
            1388–1422   1401–1437   1400–1461
            (r. from 1413)

                           Jasper Tudor
                           1431–1495

                                        Edmund Tudor [2] = Margaret Beaufort [1] = John de la Pole
                                        Earl of Richmond   1443–1509   [3]
                                        1430–1456   = Henry Stafford
                                                                                 d. 1481
                                                                             [4]
                                                                             = Thomas Stanley
                                                                                 d. 1504
Margaret of Anjou = HENRY VI
1430–1482   1421–1471
                    (r. 1422–61 &
                    1470–71)

        Edward   HENRY VI! = Elizabeth of York
        Prince of Wales   1457–1509   1466–1503
        1453–1471   (r. from 1485)

MARGARET BEAUFORT AND THE TUDOR LINE OF SUCCESSION

r. = reigned

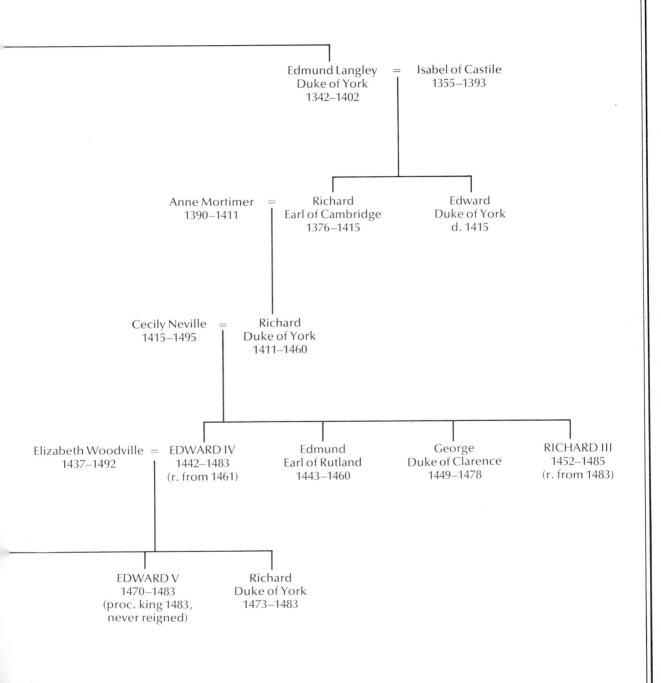

Edmund Langley
Duke of York
1342–1402
= Isabel of Castile
1355–1393

Anne Mortimer
1390–1411
= Richard
Earl of Cambridge
1376–1415

Edward
Duke of York
d. 1415

Cecily Neville
1415–1495
= Richard
Duke of York
1411–1460

Elizabeth Woodville
1437–1492
= EDWARD IV
1442–1483
(r. from 1461)

Edmund
Earl of Rutland
1443–1460

George
Duke of Clarence
1449–1478

RICHARD III
1452–1485
(r. from 1483)

EDWARD V
1470–1483
(proc. king 1483,
never reigned)

Richard
Duke of York
1473–1483

disgrace from a disastrous campaign in France. While still a child she was married to John de la Pole, son and heir of Henry VI's chief minister, the Marquess of Suffolk. Distrust of Suffolk's ambition led to the accusation that he was planning to exploit Margaret's Beaufort blood in order to make his son king should Henry VI remain as incompetent and as luckless in bed as in every other sphere of life. But during the course of Cade's revolt (1450) her father-in-law was murdered and the plan, if it had ever existed, was soon forgotten. Her first marriage was annulled early in 1453, probably so that she could marry one of the king's half-brothers, Edmund, Earl of Richmond. Edmund and his brother Jasper, Earl of Pembroke, were the children of the remarkable liaison between Henry V's widow, Katherine of Valois, and a Welsh gentleman, Owen Tudor. During Katherine's lifetime their marriage was kept secret: sufficient grounds for Richard III's feverishly moralizing imagination to assert that Henry Tudor was 'descended of bastard blood both of father's side and of mother's side'.

Unfortunately in the early 1450s Henry VI was rapidly losing both his reason and the loyalty of his cousin, the Duke of York. Margaret's second husband was to be an early victim of the struggle later known as the Wars of the Roses. Captured by the Yorkists, he was imprisoned in Carmarthen Castle and died (1 November 1456) soon after his release. His widow was installed in Pembroke, the principal castle of her brother-in-law's earldom and here on 28 January 1457 she bore a son. He was named Henry in honour of his uncle the King. (Though according to later Welsh tradition, determined to turn Henry into a son of Wales, he was originally baptized Owen.)

A few months later, in April 1457, the Bishop of Hereford gave permission for the young mother, still not quite fourteen years old, to marry her third husband, Henry Stafford, son of the Duke of Buckingham. Three years later her new father-in-law was killed at the Battle of Northampton (July 1460). Nonetheless, the next ten years brought the first substantial period of stability in Margaret's life. She and her husband were together a great deal and they found it easy to be reconciled with the new Yorkist regime. Edward IV was a king with whom it was easy to be reconciled. Presumably it was in these years that she began to develop an effective will of her own. Up till then she had been little more than a pawn in the game of politics.

But she can only have seen her son rarely. He had been made a ward of William Herbert, one of the architects of the Yorkist victory, and consequently he spent most of the decade at Raglan Castle. The Lancastrian restoration of autumn 1470 made it look as though mother and son might be brought together again but this possibility was quickly shattered by the stunning success of Edward IV's come-back campaign in the following spring. While Margaret stayed in England, Henry and his uncle Jasper took ship for France.

In 1471 three men died whose deaths were to have an immense effect on Margaret's late life. The deaths of Edward, Prince of Wales, at the Battle of Tewkesbury and of his father Henry VI in the Tower meant that if a Beaufort could transmit a claim to the throne then her son was now the Lancastrian candidate. In strictly dynastic terms it should have been Margaret herself, but this seems to have occurred to no

Margaret Beaufort, with the Tudor Rose above her head and the Beaufort portcullis behind her.

one at the time. Perhaps the turbulent consequences of the claim to the throne of Matilda, Henry I's daughter, in the mid-twelfth century had still not been forgotten; or perhaps it was the more recent experience of a woman in power, the rule of Margaret of Anjou in the late 1450s, which made it unthinkable. Although Henry VII's court historian, Bernard André, was later to portray Margaret as a life-long Lancastrian it is clear that this was a polite fiction. In law the Beaufort claim was always a weak one; in 1471 it was, in political terms, a non-starter, and Margaret accepted this. Until 1483 her best hope was that her son might be permitted to return from exile, succeed to her estates and make a good marriage, conceivably to one of Edward IV's daughters.

The third death was that of her third husband. Within a year she had married again, and this time we may assume that she had had a say in the matter. Her new husband was Thomas Stanley. Since he was steward of the royal household, this was a marriage which strengthened her ties with the Yorkist court. Moreover Stanley possessed one of the shrewdest political brains of the century. We will never know what Henry Stafford, had he lived, might have done, but what is certain is that in the great crisis of 1483–5 Margaret owed much to Stanley's power and good sense.

Richard III was crowned King on 6 July 1483. An attempt to rescue the Princes failed and soon afterwards rumours began to circulate that they were dead. Richard's failure to put them on parade in order to scotch a story so damaging to his shaky reputation is a clear indication of the truth of the rumour. All this had the effect of throwing the Yorkist political system into total disarray. For Margaret Beaufort it meant the realization that her son,

after years of waiting in the wings as an obscure exile in Brittany, had suddenly become a potential contender for the throne. Early in August her half-brother, John Welles, led an abortive rising in Northamptonshire and then fled to Brittany. Margaret herself became the central figure in a complex web of conspiracy. She borrowed money in the City of London and sent it to her son. Reginald Bray, an old Stafford servant, made contact with her third husband's nephew, the Duke of Buckingham. Her physician, Lewis Caerleon, had also attended Elizabeth Woodville, Edward IV's wife, and presumably it was as the widowed Queen's doctor that Richard III's guards allowed him to enter the sanctuary at Westminster which had served as her refuge ever since Richard had kidnapped her eldest son. In these circumstances the old idea of Margaret's son marrying one of Elizabeth's daughters took on an entirely new significance.

But Buckingham's rising was a disastrous flop – perhaps predictably so since only three months earlier he had been Richard's greatest supporter – and the rebellion of 1483 petered out in the shock-waves of this collapse. Those who had already committed themselves fled to Brittany; those who had held their hand, like Thomas Stanley, reaffirmed their loyalty to the King. Stanley's calculated allegiance to Richard at this juncture not only brought him rich rewards, it also saved his wife from suffering the penalties of treason. She was not imprisoned and, although her estates were confiscated, they were granted to her husband. All in all she escaped very lightly.

In 1485 Margaret took a back seat but the timing of her son's decision to invade and his campaign strategy were both determined by the encouragement he received from the Stan-

Henry VII, the son whom Margaret brought to the throne, painted by M. Sittow in 1505.

leys and their circle. His wife's attitude and prospects must have been one of the things in Thomas Stanley's mind when at the crucial moment at the battle of Bosworth he decided to throw in his lot with Henry Tudor – and this despite the fact that his heir was a hostage in Richard's camp. When her son was crowned, Margaret, in her confessor's words, 'wept marvellously, for she never was in that prosperity but the greater it was, the more she always dreaded the adversity'. After her childhood and after the strains of 1483–5 it is hardly surprising.

From 1485 onwards Margaret was a paramount figure at the Tudor court. Despite the fact that mother and son had hardly ever seen each other, there was clearly a strong bond between them. The Spanish ambassador noted that 'the King is much influenced by his mother' and added that 'the Queen, as is generally the case, does not like it'. As an exceptionally wealthy landowner with full control over her own household and her own estates, she was efficient and businesslike –

qualities her son inherited and put to good use.

At this stage of her life her main contribution to English history was as a notable patron of education. She founded the Lady Margaret readerships in divinity at both Oxford and Cambridge universities, but it was Cambridge, whose prestige was now beginning to match that of its older rival, which benefited most. She was a generous benefactor to both Jesus and Queen's Colleges and the virtual founder of Christ's College. In her will she arranged for the establishment of St John's College at Cambridge and of a grammar school at Wimborne Minster (Dorset) where her parents were buried. Undoubtedly much of the inspiration for her educational endowments came from her deep piety. That her faith mattered a great deal is indicated by her choice of John Fisher, later Bishop of Rochester, and one of the outstanding men of the age, as her confessor. Hers was a rigorous regime of daily prayer; in later life she took a vow of chastity. She commissioned a prayer book from Caxton, sermons and Walter Hilton's *Ladder of Perfection* from Wynkyn de Worde. She even made some translations of her own: the fourth book of the *Imitation of Christ* and the *Mirror of Gold for the Sinful Soul*. But she was no kill-joy. Her cupbearer described her conversation as 'joyous' and her first commission to Caxton was to translate and publish a French romance, *Blanchardine and Eglantine*. When she died on 29 June 1509, just two months after the son whom she had brought to the throne, she was mourned, said Fisher, by all: the commons for whom she acted as mediator, the nobility to whom she was an example of honour, the clergy whom she protected, the religious with whom she conversed, and the students and learned men because she was their patron.

HENRY VIII

1491–1547

LIKE CHARLES I, Henry VIII became heir presumptive, Prince of Wales and eventually King because of the premature death of an elder brother. Once King, though, he displayed the innate sense of regality of one destined for the throne. Born on 28 June 1491, he was almost eighteen when Henry VII died (21 April 1509) so there was no question of a regency during a minority. If there had been, it is unlikely that Henry would have accepted it. He resented immediately the well-meant attempts of Bishop Foxe, whom he had inherited as chief adviser, to restrain his youthfully exuberant urge to rule as well as to reign.

Physically and mentally the new King was in tip-top condition. His legs were reputed to be the finest in Europe; he excelled in dancing and the joust. In music he was a performer and a composer, though not, as reputed, of 'Greensleeves'. He set out, indeed, to be a Renaissance prince, an all-rounder, a combination of the hearty and the arty. Something of an intellectual, he would cultivate theology and was stimulated by the developments which were bringing about what became the Reformation both in Europe and England, to which he made by words and deeds his own peculiar contribution. He would reign for nearly forty years, but long before his life had run its course he had lost almost every one of the fine qualities which had ensured that he was greeted with

enthusiasm and uncritical loyalty on his accession. The legs were ulcerated, the handsome body bloated, the good taste overlaid with lechery, the sharp intellect blunted by bigotry and petulance; he was no longer *mens sana in corpore sano*. Medically he had become a very difficult patient, racked with pain, one for whom death when it came was a happy release for himself, and for his people. But all that was a long way off in 1509 when to be young and royal was very heaven. He intended to get a lot of pleasure out of ruling and, never inclined to do anything by halves, for a long while he did.

Henry's first major political act was to marry. Within seven weeks he wedded his brother Arthur's widow, Catherine of Aragon, in accordance with his father's wish but also perhaps to maintain for himself the link with the most powerful house in Europe, the Habsburgs. It called for a papal dispensation even though the marriage with Arthur had almost certainly not been consummated. Catherine was nearly six years older than Henry and passion could hardly have entered into their initial relationship, although for some years they got along very well. The diplomatic advantages of having children by a Spanish princess were obvious, indeed it was to his

Holbein's powerful full-length painting of Henry VIII in characteristic stance, 1537.

European reputation that Henry's energies first turned.

The foreign policy conducted in the 1510s and 1520s in association with Bishop (later Cardinal, Papal Legate and Lord Chancellor) Thomas Wolsey was tortuous and shot through with the self-interest of its two protagonists, each eager for glory. It had, however, as many failures as successes. The victorious battles of Flodden and of the Spurs, the

The title page of Assertio Septem Sacramentorum, *1521, in which Henry attacked the ideas of Luther.*

capture of Tournai and the Field of the Cloth of Gold were balanced by the unsteadiness of the alliances, unwelcome domestic reactions to high taxation and the almost universal hatred and distrust engendered by Wolsey's influence. Certainly Henry left a lot to the Cardinal but he was no *roi fainéant*. In nothing did he ever forget, nor let anyone else, even Wolsey, forget for long, that Henry Tudor was king; he was capable of taking advice but he always made his own decisions. Loyalty he took for granted and effectiveness was of the essence. His generosity, never prodigal, did not extend to reinforcing failure or condoning what he took to be disobedience. Sir Thomas More, who became Lord Chancellor after Wolsey, recognized that the royal arm flung loosely around his neck in condescending friendship could tighten into a stranglehold if Henry thought he could gain anything by it. More was only one of many victims of Henry's easy wrath. Rebellion was met with savage punishments, all justified by the inordinately 'tender conscience' of a king charged with divine responsibility for, though not answerable to, England.

Wolsey's problems began with Henry's fears for a break in the Tudor succession. In 1516 Catherine of Aragon produced a healthy girl, the Princess Mary, but as her child-bearing days petered out it became clear that she would never have a son – and it was a son that Henry, in common with most rulers of an age doubtful of the feasibility of rule by a woman, had set his heart on. His unease was understandable. For many, his father had been a usurper and there were still survivors of the dynastic conflicts of the fifteenth century with plausible claims. For a son-less Tudor a trace of royal blood elsewhere was criminal. In 1521 Edward, Duke of Buckingham, was found guilty of treason by peers more impressed by Henry's determination to get rid of him than by the evidence. Henry's ruthlessness extended even to the execution of the eighty-year-old (though it must be admitted still sprightly) Countess of Salisbury.

By then Henry had already ceased to sleep with Catherine. A succession of mistresses assuaged his exuberant sexuality. (His bastard son, the Earl of Richmond, testified that he was not impotent.) But, to a monarch who equated the interests of his realm with his own, something more permanent was required. In the later 1520s a queasy conscience, aroused by a biblical injunction forbidding marriage with a brother's widow, made him suspect that Pope Julius II's dispensation had been against 'God's law and precept'. That suspicion chimed with his love and lust for a court lady, Anne Boleyn (sister of a discarded mistress), who boldly held out for a wedding ring. The first result of these mixed motivations was 'the King's Great Matter' – the quest for a recognized nullity of the Aragon union. The quite unintended consequence was the English Reformation – the central fact of Henry's reign which had significances religious, political, constitutional, economic and cultural and was bound up with the rise and fall of a cohort of personalities. First to go was Wolsey, who for all his skills and influence could not achieve a European solution to the matrimonial problem and could not think of an English one.

Henry called a Parliament in 1529 to apply such pressure as seemed appropriate on the English clergy and beyond, on to the Papacy, but he seems to have floundered for a couple of years until, from 1531, a systematic onslaught on the problem was made by Thomas Cromwell, who had once served Wolsey. Cromwell,

Cardinal Wolsey, whose fifteen years of power ended when he failed to solve the problem of Henry's divorce.

clear-sighted and practical, had a programme not only for 'the divorce' but for bureaucratic changes which have been called 'a Tudor revolution in government'. The instrument was a parliamentary statute asserting royal supremacy over the Church in an England declared an Empire; it was to be free of limitation by any outside authority, even that of the Pope, who was *en passant* reduced to the status of Bishop of Rome. There was some urgency. By 1532 Anne Boleyn had yielded her quaint honour to Henry and was pregnant. Married in secret in May, on 7 September she bore a girl, the future Elizabeth I. Henry's enemies mocked this ironical outcome. But Anne was young and sons would surely follow.

Meanwhile, the break with Rome, and Reformation by act of state, proceeded, clinched by legislation well devised and directed by Cromwell, and accompanied by a vernacular Bible and liturgy. The latter, revised many times but always compelling, was the work of

The King processing to Parliament accompanied by his temporal and spiritual lords, painted c. 1512.

Archbishop Thomas Cranmer, a genuine divine, who was deeply affected by theological considerations, but who would go along with numerous religious changes until his moment of truth in martyrdom during the Counter-Reformation of the 1550s. Part of the Reformation process under Henry involved the dissolution of the monasteries and the dispersal of lands and assets, which amounted to the biggest and most permanent land upheaval since the Conquest. A great deal of this was not perhaps directly the work of the King himself but he could recognize the immediate advantages. Still preoccupied with his succession

and marital problems, he was the man behind the Reformation, although he never let himself fall too far behind events and drew on his theological prejudices, which were conservative, in seeking to control it both by policy and policing.

In 1536 Catherine of Aragon died and Anne miscarried of a male child. By then Henry's infatuation was gone. Anne, overlooking the deeply suspicious nature of her increasingly gross husband and of the watchfulness of her own and her family's enemies at court, grew careless about her relationships. It was simple to accuse her of incontinent adultery, though the accusation of a lascivious affair with her own brother seems particularly ingenious. She was quickly executed, incredibly dying with praise on her lips for her 'mild and gracious' consort.

Henry soon bedded a new wife – Jane Seymour – who quickly gave him the necessary son, Edward, but herself died in childbirth. Princesses Mary and Elizabeth could now be bastardized, although there were to be bewildering changes in their status depending on Henry's moods. He would have three more wives. Six marriages have led to prurient curiosity about his private life, but of course

royal relationships always carry wider implications. In each coupling it is possible to glimpse some aspect of the public interest, such as foreign policy and diplomacy, court factions or religious trends. Jane's plain successor, Anne of Cleves, was wished on Henry by Cromwell as part of a political deal with the Lutheran princes of Germany. She did not appeal, and Henry rejected her. Cromwell fell, a victim of royal petulance and the ceaseless machinations of court factions, and was executed in 1540.

The last seven years of Henry's reign have been characterized as the very definition of tyranny. Determined to check the drift towards Protestantism which for him at least, *defensor fidei* (Defender of the Faith) against Martin

Luther, was unwelcome, Henry was fierce in his onslaught upon heresy, as for instance with the fundamentally Catholic Act of Six Articles and the King's and Bishop's Books, which defined doctrine for a Christian man. At best these were a slipping brake in the gathering momentum of the Reformation.

To console himself for Anne of Cleves, Henry married Catherine Howard, an empty-headed girl with an appetite for tall, handsome young men who saw no reason why she should give them up. It is a mystery that the Howard 'clan', whose tool she was, were themselves not more apprehensive. The King, of course, received embellished accounts, and the bright thread of Catherine's life was snapped, Henry no doubt reflecting (rightly) how much better a judge of men he was than of women. Undeterred he went on to Catherine Parr, a safe haven at last, a no-nonsense woman with the patience and capacity to survive.

Henry died on 28 January 1547 in his bed, a happy release. His son succeeded as Edward VI. The next decade has been described as 'the mid-Tudor crisis' with a minority rule (1547–1553) succeeded by the brief disturbed 'regiment' of his papist elder daughter Mary. The Tudor regime was tested, but in 1558 Elizabeth came peaceably to the throne and proved it true. The commonwealth had been sick, though not chronically. Henry VIII had presided over the revolution of the Reformation, survived all manner of rebellions and factions, and indeed survived the comparative failure of expensive wars and diplomacy. As a man, he was selfish, devious, cruel, ungrateful, but fiercely intelligent. The breaker of an old mould, he was a maker of a new one for England, which apart from a few jaunts to France or Flanders he never left.

An engraving by G. Matsys of Henry in the last years of his life.

THOMAS MORE

1477–1535

'A MAN for all seasons' – such is the popular image of Sir Thomas More, fostered by his good friend, the humanist Erasmus. It is an assessment enhanced by More's noble performance on the scaffold, by his son-in-law John Roper's loving *Life*, and by a host of admiring biographers, not all of them Catholics but all impressed by his noble qualities. In this century the most influential life, by R.W. Chambers, which is almost hagiographical, has been fleshed out in a play and a film by Robert Bolt. But lately more objective appraisals, putting the man more firmly into the context of his age, have been made possible by the collective enterprise of the Yale edition of his works. The results are somewhat surprising but ought not to have been. Historians have known that to be (as he was) a courtier and a politician, he had to be ambitious and tactful, even a flatterer. He was Sir Thomas (1521) three-and-a-half centuries before he was St Thomas (1886). He now appears a 'complex, haunted and not altogether admirable man', caught between two worlds, the secular and the spiritual, completely at home in neither. He was also a creature of two eras – the Middle Ages and the northern Renaissance or Reformation.

Thomas More was born on 7 February 1477 in Cheapside, London, and, apart from two years at Oxford, was also educated in London – in a City grammar school, in the household of Cardinal Morton, Henry VII's Chancellor, and at the Inns of Court (New Inn and Lincoln's Inn). In taking to the law he followed his father, Judge John, whom he greatly respected. Morton's household, where the secular overlaid the ecclesiastical, must have been formative of a political outlook, while the three years he chose to stay as a 'guest' in the Carthusian monastery next to Lincoln's Inn aroused a religious ardour. A third strand was spun by a classical grammar school curriculum and Oxford humanism. By the dawn of the sixteenth century young Thomas was open to the not entirely compatible influences of wide reading and a growing circle of friends. In him they mingled but never quite made a genuine compound.

Humanism should have encouraged an optimistic view of man's potential, but pious introspection imbued More with an awareness of human depravity in general and in himself in particular, expressed in a struggle with his own sexuality which seems to have occasioned a deep crisis around 1505. Welcoming asceticism, he may even have contemplated becoming a monk. But, despite his piety, he recognized within himself a powerful drive towards sexual intercourse, which for him could only be acceptable in wedlock. In the event he married. As Erasmus put it, 'he chose rather to be a chaste husband than an impure priest.' He selected with some care Jane Colt who, before she died in 1511, compliantly and quickly gave him four children (three daughters and a son), whom he loved and who loved him. Within a month the widower had married again. Alice Middleton was a merchant's widow, six years older than Thomas, plain, a good housekeeper, apparently none too easy-going, but rich. It shows another facet of More, who was enough a man of his time to regard marriage as an economic bond. It has been suggested that, since Alice was most likely past the menopause and therefore incapable of conceiving, More, no doubt revolted by the notion of intercourse merely for pleasure, could by such a union bind himself to sexual abstinence. But he was still in his early thirties and the self-imposed strain must have been intense. This may go some way towards accounting for the prurience and scatology of much of his polemical writing

BELOW *Sir Thomas More by Hans Holbein, 1527.*

against heretics, who wanted to abolish clerical celibacy. There is more than a hint of misogyny in his attitude, which was sometimes patronizing and mocking, but at other times full of sheer hatred. Living with a woman whom he could not touch must have thrown him into that rage for work that marked the rest of his career. The man for all seasons may have had such a divided heart and mind that he may in reality have been right for none.

The first decade of the sixteenth century found him developing friendships with humanists like Erasmus and Colet, learning and translating Greek, writing his first poetry – of a kind that stressed his readiness to play the courtier. He was rising, too, in his profession as a barrister, for which by learning, voice and histrionic talents he was well suited. More, it has been noted, was a natural actor who fell into any role that came his way. He greeted the accession of Henry VIII, after the bleak years of Henry VII, with a Latin paean of joy. The year 1509 was indeed something of a turning-point for More, who then took an office as a London undersheriff, presiding over a municipal court and representing the City in the national law courts. He would serve as well on various commissions – of sewers, for London Bridge – and as an arbitrator. In this way he came to the attention of the powerful Lord Chancellor, Cardinal Thomas Wolsey, who sent him to Bruges in 1515 on a trade mission. Negotiations dragged. Idleness found work for his itching pen. The result was the bulk of *Utopia* (Greek for 'nowhere') – that description of, and commentary upon, an imaginary commonwealth, the most famous and perhaps least understood of his writings

RIGHT *The frontispiece to More's* Utopia.

UTOPIAE INSVLAE FIGVRA

Sir Thomas More and his family by R. Lockey, 1593.

(published 1516). It is also the least typical. Nowhere else does he show such an interest in such mundane socio-economic problems as poverty. His Utopia has attractive features but its total effect is rather repellent, a quality it shares with most other regulated ideal states.

Before *Utopia*, More had composed his *History of King Richard III* (unfinished and not published in his lifetime), which helped to establish the traditional image of the usurper clinched by Shakespeare's later physical and moral monster. This remarkable work is not just Tudor propaganda, but a story with a familiar moral – that tyrants all must come to a bad end. God will not be mocked. At about the same time More was led to write *A Dialogue Concerning Heresies*, sparked off by the notorious case of the murder (or possible suicide) of Richard Hunne, which involved a Lollard, a

dead child, a winding-sheet, a parish priest and the Bishop of London. This is the first of a long run of assaults upon heresy, works usually underplayed by More's admirers. If referred to at all, they are described as 'written in a popular style which unites learning with wit and humour' and showing a 'command of direct and virile English'. This is correct – up to a point. But they are also often brutal, scatological, contemptuous, even at times hysterical. The More who fears for his own soul and the souls of humanity takes over, with appalling consequences. This judicious lawyer, sage councillor and humanist is revealed as deeply disturbed, terrified of Protestantism, which, in its rejection of many centuries of Catholicism, would endanger the communion of souls in favour of a selfish individualism and make 'a nose of wax' out of the fine Roman one. Over the next two decades Lutheranism grew and continental heresy seeped into England to merge into native Lollardy. More's tone became more urgent and aggressive as he saw the Mass, the essence of his personal religion and of Catholicism itself, as under fire, while clerical marriage, 'filthy and incestuous', led to sexual licence. The gates of hell were opening.

Yet all the while More was a true courtier, a politician who, despite the hair shirt under the finery, was ambitious to get on and acquire honour. A privy councillor in 1518, he soon became a judge in the prerogative Court of Requests, then assistant to the King's principal secretary and a sort of private secretary himself to Henry VIII, who took a liking to him. More expressed some reluctance as these posts came his way, but in fact one feels that he really welcomed their demands and their profits. It would be harsh to call him a time-server, but he was not averse to practising the art of winning friends and influencing people, particularly people who influenced other people. He helped Henry VIII with the *Assertio septem Sacramentorum adversus Lutherum* ('Defence of the Seven Sacraments against Luther'), which won that enthusiastic amateur theologian the title of Defender of the Faith. As Speaker of the Commons in 1525, he played consummately the difficult role of being both the voice of the House to the King and of the King to the Commons. He asked and got confirmation of the privilege of freedom of speech but also saw the tax bill through.

In 1527 he went with Wolsey, to whom he was ostentatiously loyal all the while the Cardinal was in power, on an embassy to France. There he found some involvement with what became 'the King's Great Matter' – the divorce or nullity suit that dominated both domestic and foreign policies for most of the next decade. Wolsey's efforts, which More must have followed with interest, failed, of course, and in 1529 Henry, losing patience, deprived him of the Great Seal. Soon the Cardinal was dead. The Chancellorship for once went to a layman, Sir Thomas More, no less; not an unlikely appointment, in fact, given his legal skills and administrative experience. What is somewhat surprising is his acceptance, knowing as he must have done that Henry would push on with his case, but he hoped perhaps that in the end something might turn up to divert Henry. Unlike John Fisher, Bishop of Rochester, who was consistently against the divorce, More kept silence. (He would speak up, though, against his old master, Wolsey, when even Thomas Cromwell would not bring himself to join in.)

To be Chancellor was no doubt the logical ambition for a man like More. It put him in a position of power to do good for causes that appealed to him. But he had also put himself in danger. His internal tensions must have intensified, even though he played down somewhat the political side and concentrated on the legal side in the Chancery and Star Chamber. Active in heresy cases, he could be confident for a while of the support of the monarch and of the conservatives at court. A somewhat distasteful aspect is his unwillingness to allow the accused the right to say nothing, yet he would claim this right at his own trial – which was admittedly not for heresy.

The rise of Thomas Cromwell meant that Henry would eventually have his way with Anne Boleyn and with the divorce, the latter through a statutory Reformation to which the Chancellor was effectively only an embarrassed spectator. This situation could hardly continue. On 16 May 1534, the day after the bishops accepted the royal supremacy over what was becoming by degrees the Church of England, More resigned at the behest of the King, who was increasingly demanding the utter loyalty of his ministers. It was the demise of a public career and the beginning of the end of a human life.

Still silent about the Great Matter on which Henry was never less than touchy, More retired to scrawl as fiercely as ever against heretics who were taking advantage of the Reformation by act of state. But it was impossible for him to be accepted merely as a private man. The Act of Succession (March 1534), authenticating Henry's marriage to Anne, made it treason not to swear to it and to all the legislation since 1529, when called to do so. Summoned to take the oath, Fisher and More demurred and were sent to the Tower. No charge was made. More continued to write – *A Treatise on the Passion, A Dialogue of Comfort against Tribulation* and *De Tristitia Christi* – works filled with the love of Jesus, containing themes apt enough for his situation and almost but not quite manifesting 'calm of mind, all passion spent'. Now and then that obsessional hatred of heresy breaks through. *A Dialogue* asserts that only a fool would imperil his soul just to save his life. More was no fool. But step by step his life crept closer to the edge of danger. His treatment in the Tower grew harsher, although visitors found him always cheerful and resilient. In May 1535 attention turned to him again and to Fisher. Quizzed about this and that, he refused to entrap himself, saying no more than that he was the King's 'true and faithful servant', wishing and doing nobody any harm. 'My poor body is at the King's pleasure. Would God my death might do him good.' Otherwise he stayed silent, aware, lawyer that he was, that the recent Statute of Treasons challenged

words spoken or written, not mere silence. But it was hard to keep things up. Eventually in a passing conversation with Sir Richard Riche about legal hypotheses More uttered what amounted to a statement that Parliament could not make such a statute as the Act of Supremacy because it went contrary to the general view of Christendom. Though not a categorical rejection of the statute, this could be and was construed at his trial (1 July 1535) as spoken 'falsely, traitorously and maliciously'. Physically weak but mentally alert, More played his penultimate role there, facing a hostile audience with dignity and professional subtlety. It was not enough. A quarter of an hour's deliberation found him guilty. Allowed grudgingly to speak before sentence, he cited Magna Carta – not often mentioned in his day – on the rights of the Church. He appealed, too, to Henry's coronation oath and, remembering his own work for London, argued that just as the City could not legislate contrary to the Parliament of England, so Parliament itself could not make a law against the traditional and general law of the community of Christendom. Sentence of execution, probably of hanging, drawing and quartering, was then passed. That was commuted to the simple axe before the final episode on Tower Hill on 6 July.

Sir Thomas, of course, made an impressive end, his final bow and finest performance in the largest auditorium. He said little, but naturally tradition has ascribed to him many eloquent phrases and much idiosyncratic behaviour. The most convincing perhaps is the quiet assertion that he would die 'the King's good servant, but God's first'. The axe rose and fell. At that moment of truth, the courtier, poet, lawyer, politician, polemicist and actor perished and the martyr was born.

ELIZABETH I

1533–1603

THE CHILD who became the last and longest reigning (1558–1603) of the Tudors was also the first fruit of the Henrician Reformation. Henry VIII's marriage to Elizabeth's mother, Ann Boleyn, in May 1532, when she was already pregnant, was expected not only to assuage his lust but to provide that male heir that would ensure continuance of Tudor rule in an age when the 'regiment of women' seemed monstrous. Elizabeth was, then, a disappointment but the next best thing to a boy. Her birth (on 7 September 1533) confirmed Anne's fecundity and Henry's potency. Sons would follow. Meanwhile, as the breach with Rome widened – the Pope finally in 1534 coming out clearly against a nullity for Henry – Elizabeth could be a useful diplomatic pawn. When she was only a year old, her marriage prospects were being canvassed. The 1534 Act of Succession recognized her as heir presumptive over her sad half-sister, Mary.

But 1536 saw one of those kaleidoscopic switches which made and marred Elizabeth's formative years. In January Catherine of Aragon died, but by then it was too late to have any significance. In the same month Queen Anne miscarried of a son. That sealed her fate. Henry's long obsession with her had withered and he was open to tales of her copious adulteries. In a few weeks Elizabeth had lost her mother and was soon to be regarded by her

father as 'the little bastard'. The birth of her half-brother Edward in 1537 eased things somewhat. She was given a first-rate education, classical and modern, responding with true Tudor intelligence, but she continued to be the victim of her father's uncaring policies.

Edward VI's accession in 1547 found her next in line after Mary and, no longer illegitimized, comfortably placed in the household of the Queen dowager, Catherine Parr. Rumours flew that Elizabeth's responses to the attentions of Thomas Seymour, Lord High Admiral, Catherine's (initially secret) second husband, were hardly innocent. If that were true, she must have quickly sensed the danger of the relationship and distanced herself from Seymour, whose execution in 1549 eased her own situation. Her circumspection already suggests that experience and intuition together were deepening her political understanding. But under Protector Warwick, regent for Edward VI, and during the reign of Mary I she was never a free agent, submitting quietly enough to talk of marrying her off at home or abroad. What would have happened had these moves become more than tentative is an open question. Mary was naturally suspicious of her half-sister, particularly when she was confronted with plots and rebellions like Wyatt's (1554). Somehow Elizabeth survived until Mary's failure to produce a child by Philip II of Spain

THE TUDORS

HENRY VII = Elizabeth of York
1457–1509   1465–1503
(r. from 1485)

Arthur   = Catherine of Aragon = [1] **HENRY VIII** = [2]   Anne Boleyn   = [3] Jane Seymour
Prince of Wales   1485–1536   1491–1547   1501–1536   1509–1537
1486–1502   (r. from 1509)

[4]
= Anne of Cleves
d. 1557

[5]
= Catherine Howard
d. 1542

[6]
= Catherine Parr
d. 1548

Philip II   =   MARY I
of Spain   1516–1558
1527–1598   (r. from 1553)

ELIZABETH I   EDWARD VI
1533–1603   1537–1553
(r. from 1558)   (r. from 1547)

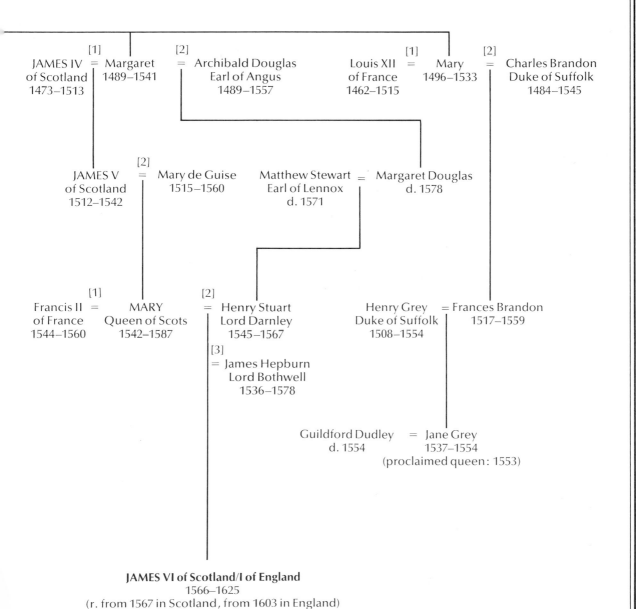

<table>
<tr><td>[1]</td><td></td><td>[2]</td><td></td><td>[1]</td><td></td><td>[2]</td></tr>
<tr><td>JAMES IV
of Scotland
1473–1513</td><td>= Margaret
1489–1541</td><td>= Archibald Douglas
Earl of Angus
1489–1557</td><td>Louis XII
of France
1462–1515</td><td>= Mary
1496–1533</td><td>= Charles Brandon
Duke of Suffolk
1484–1545</td></tr>
</table>

[2]

JAMES V = Mary de Guise   Matthew Stewart = Margaret Douglas
of Scotland   1515–1560   Earl of Lennox   d. 1578
1512–1542   d. 1571

[1]   [2]

Francis II = MARY   = Henry Stuart   Henry Grey = Frances Brandon
of France   Queen of Scots   Lord Darnley   Duke of Suffolk   1517–1559
1544–1560   1542–1587   1545–1567   1508–1554

                             [3]
                             = James Hepburn
                               Lord Bothwell
                               1536–1578

                    Guildford Dudley = Jane Grey
                         d. 1554   1537–1554
                                  (proclaimed queen: 1553)

JAMES VI of Scotland/I of England
1566–1625
(r. from 1567 in Scotland, from 1603 in England)

and her death left Elizabeth the obvious successor. The best alternative was Mary Stuart, Queen of Scots, then in the pocket of France and therefore quite unacceptable to Philip as well as to most Englishmen.

Elizabeth's accession (17 November 1558) was a happy one, celebrated then and for many years afterwards on its anniversary with bonfires and 'pope-burning' processions. At the age of twenty-six, red-haired, vivacious, English, she encouragingly represented the Tudor House, which seemed the sole shield against the recrudescence of the dynastic conflicts of the fifteenth century, whose dangers had been sedulously exaggerated. Elizabeth herself cultivated the image of the great deliverer from the evils of a too rapid expansion (for some) of Protestantism under Edward and a too abrupt (for others) reversal to Catholicism under Mary. The new Queen had no direct experience of government but plenty of coping with those who had. She might well feel she had been 'taught by masters'. Once on the throne, Elizabeth, like her father, knew she was meant to rule and did. Although Mary's reign had, in fact, been far from sterile, it had done little to dispel doubts of petticoat regality. But Elizabeth, a first-rate actor of majesty, put over her will and her personality not to all of her people all the time, certainly, but to a great many of them for most of it. She played the part so consummately, large gestures mingling with subtle nuances, that posterity has been inclined to see her as 'the matchless pattern' of sovereignty – Gloriana, the (possibly) 'Virgin Queen' presiding over a golden age. Even in the regicide Commonwealth Oliver Cromwell would see her as 'that Lady of famous memory. We need not be ashamed to call her so.' (He was thinking of her long resistance to Spain and of

her – presumed – championship of Protestantism at home and abroad.) Like her father she portrayed herself as the embodiment of England and, indeed, never once left the country.

On the accession of the second Elizabeth we were urged to be 'good Elizabethans', as if to call up the ghost of the first would automatically lead us into a golden era. The fact that the last thirty years or so have not turned out like that seems to be reflected in the current appraisal of Elizabeth Tudor's reign, for she and her age are under the same sort of revisionist scrutiny that has struck the early Stuarts and the mid-eighteenth century. The idea of 'Elizabeth triumphant' will no longer do for the representation of an age of problems, not all of which were resolved by the time of her death in 1603. And perhaps even with those difficult situations through which she successfully led the nation there was as much luck as judgment, although in politics luck often goes to those that deserve it.

Religious conflict may serve as an example. 'A discreet beginning' in a workable settlement was essential after the rapid oscillations between Protestantism and Catholicism in the 1540s and 1550s. The Queen's own origins argued for something with some Protestantism in it, something clearly guided by the state between the two extremes of Puritanism and popery. The mass of the population, who, as Elizabeth and her advisers sensed, were keenly conservative in practically everything, would only slowly take to new ways. The statutory religious settlement of 1559 was, however you look at it, a compromise, nowadays taken as one between a certainly Protestant regime and

'The Rainbow Portrait' of Elizabeth I, named after its inscription 'No rainbow without a sun'.

a trenchantly Catholic House of Lords rather than between a reluctantly Protestant regime and a dynamically Protestant House of Commons. Perhaps it was a little of both. In any event, its actual implementation was a complex and changeable process, which tended to reflect prevailing conditions and circumstances. The Queen's attitude combined conservatism and scepticism with an unflagging determination to maintain her authority. (Wayward as she often was, this was her most consistent objective.) One difficulty was that some of her more zealous supporters against Romanism – a few of them indispensable in her Privy Council – felt reluctant to wait for her to act. That, in the end, there was a genuine Church of England, infused with 'the religion of Protestants', may have owed more to providence than to what admirers have elevated into a monarch's masterly *politique*. Elizabeth, in fact, tested the patience and loyalty of even her closest confidants. It was fortunate that in religion, as in everything else, the Elizabethan state lacked the means to impose the royal will forcibly.

Foreign policy, which was inextricably bound up with religion, was a major preoccupation. The European situation remained fluid throughout the reign, with the Peace of Cateau-Cambrésis (1559) towards the beginning of the period ostensibly ending the Habsburg-Valois wars which had dominated the first half of the century. Did that presage a combined Habsburg and Valois Counter-Reformation offensive? Many thought it did and argued for the emergence of England as the champion of Protestantism. Elizabeth was more cautious. If her tergiversations concealed

Elizabeth I dancing with one of her favourites, Robert Dudley, Earl of Leicester.

The execution of Mary Queen of Scots, 8 February 1587.

Religion and foreign policy complicated the succession problem, which, like the Irish problem of the nineteenth and twentieth centuries, remained alive throughout the Tudor period by continually changing. It was a problem which faced Elizabeth immediately in 1558. If she should die (or be killed) without a direct heir, who should succeed? The obvious nominee was Mary Stuart, Queen of Scots, then very much under French influence. Indeed, she claimed the throne itself. The field after her was open. Everything argued for Elizabeth's early marriage – or so it seemed. But to whom? If to one of her subjects, factionalism would be stimulated – and, besides, what of the customary subordination of a woman in wedlock? If to a foreigner, would Queen and country be sucked (as under Mary) into unwelcome alliances, even into war? Such considerations surely underlay Elizabeth's ultimate failure to marry, reinforced perhaps by the memory of her own mother's fate.

Elizabeth was not averse to courtship. She liked men, particularly handsome men like Robert Dudley, Earl of Leicester, and Robert Devereux, Earl of Essex. But she surely never seriously contemplated wedlock with either. In the diplomatic matches which she kept in train, she 'took delight and made profit in simulation and dissimulation' while allowing an open succession to underline her own indispensability. In effect, she let the safety of her realm, to which she claimed to be wedded, depend upon her own survival. In this way she made a strength out of a weakness, although it brought some of her advisers and Members of Parliament to the point of exasperation. Her treatment of Mary Stuart, whom she kept in honourable captivity but never actually met, is a case in point. She said she could never 'love

a consistent policy, it did not go far beyond the simple objectives of staying alive and reigning in a country free of foreign influence. Unwilling to raise and spend money to stiffen the sinews of war, Elizabeth lived from hand to mouth, incurring as many risks as she avoided. Fortunately Philip II, who seemed the greatest threat, was a slow-burner who could react mildly to the predatory incursions of English 'sea-dogs' and privateers like Drake – and even a few traders – on the Spanish main and beyond. Elizabeth herself disclaimed any responsibility. There are three prime facts about the Spanish Armada – it came as late as 1588, thirty years after Elizabeth's accession; its defeat was by no means inevitable; and victory over it did not win the war for England. The war became one of attrition, which drifted on throughout the perilous 1590s and finally ended in 1604 to the relief of both governments, if not of all their subjects.

her own winding-sheet' (such was the threat that Mary seemed to embody), but could never bring herself to condemn her, until in 1587 she was momentarily caught off guard. Even when she was long past child-bearing and it became obvious, especially to him, that the heir must be James VI of Scotland, she refused to name 'that false Scots urchin', even on her death-bed. But, confounding Francis Bacon's fear of 'perturbations and interreigns', James succeeded quietly, gleefully gaining at last the title which he had said he must prefer over the life of his mother, Mary, Queen of Scots, whom he laconically referred to as 'the defunct'. His coming was greeted almost with relief in England after a long reign when security was never certain and by the end of which Elizabeth herself, a recluse who had outlived all of her own generation, had become a crabbed old woman, bald, gap-toothed and blatantly painted, her once enchanting 'love tricks' now seeming obscene.

The last decade was particularly bleak, though throughout 'the spacious days' of her reign there was always a darker side, slumps, an increasing pauperization of the poor, the continuing uncertainties of life threatened by plague, superstition, bigotry, and an unruly people whose very games, like football, were murderous. The poetry of the time was as much obsessed with death as with love, as for instance Thomas Nashe's *Timor mortis conturbat me* ('The fear of death oppresses me'), or marked by cynicism like Ralegh's *The Farewell*. Good taste was often interlarded with sheer vulgarity.

What of the Queen herself? Her tolerance can be equated with indifference, her determination with mere obstinacy, her good housekeeping with miserliness, and subtle trimming with shiftiness. Every coin has an obverse and a reverse. But to the last this woman retained the rare fusion of majesty and humanity which informed her golden speeches to Parliament:

> To be a king and wear a crown is more glorious to them that see it than it is a pleasure to them that wear it. For myself I was never so much enticed with the glorious name of a king or royal authority of a queen as delighted that God hath made me his instrument to maintain his truth and glory and to defend this kingdom ... from peril, dishonour, tyranny and oppression.... Though you have had and may have many princes more mighty and wise sitting in this seat, yet you never had or shall have any that will be more careful and loving.

That was said in 1603. What can today's great communicators, fed by committee-compiled and auto-cued effusions, put alongside it?

An allegorical portrait of Elizabeth with Time and Death, painted after her death by an unknown artist.

WILLIAM SHAKESPEARE
1564–1616

SHAKESPEARE is Britain's greatest artistic asset and best-appreciated contribution to world culture. His plays are performed and read, and his works studied, all over the world. For him there are no Iron Curtains – he helps to bring people together. It is true that in Mao's China his plays were censored, but since then the Chinese have flocked in thousands to see them.

Shakespeare had the good fortune to live in the Elizabethan Age, which in many ways was one of the most exciting and creative periods in English history. Although a small country of only some five million inhabitants, England was experiencing a period of exceptional progress and development, and new horizons were opening out – especially in America and the New World. Similarly, new horizons were opening out for Shakespeare, to which he gave unequalled expression in his plays.

His life and career were typical of the age. He started from small beginnings, had a hard and strenuous apprenticeship, then won through to become the most popular and famous dramatist of the age, the favourite playwright of both Elizabeth I and James I. And that was at a time when English drama was the best in Europe; foreigners flocked to see the plays staged in London, and English actors were favourites in northern Europe, especially the Netherlands, Germany and Denmark. The court was a prime patron of the theatre, and Shakespeare's company – the Lord Chamberlain's, later the King's Men – the choice and most frequent performers at court.

Shakespeare was baptized William, in the splendid church of Holy Trinity at Stratford-upon-Avon in Warwickshire, on 26 April 1564. Children were baptized a few days after birth then, so his birthday is kept appropriately on St George's Day, 23 April. He died on that day in 1616.

His people, and he himself, were very much Warwickshire folk. His father John Shakespeare, a glover, was an alderman of the town and became bailiff (equivalent to mayor). His mother, Mary Arden, came from a family of small gentry in the 'Forest of Arden', with an inheritance of her own, so they were among the town's leading citizens. John Shakespeare devoted so much time to the town's affairs that his own went downhill. William added to his difficulties by having to marry Anne Hathaway when he was only nineteen; their clever elder daughter, Susanna, was born five months later. Then followed twins, Hamnet and Judith, in 1585. By twenty-one William had a family of three children to support.

He had a good education, such as was provided by the grammar schools of the time, which concentrated on Latin grammar and poetry, along with study of the Bible and Prayer book – all fully reflected in his work. He did not go on to university: life itself was his university. For a short time he taught in a country school; but there was no future in that without a degree, so he joined a travelling troupe and became an actor – a good one, it is said. As an actor he was on a moving escalator; for the theatre, like everything else, was on the upward rise, and he was ambitious to make the most of it.

In that age it was thought grander to be a poet, and he staked his claim with two long poems, *Venus and Adonis* (published 1593) and *The Rape of Lucrece* (published 1594). Both were publicly dedicated to his one and only patron, the young Earl of Southampton. Privately he owed an enormous amount to him – and acknowledged it – for encouragement, inspiration and support. For him he wrote the famous *Sonnets* during the same period, 1592–4, although they were not published until years later, 1609, and then not by Shakespeare – they were too intimate. (Mr W.H., the dedicatee, was the publisher's, not Shakespeare's, dedicatee and was also not the young man of the poems, who like the 'dark lady' is not specifically named.)

In 1594 the Lord Chamberlain's company was formed with Richard Burbage as its chief actor, and Southampton enabled Shakespeare to purchase a share and become a founder member. Lord Chamberlain Hunsdon, first cousin of the Queen, was the patron; his discarded young mistress was the musical half-Italian Emilia Bassano, Mrs Lanier. She was, in my view, the dark lady of the Sonnets, with whom Shakespeare was infatuated. Socially superior, a strong personality, but of equivocal character, she was an educated, temperamental lady, who eventually proved to be a good poet herself.

In both acting and writing Shakespeare had a long apprenticeship, beginning with such plays as *Titus Andronicus* and *The Comedy of Errors*, and a poem for Southampton, 'A Lover's Complaint'. He had his first popular success with the new vogue of plays on English history, the trilogy of *Henry VI*. In time he wrote a whole series of historical plays: *King John*, *Richard II*, *Richard III*, the two parts of *Henry IV* (which with Falstaff, the greatest of English comic characters, was the finest of them all), followed by *Henry V*. At the end of

Title page of the first collected edition of Shakespeare's plays known as the First Folio, 1623.

Mr. WILLIAM
SHAKESPEARES
COMEDIES,
HISTORIES, &
TRAGEDIES.
Published according to the True Originall Copies.

LONDON
Printed by Isaac Iaggard, and Ed. Blount. 1623.

at an international level as well – in music, opera, painting and the visual arts.

With the Lord Chamberlain's company Shakespeare was at last on firm ground and he helped to make it the premier company of the time. These were the men with whom he worked intensely hard for the rest of his life – acting, touring, producing, and writing usually two plays a year. In London he lived at first in Shoreditch and then in Bishopsgate, which was convenient for Burbage's 'Theatre' outside the City Wall. When Burbage moved, to build the Globe on the South Bank, Shakespeare moved over to Southwark. He always retained a home at Stratford, in Henley Street – his birthplace – until 1597, by which time he had prospered sufficiently to buy the best house in the town, New Place. He then marked his success by taking out a coat-of-arms as a gentleman. The younger playwright, Ben Jonson, laughed at this, but William Shakespeare was always very much the gentleman and behaved like one. He was socially conservative, and thought that undermining the social order led to anarchy and only more suffering for people than before – the message contained in all his historical and political plays. He had a firmer and truer view of society than any other writer, partly because he had a deeper and wider knowledge of human nature.

This appreciation of human nature appears no less in his comedies. He had a wonderful eye for human quirks and oddities, weaknesses and foibles, and the entanglements, especially sexual, which people get into (a knowledge gained from his own experience). Love interest is dominant in all his comedies, including the autobiographical *Two Gentlemen of Verona*, which reflects the conflict between love and friendship in the rivalry between him and his

The Globe theatre, built in Southwark in 1598.

his career came *Henry VIII*, which contains his valediction to the age in Cranmer's speech on the baptism of the baby who was to become Elizabeth I. It was in these plays that Shakespeare introduced the mixture of history and fiction, which was the origin of the historical novel. His creative influence can also be seen –

young patron for Emilia. This dark lady appears again in *Love's Labour's Lost*, a private play for Southampton in which she is described in practically the same language as in the Sonnets. *A Midsummer Night's Dream* was produced first for the occasion of Southampton's mother's second marriage. Then followed the splendid sequence of *The Merchant of Venice* with its Italian-Jewish theme (the Bassanos were probably Jewish), *As You Like It*, with several recognizable references to Marlowe, and finally *Twelfth Night*.

The tragedies were written in the early 1600s. *Hamlet* and *King Lear* are about the greatest and most enduring plays in the world, *Macbeth* and *Othello*, shorter and more concentrated, are hardly less so and have the atmospheric effect of opera. The Roman plays appeared at about the same time: *Julius Caesar*, Shakespeare's chaste and classic model of a play; *Antony and Cleopatra*, the richest in sheer language and poetry that he ever wrote; and *Coriolanus*, again severe and classic, with its political message. Still more stark and uncompromising in its disillusioned strictures is *Troilus and Cressida*, a brilliant play but hardly a popular one, almost a satire on love and war. People were wearying of the twenty-year long war with Spain; when peace came they were disenchanted, and Shakespeare – the most sensitive register of the age – reflected this in the 'bitter' tragi-comedies, *All's Well that Ends Well* and *Measure for Measure*.

In his last plays he came back to romance and love, but with new tones of reconciliation and forgiveness after sorrow and grief. Of these the most beautiful are *The Winter's Tale* and *The Tempest*. By this time, from 1609, he was living more at Stratford, a semi-retired country gentleman of property. Even in his busiest

Popular figures of Shakespeare's time in a 1673 print.

years he had always gone back to his family each summer; but in 1596 his only boy died – his grief is reflected in the mother's lament for her boy Arthur in *King John*. Of his direct progeny there remained only his granddaughter, Elizabeth, who became a lady of title, Lady Barnard. At her husband's death the house in Stratford was sold, and all the old lumber of books and papers there destroyed.

But Shakespeare's work lives on everywhere – not only on the stage and in literature, but in history and in real life. I know that when people are in trouble they find consolation in it; and in time of danger they find inspiration. When London was being bombed in 1941 and the theatres were closed at night, people crowded in in the afternoons to hear Edith Evans recite the noble patriotic speeches of *Henry V*. When a landing-craft was approaching the coast of Normandy on D-day 1944, a gallant Yorkshire captain recited to his men Henry V's wonderful speech before Agincourt.

This was President Kennedy's favourite piece of Shakespeare, too.

Mention has already been made of Shakespeare's ever-potent influence in literature and the arts, in the historical novel and on so many English poets – Milton and Dryden, Scott, Keats, Tennyson and Hardy especially. He has also inspired and encouraged people in other areas of human endeavour, men such as William Pitt and Winston Churchill, whose ancestor the Duke of Marlborough, first of English soldiers, said that Shakespeare's plays taught him all the history he knew. Shakespeare offers the fullest understanding of humanity, as well as inspiration and consolation, to men and women in all walks of life, of whatever class or race, all over the world.

Shakespeare's patron, the Earl of Southampton, for whom he wrote the Sonnets, *by Jan de Critz.*

The Chandos portrait of Shakespeare. Of doubtful authenticity, it is named after a former owner.

FRANCIS DRAKE

c.1540–1596

THE TUDOR century was the first great age of English sea-power, with English ships, captains and crews appearing on all the world's oceans and growing ever more skilled and ambitious. The claim that Englishmen discovered North America a decade or so before Columbus reached the Caribbean is not implausible. The monopoly of the New World, blandly allotted by the papacy to Spain and Portugal, was unacceptable to some Englishmen even before the Reformation. Deep-sea fishing, trade, exploration and, above all, plunder were their objectives. As hostility grew towards Spain, which absorbed Portugal and its empire in 1580, blatant piracy, combined with slave-trading (on ships with names like *Jesus*), became infused with patriotism and Protestantism. The legend of the English 'sea-dogs' was born, with epic tales of cockleshell ships taking on Spain's lumbering galleons with the same courage that met winds and waves. The story told contemporaneously in Hakluyt's *Voyages of the English Nation* has been renewed ever since in novels like *Westward Ho!*, songs like *Drake's Drum* and (almost as romantically) by loyal historians.

Drake may serve as the epitome of all the heroes – Hawkins, Grenville, Norris, Frobisher and even Ralegh. He was certainly among the most dynamic, persistent and arrogant. His circumnavigation of the globe provides a set-piece of enterprise and fortitude. Like most of the Elizabethan master-mariners he was a south-westerner, born *c.*1540 near Tavistock, though toughened by a boyhood spent on the Medway, where winters were harsher. Returning home, he served an apprenticeship in coastal trading, until ambition pointed him towards the high seas. Contacts with the already experienced John Hawkins gave him

Sir Francis Drake by an unknown artist, dated 1591.

his first opportunity, in 1567, to voyage to the Spanish Main. Hawkins had established that there was an eager, if illicit, market for African slaves in the West Indies; if the risks were high, so were the profits, particularly if slaving went with plundering.

As it happened, the first voyage was not a success. A fight at St Juan de Ulua separated the ships. Drake quickly made for home, leaving Hawkins to extricate himself. That episode might have ended their friendship, but, finding a common source of inspiration in their religious, political and economic aversion to Spain, they were soon together again. Drake in particular saw himself as one of God's Englishmen, fighting a personal campaign against popery. Although back in Europe England was not yet at war with Spain, and Philip II was remarkably patient with Elizabeth I, men like Drake knew in their bones that open war must come. Meanwhile there were golden opportunities in western waters.

Drake and others like him knew their Queen, to whom they professed utter loyalty, would repudiate them without a blush if they were caught. But Drake, outwardly genial and bluff, yet with a keen brain and as tough on himself as on his subordinates, had tasted blood and booty, and he could hardly wait to go travelling again. Even his marriage in 1570 could not hold him back and that same year he took off to Panama, the collecting-point for the output of silver and gold from New World mines. This time he was there chiefly to gather information about the treasure-fleets plodding annually to Seville. But in 1572 he was back,

An engraving by Boazzio depicting Drake's attack on Cartagena, on the north coast of Colombia, during his expedition to the Caribbean in 1572.

The launch of the British fireships against the Spanish Armada, 1588.

ready now for action; at Nombre de Dios, and at Cartagena, he preyed on whatever shipping came along, Spanish or not. There were some setbacks. His brother John was killed in a landing party and fever was endemic. He was home in Devon by August 1573, having made the long haul from Florida to the Scillies in little more than three weeks.

By now he had acquired a national reputation. Too restless to stay long at home, he went as captain of a troopship on the Earl of Essex's punitive colonizing 'adventure' in popish Ireland. Evidently Drake, like most of his contemporaries, despised the Irish for their 'barbarity' and popery. As Essex's forces chalked up the usual crop of atrocities, Drake made his own contribution in July 1575 by massacring some 600 men, women and children – the whole population of Rathlin Island – an episode, however, which was quite consistent with his worship of both God and Mammon.

With the death of Essex the sorry affair came to an abrupt end. Drake returned to England, no doubt convinced that for quick returns and plunder Ireland was a poor prospect. Through Thomas Doughty, whom he had met in Ireland, he became involved in a scheme originally devised by Sir Richard Grenville and a syndicate of courtiers (men never slow to scent a profit). This was to be an expedition, ostensibly of exploration, to see if there really was a *terra australis incognita* in southern seas beyond the Horn. Whatever the outcome, there would certainly be booty to be won along the extensive western seaboard of South America where Spanish colonies and shipping were already flourishing. Doughty, gentleman-born, impressed the parvenu Drake by his plausibility, which, however, concealed a very devious character. It was probably Doughty's court contacts which got Drake a private interview with the Queen, during which she hinted that she would give the project covert encouragement, though its true purpose must be kept as secret from her cautious leading minister, Lord Burghley, as from Spain itself. Drake was flattered. It was given out that he would take some ships to trade in the Levant, while in reality making his way south and west through the Straits of Magellan into the Pacific. The prospect of booty was much more to Drake's liking than hanging about in the Mediterranean.

In the late summer of 1577 Drake had no great difficulty in getting together half-a-dozen small but well-armed ships, headed by his own *Pelican* of some 120 tons and eighteen guns. Captains and crews were mostly experienced old acquaintances, but they included Doughty, who soon aroused Drake's suspicion that he was deliberately fostering low morale. Doughty was, indeed, fast becoming a nuisance and a danger. At Port St Julian Drake decided on a court-martial, confounding Doughty by producing a warrant from the Queen authorizing him to put wrongdoers to death. A jury found Doughty guilty of mutiny. Curiously, the two men dined and took Communion together the night before Doughty was executed. By his determined gesture Drake managed to check the rot among the rest of the ship's companies.

Soon they were in the Straits of Magellan, those stormy channels beset with shoals, currents, tides and rocks. The ships scattered. Only the *Pelican* actually made the passage.

Proudly renamed the *Golden Hind*, from November 1578 she began to sail up the Chilean coast, taking prizes at sea and raiding settlements. The sudden appearance of an English pirate-ship in these remote waters sent a frisson of alarm ahead. No ship was safe from this predator. March 1579 found her off Ecuador, where a huge treasure-ship, the *Nuestra Señora de la Concepción*, irreverently nicknamed *Cacafuego* (shit-fire), was seized. Thence Drake sailed still further northwards to what would become California, where he landed to refit. There at an unknown spot he claimed the region for Queen Elizabeth, naming it New Albion, on the grounds that 'as the main ocean is the Lord's alone [it is] by nature left free to all men to deal withal . . .' – a line he unhesitatingly pursued throughout his career. A brass plaque was made recording the visit and claim. In 1937 one fitting the known description was found at a likely place, but its authenticity remains a matter of controversy.

If Drake had originally intended to continue through a north-eastern passage he abandoned it now. Instead in July 1579 the *Golden Hind*, laden with booty, set off westwards across the Pacific. October found it at the Moluccas, where a spice treaty was negotiated, to be taken up years afterwards by the East India Company. The Cape of Good Hope was rounded in March 1580 and at the end of September the travel-worn ship made her way into Plymouth Sound. Drake's first words on making landfall were, 'Is the Queen alive and well?' It sounds like a loyal subject's solicitude, but more likely reveals his worry that there might have been a change of ruler and thus of foreign policy. But Elizabeth was still there, and relationships with Spain were still worsening, though they had not yet turned into open warfare. The

Another scene from the Battle of the Armada, probably off Portland in early August, 1588.

enormous proceeds of the voyage were sent up overland to London, pending a share-out, in which the Queen herself graciously took part. At length the *Golden Hind* was summoned to London and at Deptford the Queen came on board to knight her captain (3 April 1581).

By now Drake was a rich man of high social standing. He stayed in Devon for a while,

becoming Mayor of Plymouth in 1581 and making nearby Buckland Abbey his seat. This he acquired through middlemen from Grenville, who would never have sold it direct to an upstart like Drake, particularly to one who had stolen his own scheme and made such a profit out of it. In 1583 Drake's first wife died. He soon married again, this time into a higher social group. He was MP for Bossiney in the 1584 Parliament and took on various official jobs, for example, as a commissioner for the

state of the Royal Navy. Sir Francis Drake had 'arrived'.

In the 1580s tension between England and Spain mounted, intensified by English support for the revolt of the Netherlands and the continuing western depredations of English pirates. Drake was at sea again in 1585. In 1587 he put on the famous 'beard-singeing' operation at Cadiz, naturally combining it with profit-taking along the coastline of Spain. Elizabeth seemed worried, but shared in the spoils. By now it was clear that war must come soon. Philip became engrossed in 'the enterprise of England' and built a vast armada, chiefly of troop-carriers, to invade and occupy England in the linked names of God and Spain. It set sail in 1588 and was, of course, a disaster. Most of Drake's part in the defeat is well-known, although it is not always remembered that in the midst of the engagement he went off on a private enterprise to seize a rich galleon as a prize.

The victory over the Armada, owing as much perhaps to favourable winds as to superior seamanship, did not conclude the war. That went on, making the 1590s a bleak period, until in 1604 James I, who lacked Elizabeth's commitment, negotiated an end to a conflict tiresome to both sides (Treaty of Hampton Court). By then Drake was dead. He had tried to continue his work for the Royal Navy and for himself, but in 1589 was blamed by the Queen for the failure of a costly expedition to Lisbon. Land-locked for four or five years, he lived the life of a country gentleman, 'improving' Buckland and showing off his new 'civility'. For the welfare of the community he supported a scheme to bring a decent water supply to

Miniature of Sir Francis Drake by Nicholas Hilliard.

Plymouth. But even here he had an eye to personal profit. Eventually he struggled back into Elizabeth's favour and with her backing he joined Hawkins in a Caribbean enterprise. It was not a success. Hawkins died and landing raids failed. Without booty, morale among the seamen faltered. Dysentery sped through the ship's companies and at the end of 1595, Drake himself, that iron constitution weakening at last, went down with a fever. On 27 January 1596 he prudently made his will. Early next morning he expired. Soon his stocky, weather-beaten body, encased in a leaden overcoat, was rolled overboard off Puerto Bello.

Drake and the other sea-dogs are still seen through chauvinistic spectacles as bravely taking on the mighty Spanish Empire and building up English sea-power to keep us free. There is some truth in the legend. Certainly there was courage in sailing round the world in tiny ships and in tapping a monopoly, for which there was very little by way of a moral justification. But these men were also greedy, self-centred and cruel. Drake's circumnavigation, the first completed since that of Magellan's ships was, of course, a remarkable achievement but its objectives were largely piratical. During its course Drake showed himself harsh in dealing even with his own men. True, he sacrificed his own comfort and risked his own life, and like Warren Hastings he must have been astonished sometimes at his own moderation in dealing with 'the enemy'. But Buckland Abbey, ironically bought and beautified out of Catholic booty, testifies to the generous rewards he allowed himself. England certainly benefited in both the short and the long run. That may even have been one of his priorities. But it is hard to believe that it was his highest.

FRANCIS BACON

1561–1626

FRANCIS BACON was a 'Jacobethan'. Like Shakespeare, Donne and Ralegh he was a denial that the accession of James I in 1603 was, in cultural terms at any rate, an abrupt break with the closing years of Elizabeth I, though, of course, like any other stretch of a few decades, the 1580s to the 1620s were a period of transition. Like the best of the rest, Bacon was not fixed for ever into a hard Elizabethan mould but had the fluidity to reshape modestly as time went by. He was in his early forties when the old Queen died, a man already with achievements but with new aspirations welling up beside the old.

Francis had had a good start. Born in London on 22 January 1561, he was the second son of Sir Nicholas Bacon, Elizabeth's first Keeper of the Great Seal, brother-in-law to Sir William Cecil, later Lord Burghley, her long-serving Secretary of State. Francis's mother, Anne Cooke, was a bluestocking of a Puritan inclination, censorious but affectionate. Initially educated at home (Gorhambury, St Albans, with which his fame is forever associated), Francis was a precocious child. In 1573 he was at Trinity College, Cambridge, then he went to Gray's Inn. (Later he showed a dislike of universities, because at them men learned 'nothing but to believe'.) Alongside an academic education, young Bacon grew up in a courtly and political environment, observing political issues tossed around among power-hungry individuals and factions. This must have had something to do with his inclination in maturity to identify various people, like his Cecil cousins and, in particular, Edward Coke, as rivals, professional and personal. (Coke galled him by winning the hand of the well-endowed Lady of Bleeding Heart Yard, Elizabeth Hatton.) Francis beat him to the Lord Chancellorship, but Coke achieved greater fame as a 'legal eagle' and parliamentarian. In marriage Bacon had to find what happiness he could with Alice Barnham, an alderman's daughter, twenty years his junior, who, even if she was not the sort of wife he described in his *Essayes* as an 'impediment to great enterprises', was still no great help to him.

At fifteen Francis went to France with his brother Anthony (who would turn out to be an oddity) in the retinue of the diplomat Amyas Paulet, earning a favourable report as a 'very able and sufficient subject', who would some-day do the Queen 'good and acceptable service'. His prospects were bright, but then his father died and he was called home to find that he had been bequeathed almost nothing with which to make his own way in the world. There was no doubt, however that he intended to do just that.

The law seemed the obvious starting point and after that Parliament. A barrister by 1582

and QC in 1596, he was an MP in 1584 and sat in the Commons for various constituencies. Here he acquired a reputation as an effective speaker, offering 'oracles rather than discourses' and with a mastery of aphorism which came to fruition in his earliest published work, *The Essayes or Counsels Civil and Moral* (1597, then revised and enlarged several times). Notable among them are 'Of Ambition' and 'Of Great Place', about which he already knew a great deal. In describing 'rising into place' as 'laborious' and 'the standing slippery', he was both commenting on experience and making a personal prophecy. It is unfortunate that he did not take his own advice: 'For corruption: do not only bind thine own hands or thy servants' hands from taking but bind the hands of suitors also from offering.'

Sometimes, as in the 1593 Parliament speaking against supply, he let his volatile tongue run away with him, incurring the Queen's open displeasure. Often in debt, he sought to rehabilitate himself by appropriate gestures, supporting the Subsidy Bill in 1597 and echoing government condemnation of land enclosures as a social scourge. In 1600 he was a violent advocate for the prosecution in the trial of the rebellious Earl of Essex, whom he had once courted and who had shown him many favours. (To be fair, Bacon had earlier gone out of his way to warn Essex off courses that he knew could only lead to disaster. It was one of the sad facts of his career that the advice he gave was so often ignored, although he would go on offering it.) Elizabeth never gave him office but under James I he became Solicitor-General (1607), Attorney-General (1612),

Sir Francis Bacon by an unknown artist. Lord Chancellor in 1618, he fell from power in 1621.

Privy Councillor (1616), and Lord Keeper (1617). He was raised to the peerage as Baron Verulam in 1618, becoming Lord Chancellor at the same time and Viscount St Albans in 1621 – a steady, consistent progress.

In notable trials – Somerset, Ralegh, Suffolk, Yelverton – he was a vigorous prosecutor and generally acquired the reputation of an advocate for the widest possible interpretation of the royal prerogative. By now he had as many enemies as friends, perhaps more, because he was widely regarded as too clever, devious and 'all for himself'. Assailed in 1621 by that medieval judicial device, impeachment, he was found guilty of bribery. (His old foe, Sir Edward Coke, was conspicuous among the prosecutors, sententiously opining that 'a corrupt judge is the grievance of grievances'.) Deprived of the seals of office Bacon went to the Tower, a crowded residence in the early seventeenth century. James I treated him leniently, knowing that Bacon, like Cranfield, had also helped the Crown in the process of looking after himself. He was soon released with his huge fine mitigated. But it was the end of his political career. He retired to continue and, he hoped, complete the great body of thinking and writing, upon which he was already well advanced. But heavily in debt, he died on 9 April 1626, of bronchitis, having caught a chill while conducting an impromptu experiment in refrigeration – stuffing a chicken with snow to see how long the carcass would retain its freshness. His death came too soon for the rehabilitation that his works, few of them published in his lifetime, would bring him. Not many of his contemporaries were in a position to grasp what it was that he was working towards. It was, in any case, probably too complex. Only with the great collected

The title page from Bacon's Advancement and Proficience of Science, *published in 1640.*

put it: 'my soul [has been] a stranger in the course of my pilgrimage.' It may be that his professional career and his writings on law, politics, history and the constitution were a necessary part of his philosophical and scientific schemes. Without position, authority, and experience, he could never have hoped to advance towards his goal of organizing and directing science, in the broad sense, for the benefit of humankind. Sir Henry Wotton saw him as 'of science, the light', while Abraham Cowley, Fellow of the Royal Society, compared him to a Moses who led science through the wilderness to the 'very border' of the promised land. Pope summed him up as 'the wisest, brightest, meanest of mankind'.

What Bacon sought was universal knowledge, a synthesis of his manifold interests into one single fabric which did not merely involve categorizing (though that was needed) but also understanding. At the centre of this scheme were human beings. Bacon had a view of 'man's unconquerable mind', which he saw as drawing on past, present and future. The past had made giant contributions – among them three fruitful inventions, the wheel, the compass and, above all, printing – but could be surpassed by the present (as it was, in fact, being surpassed by Bacon himself) and by the future for which he had taken it upon himself 'to ring a bell to call the wits together'. Cheerfulness was forever breaking in. Unlike Newton to whom humour was otiose, Bacon loved 'a laughing face'. He recognized that there were and always would be tensions between past, present and future, between science and society, between the advancement of learning and the urge to revere received opinion, including particularly, perhaps, religious beliefs and prejudices, between the

edition and life by Spedding in the mid–nineteenth century, brought out partly in reaction to Macaulay's sneering *Essay on Bacon*, was it possible to appreciate the adventurousness and comprehensiveness of Bacon's aspirations and achievements.

Bacon has been compared to Icarus, flying too close to the sun. The truth may be that he had too many interests and a flawed character – 'a divided heart', it has been said. He himself

mere accumulation of facts and the interpretation of their utility and significance, between the pure and the applied – all these he believed could be overcome because in the end, for the future of mankind, they must be overcome. Most of these tensions remain in our present, his future; indeed, they are intensified in an age in which knowledge and technology are outstripping understanding and humane values.

Was Bacon, then, a false prophet? Time, whose daughter is truth, will tell. Bacon, as he modestly and presciently saw himself, has long been overtaken and his influence, if valued at all, has been reckoned as only one among many pushing along the rim of the wheel of the scientific revolution. But it may be that he is too readily brushed aside, the victim of his own diversity and of his respect, currently unfashionable, for comprehensiveness. Yet the wheel can move again or, more simply, we can read again, and more closely, what this 'first statesman of science' actually wrote.

Bacon's scheme for the advancement of learning and its application was reinforced by setting out a method of discovery – a combination of experiment and 'reasoning and true induction' to find the laws by which nature operates and then going on to devise further experiments from knowledge of those laws. (Nature is very important to Bacon: 'the empire of man over things depends wholly on the arts and sciences ... we cannot command Nature except by obeying her.') Everything should be done as systematically as possible, but he does allow room for the use of intuition and imagination. There will be errors, but 'truth ... ['the sovereign good of human nature'] ... will sooner come from error than from confusion.' (This is not far perhaps from someone else's aphorism: 'Better a fertile error than a sterile truth.') Bacon's definition of truth amounted to something like what is left when everything else that is not applicable to the topic under review has been eliminated. In the process of coming to his method he contemplated a series of 'instances', which he categorized into some twenty-seven differences. In this process he came very close to anticipating a fair number of later theories or discoveries. That of the Continental Drift is an example: 'Take Africa and the region of Peru with the continent stretching to the Straits of Magellan, in each of which tracts there are similar isthmuses and similar promontories, which can hardly be by accident.'

Bacon's vision surprises, appeals, impresses and often convinces, not solely because of the content but also because of the manner in which it is conveyed. Few writers are so immediately accessible. The style has been characterized as 'neat and polite, clear, masculine, apt'. Shelley described Bacon as a poet – though that was perhaps more in reference to his own view of poets as 'unacknowledged legislators' than to Bacon's capacity to compose verses, which was in fact rather weak. This fact in itself, rather then any scepticism about the existence in Shakespeare's works of cryptograms and anagrams – which were, it is true, much used and respected in his times – should disabuse us of any notion that Bacon 'wrote Shakespeare'. His own prose style is *sui generis*, a combination of natural and schooled eloquence, the generous flow of the former stemmed by the latter, seeking precision, economy, clarity, limpidity, not just for literary effect but because his whole philosophy and system demanded it. The bell he rang to summon the wits still rings true, flawed though the campanologist himself may have been.

JAMES VI AND I
1566–1625

JAMES I came to rule in England as 'an old and experienced king' – James VI of Scotland. Born on 19 June 1566 posthumously to his father, Henry Stewart (Lord Darnley), Mary's murdered husband, he had reigned from her deposition (1567), first with a regency and then, from the early 1580s, on his own account. He was given a thorough academic education by distinguished tutors like the Latinist, George Buchanan, proving himself an apt pupil, quick to pick up and to pick at an argument, and capable of pouring out quotations to show off his memory and learning. The circumstances of his life were uneasy for more than a decade as Scotland was torn apart by faction-fighting between the Queen's men, who wanted Mary back, not so much for her sake as for their own, and the King's men, who aimed – through young James – to control the kingdom, and in particular to dispense among themselves royal patronage.

All the while, the Scottish Reformation was proceeding more fiercely than the English. James, who enjoyed political philosophy as an intellectual exercise, interwove it with practical politics, creating the 'Kingcraft' (as he called it) with which he was eventually able to control the Scottish nobility. James proved allergic to some of the ideas that were fed to him about the relationship of subject and sovereign, Church and state. Almost by instinct he favoured the principle of *cuius regio eius religio* ('whose region, his religion'), and soon felt that he had enough of a Presbyterian kirk which would tell a king – 'God's silly vassal' – what to do. Much of his success in Scotland lay in the intelligent application of 'divide and rule.'

As James VI extricated himself from tutors and regents and tasted independence, his ambitions and horizons widened. His eye was on a succession to the English throne even before his mother was executed (1587). Indeed, his confidence in his prospects during the 1590s, was so blatant that Elizabeth I, who never met him and never named him as heir, reprimanded him. His English contacts, like Robert Cecil, Earl of Leicester, who could visualize no alternative to him although there were a dozen with some sort of claim, advised tact and patience. James listened. Consequently his succession was quickly effected by the men on the spot who, of course, expected their reward.

Elizabeth died on 25 March 1603, not unexpectedly. James was already prepared and, as soon as the news arrived by a breathless messenger, he was on his way down to London, which he had already decided would be his capital once the union of the crowns of his two kingdoms had, as he intended, brought about the single state of Great Britain. This aspiration was more than an expression of his personal conceit. Like every other contemporary ruler over heterogeneous territories – Spain, the Netherlands, France – he was trying to bring them together for the convenience of effective rule. He failed, largely because of English Scottophobia, which was reinforced by James's initial predilection for his fellow countrymen, who flocked into England, as someone said, like famished cattle into lush meadows, and among whom – until the rise of George Villiers, his last and most beloved – he found his favourites.

How far was James VI an asset to James I? Generally the answer has been 'not much'. Experience is certainly useful, but only where it is or is made relevant. England and Scotland were very different. James was shrewd enough to glimpse that, but never dedicated enough to act on it. Although he only once went back to Scotland (1618), he always seemed a foreigner in England, after the cultivated 'mere Englishness' of his predecessor. He never lost interest in his northern kingdom and, though he ruled there more or less by proxy through his Privy Council, the chief decisions were his and their achievements considerable. He maintained a control of the Scottish Parliament which was superior to that which he had over the English Parliament – a very different institution. Although there was no longer in any real sense a Scottish court, there was still some cultural vitality in Edinburgh. James's ecclesiastical policy, which involved pushing episcopacy back into everyday life, was at least half successful. He would have had a more positive impact in Scotland if he had not made it so plain that his policy there was really one of Anglicization, although he had enough intelligence not to go too far too fast. It was left to his son, Charles I – who has been described as suffering

from too much energy – to ruin things by over-precipitate action.

All this meant that James, whose greatest faults were laziness and impatience, could give rather less attention to England than he might have done. A passion for hunting led him to rely too much on his ministers. He had some loyal and able ones, some whose loyalty outstripped their capacity, and some whose personal ambitions inhibited their devotion. After 1612 when Salisbury, who had served the King as well as he served himself – which was very well – died, James's Privy Council was more than ever prone to faction as favourites rose and fell. A peak was reached in the gorgeous person of George Villiers – successively Viscount, Marquess, and Duke of Buckingham – who became 'the gilded bottleneck of

King James aged fifty-four by Jan de Critz, Sergeant Painter to the Crown, 1620.

patronage'; the free flow of patronage was desirable, indeed necessary, for unity. Such able servants as James did have were constantly under fire. Lord Chancellor Francis Bacon, whose advice could be sage, was successfully impeached for bribery in 1621, as was Lord Treasurer Lionel Cranfield in 1624 – a victim of Buckingham and of James's heir, Charles, the Prince of Wales since the death of his glamorous brother, Henry, in 1612. Buckingham and Charles were advocates of a war with Spain which would have made nonsense of James's pacific Hispanophile foreign policy and havoc of Cranfield's economies. As James ruefully remarked, any treasurer who served his master well was bound to be hated.

Foreign policy ran through all the politics of James's reign. He saw himself as a wise statesman like a Solon or Solomon, but most of all as the peacemaker of a Europe where war was endemic. His love of peace was as genuine as his desire for reputation, and it was intellectually as well as emotionally based. Peace was made with Spain in 1604, and from then on he saw increasing English friendship with Spain (to be sealed with a marriage alliance) as the best way to make a European impact. Not all of his subjects agreed, though some – traders with the Spanish Netherlands or with the Iberian peninsula itself – did. The outbreak of what became the Thirty Years War, with James's ambitious son-in-law, Frederick of the Palatinate – 'champion of German Protestantism' – driven from his hereditary lands, led to strains in English domestic politics, and this made the 1620s a troubled decade after nearly twenty years of what revisionist historians judge as being a quietly successful search for a national consensus.

The historiographical situation is in fact

The Somerset House Conference by Marcus Gheeraerts the Younger. The conference, held in 1604, at which the Spanish peace was negotiated, was attended by six Spanish/Flemish delegates (on the left) and five English delegates (right, from the window): Thomas Sackville, Charles Howard, Charles Blount, Henry Howard and Robert Cecil.

fluid and likely to remain so. It has proved easy to play down the significance of Parliaments before 1621. There were only two. The first sat intermittently from 1604 to 1610, surviving the drastic threat of the popish conspiracy forever associated with Guy Fawkes (1605), some tense matters such as a well-meant but chimerical scheme to put royal finances on a firmer basis

by a Great Contract with Parliament, and a contest over the determination of disputed election returns. The second Parliament, sitting for a couple of weeks in 1614, was addled – in other words it passed no legislation at all. Its impact upon the drift and pace of politics was negligible. In those years, too, the notion of a religious conflict arising out of the Hampton Court Conference (1604), called to discuss moderate reforms of a Puritan sort, has been overstressed – too tightly tied to James's growl about 'no bishop, no king'. Neither in fact was under fire. There were a few ejections of unconformable clerics, and some laymen, who were 'vexed and troubled' about the (generally

acceptable) 'religion of Protestants', went abroad either to the United Provinces or, at length, as Pilgrim Fathers to 'the howling wilderness' of New England, to reinforce the burgeoning English colonization of North America. But to lump these and other critics of this or that part of the government into something called 'the opposition', inside or outside Parliament, is to mislead.

However, sporadic opposition to specific items there certainly was, some of which found a focus in Parliament. James's third assembly (1621) irritated him by attempts in the Commons – the Lords were generally more conciliatory – to discuss, under privilege, 'mysteries of state' like foreign policy. There were fraught moments but there was no sharp cleavage, even when James tore a page out of the *Commons Journal*. The fourth Parliament (1624) met under different circumstances. Buckingham had taken 'Baby Charles' off to Madrid in 1623 to woo, on the spot, an Infanta. It was against James's wishes, but his grip on affairs was relaxing. (He seemed to be becoming prematurely senile.) The trip was a disaster. The two 'boys' came back calling for war. The 'Prince's Parliament', as it was called, was enthusiastic. Twenty years of James's delicate (as he saw them) negotiations had been wasted, but he was so pleased to have both his son and his favourite back safe that he could not bring himself to frustrate their plans for a war. On 27 March 1625 James died quietly in his bed – an unusually natural event for a Stuart. 'The joy of the people devoured their mourning', as the new young King, still an unknown quantity, succeeded, but it was hardly a true augury. Charles was overshadowed by the favourite, Buckingham, who was determined to show that he was something more than just a pretty

211

A COVNTERBLASTE
TO *TOBACCO*.

TO THE READER.

AS euery humane body (deare Countrey men) how wholesome soeuer, is notwithstanding subiect, or at least naturally inclined to some sorts of diseases, or infirmities: so is there no Commonwealth, or Body-politicke, how well gouerned, or peaceable soeuer it be, that lackes the owne popular errors, and naturally inclined corruptions: and therefore is it no wonder, although this our Countrey and Common-wealth, though peaceable, though wealthy, though long flourishing in both, be amongst the rest, subiect to the owne naturall infirmities. We are of all Nations the people most louing, and most reuerently obedient to our Prince, yet are we (as time hath often borne witnesse) too easie to be seduced to make Rebellion vpon very slight grounds. Our fortunate and oft proued valour in warres abroad, our heartie and reuerent obedience to our Princes at home, hath bred vs a long, and a thrice happie peace: Our peace hath bred wealth: And peace and wealth hath brought forth a generall sluggishnesse, which makes vs wallow in all sorts of idle delights, and soft delicacies, the first seedes

ABOVE *The title page of King James's* Counterblast to Tobacco. *Published anonymously in 1604, it sets out his own heartfelt arguments against smoking.*

RIGHT *A contemporary Dutch engraving of the Gunpowder Plot, 1605. It shows (above) the conspirators – a group of Catholics, including Robert Catesby and Guy Fawkes – angered by James's refusal to grant more religious tolerance, and (below) their gruesome deaths after the plot had been discovered.*

face, and who was prepared to take England to war with Spain – and soon with France, also – to prove it.

Traditionally James I has had a bad press. Potentates live by acting. James was a poor actor, not even a 'ham'. Lacking that blend of humanity and regality cultivated by Elizabeth I, scruffy in his dress, loquacious – and in a thick Scots accent at that – impatient, extravagant, sometimes maudlin, too inclined to let his academic intellect overlay his political

James's favourite, George Villiers, Duke of Buckingham, by Daniel Mytens.

nous, James was certainly an oddity. His correspondence with Buckingham is astonishing, swapping four-letter words and allowing his subject to end letters to him with remarks like 'I kiss your dirty hands'. (They were, in fact, dirty.) But historians can point to some positive aspects of his reign, as, for instance, his relations with his Parliaments, from whom he unfailingly got such subsidies as he asked for, or the broad unity of the Church of England, which would only be shattered in his son's reign. If the civil wars to come were England's Wars of Religion, they certainly cannot be blamed either on James's personality or on the general thrust of his reign.

The cultural achievements of these years were considerable. James presided over no secondary age of English civilization. Much of what is popularly ascribed to the golden years of Elizabeth I was really Jacobean. Not only Sir Walter Ralegh – that demonstration that a man can be at once a crook and scarcely less than an angel – but also Shakespeare, Donne, Bacon, Jonson and many more luminaries were at their peak in the early years of the seventeenth century. James appreciated at least some of them. But how far his sleazy court – which for Ralegh 'glowed and shone like rotten wood' – contributed to this more wholesome effulgence remains an open question. But it is evidently too soon to halt the rehabilitation of this most scribacious of monarchs, who wrote intelligently on the divine right of kings and on witchcraft, who gave advice to his heir in his *Basilikon Doron* and who presented a forceful government health warning on tobacco. Perhaps Lord Herbert of Cherbury, who had so many doubts about the worth of Henry VIII, was right about James VI and I – that he 'did live/At once king and shepherd of his sheep'.

OLIVER CROMWELL

1599–1658

IF OLIVER CROMWELL was 'great ere fortune made him so' – as Dryden, to his later regret, wrote in 1658 – little in his early life marked him out from the common run of East Anglian gentry. Born on 25 April 1599, he was a 'Jacobethan', more Elizabethan perhaps than Jacobean. His grammar school at Huntingdon may have moulded him as a Puritan, but it was in the 1620s that he went through 'conversion', that spiritual crisis which makes for a born-again Christian. Afterwards he would boast of having been the greatest of sinners, but was probably just an ordinary young man who after a single, possibly formative, year at Sidney Sussex College, Cambridge, faced the responsibilities of family life.

Cromwell's marriage (1620) to Elizabeth Bourchier, of London merchant stock, was a happy one, producing eight children living in decent comfort in Ely. (After the Restoration Lady Elizabeth Dyott claimed to have been his mistress and there are allusions to an 'M. Cleveland', a natural son. Neither is to be believed.) Legend has Oliver earning from grateful Fenmen, their way of life threatened by draining, the soubriquet 'Lord of the Fens'. He sat, though inconspicuously, in the 1628–29 (Petition of Right) Parliament. In fact, before 1640, he was very much 'a private man'.

In the Short and Long Parliaments elected in 1640, Cromwell appeared for Cambridge town.

In 1641 he spoke up for the religious dissident, John Lilburne, later the unpleasingly stentorian leader of the more or less radical Levellers. Oliver also supported root-and-branch extirpation of episcopacy. In 1642, a good horseman though without military experience, he volunteered for 'King and Parliament', enthusiastic for a cause whose objectives still elude the historian. Currently, the conflicts of the 1640s are taken to be 'England's wars of religion', something like the sixteenth-century French wars of religion. Cromwell himself said that 'religion was not the thing at first contested for, but it came to that in the end'. Anyway, he argued that if a war was to be fought it must be fought hard by men of military talent. Starting with a cavalry troop he soon won a name and promotion in what became the Army of the Eastern Association. In 1645 he became second-in-command of the New Model Army – a professional body, weaned away from the localism that clogged effort on both sides in the conflict. He and his Ironsides were vital at Naseby (14 June 1645) which ensured Parliament's victory in the first civil war.

The shooting war over, Charles I set out to win the peace, finding scope for a divide-and-rule policy within the shaky coalition called Parliament – Presbyterian against Independent, civilian against army, conservative against radical. That determination to 'be king again' underlined the significance of a man like Cromwell – an MP but also a soldier. He came forward as a link between different outlooks, to some a reconciler, to others a fomenter of trouble. This sharp differing of interpretations points to one of Cromwell's enduring qualities – an ambivalence which led him to be taken, notably by friends turned enemies, as a dissembler, a hypocrite. Between 1646 and 1649, with Charles a prisoner successively of the Scots, Parliament and the army (which, meeting resistance to its claims for redress of grievances, was becoming increasingly 'politicized'), Cromwell evolved into 'our chief of men', as Milton called him, thanks less to his initiatives than to his recognition of opportunities. At one moment he appeared to be holding aloof, seemingly inert, and at the next he was abruptly dynamic and decisive in action. 'Waiting on the Lord', he called it, waiting until the finger of Providence pointed out what must be done. This behaviour might be natural, that of a manic-depressive or a latent epileptic, or it might be that of a consummate Machiavellian. Either way it was effective in drawing attention to himself. During his waiting periods he was not solely communicating with God, but listening – he was always a good listener – to more secular counsels. To Providence he was never supine. The Lord, he said, helped only 'tried wrestlers'. In his famous phrase 'trust in God and keep your powder dry', the critical word is 'and'. It cannot be replaced by 'to'. There is reciprocity between the seeker and Providence. And it was this sense of being the recipient of a special dispensation that kept Cromwell going over the next decade; he was the taker and maker of opportunities and for his last five years the *sine qua non* of stability.

All that was a long way off in 1647, but his qualities were revealed in his chairmanship of the 'Putney Debates' (autumn 1647), when the fundamentals of citizenship were discussed, and in his weakening and ultimate destruction (1649) of Levellerism in the name of military discipline. By then Charles I had precipitated a second civil war (1648), which was fiercely fought, not least by Cromwell. When a majority in the Commons pressed to continue negotiations with 'Charles Stuart', an army group organized the Pride's Purge (December 1648) of these members, in order to clear the way to bringing 'that man of blood' to a fitting punishment. Cromwell accepted the Purge *ex post facto* and, though slow to support trial and execution, once he had made up his mind – or Providence had made it up for him – was forceful in bringing them about. At the signing of the death warrant he was elated, like a man 'who had had a cup too many' – a sign of relief from the enormous strain that had preceded a decision.

The Rump of the Commons (what was left after the Purge) went on to abolish monarchy and the House of Lords, as 'useless and dangerous'. The regicide Commonwealth, run by moderate, even conservative men, was beset by enemies, internal and abroad. Cromwell was required to deal with most of them and did, very effectively, stressing his indispensability. Mutinous Levellers in the army were cut to pieces. Catholic Irish, in rebellion since 1641 and now associated with exiled royalists, were battered in a ruthless campaign, with the garrison massacres at Drogheda and Wexford that have made the name 'Cromwell' a curse there ever since. The truth is that Cromwell

Oliver Cromwell, by or after Robert Walker.

*Edward Bower's portrait of Charles I at his trial, 1648.
Found guilty of treason, he was executed in 1649.*

behaved there no worse than most Englishmen of his generation to whom Irish popery and 'incivility' put them literally beyond the pale. On his return, celebrated in Marvell's prophetic *Horatian Ode*, he was sent to Scotland, where the Prince of Wales had been made king. The Stuarts, after all, were a Scottish dynasty. Cromwell won a sharp engagement at Dunbar (3 September 1650), where the help of the Lord was secured by singing the shortest psalm as a preliminary.

A year later to the day Charles was thwarted again in Cromwell's 'crowning mercy' at Worcester. The Prince made a romantic escape to what might have been unending exile. Scotland now lay open to English control but was treated more leniently than Ireland. Meanwhile France and Spain, who might have been expected to intervene against the regicide republic, held off, locked as they were and would be in war against each other till 1659. So the Commonwealth was ostensibly safe but also vulnerable, facing a critical, largely idle army and a dominant Lord General demanding reforms and 'a new representative'. The army was more impatient than its general who once again was the go-between, the honest broker – or the *provocateur*.

Suddenly on 20 April 1653 Cromwell strode into the House of Commons, where they were briskly debating a bill for a new representative body contrary to an agreement reached with the officers the day before. Shouting that they were no Parliament, Oliver had soldiers clear the chamber, ignoring cries that what he was doing was 'against conscience'. Soon afterwards Cromwell and his Council of Officers claimed in a formal declaration that the Rump would have perpetuated itself into the new representative – a charge long accepted by historians and not denied point blank even by the Rumpers themselves. Circumstantial evidence suggests that the truth was rather more complex, but it has yet to show itself clearly. The bill certainly must have had something in it detrimental to the army's and Cromwell's own position.

The Rump was replaced by an Assembly nominated by the Council of Officers (July–December 1653). This new-fangled body was of diverse membership, but not all were par-

Oliver Cromwell, the Lord Protector, portrayed as the saviour of England in a contemporary broadside.

venus or the religious fanatics suggested by the nickname 'Barebones Parliament' after Praise-God Barbon, a London leather-seller, and they did bring in some sensible reforms. But when a minority of radicals threatened legal vested interests and tithes, the moderates engineered a

A Royalist satire on Cromwell and his followers which depicts them consulting with the Devil.

resignation of authority back to Cromwell, who later called the entire experiment 'a story of [his] own weakness and folly'.

A new device was to hand – a Protectorate working within a written constitution, *The Instrument of Government* (December 1653), compiled by Gen. John Lambert, who had helped with the Army Grandees' *Heads of the Proposals* to Charles I in 1647. The Protector was (who else?) Cromwell. He was to be no dictator. The constitution envisaged checks upon the legislature (a single-chamber triennial parliament) and on the head of the executive. The key lay in a Council of State of nominated civilians and swordsmen, among them, not surprisingly, Lambert, regarded by many as Cromwell's understudy. Oliver welcomed 'bounding' of his power, glimpsing beyond the Instrument a settlement within which he might revert to his civilian self. In the meantime he would be 'a good constable to keep the peace of the parish'. But this was not easy, proving the truth of Marvell's prediction that he would have to 'keep the sword erect' since

> The same arts that did gain
> A power must it maintain.

Even after being purged, the first Protectorate Parliament (September 1654 – January 1655) assailed the Instrument and Cromwell's division of its contents into 'fundamentals' (unalterable) and 'circumstantials' (open to amendment). Exasperated, he dissolved it, though, determined to stick to the letter of the constitution, not until it had sat for the stipulated minimum of five months, reckoned as lunar – or 'soldier's' – months of twenty-eight days. There followed immediately a royalist rising in the south-west meant to be part of a nationwide effort. That was enough to justify carving England and Wales into a dozen 'cantons', each under a major-general and a militia, with detailed instructions to provide for security and to tighten up local administration. 'Cromwell's major-generals' – though the scheme was hardly of his devising and he showed little direct interest in it – were not popular with the gentry who had been creeping back as the 'natural rulers' in the localities. Parliament, which had been called in 1656 to vote supply for a war with Spain,

A Dutch engraving of Cromwell's dissolution of the Rump of the Long Parliament on 20 April 1653.

deplored the system. After a perfunctory defence of such 'a little inspection upon the people', Cromwell dropped it without compunction – a striking instance of his pragmatism and continuing urge for a more civilian government. The first session of this Parliament, somewhat purged of known recalcitrants, notably 'Commonwealthsmen' (republicans), proved comparatively amenable. In the case of James Nayler, however, tried within the Commons for 'horrid blasphemy', it impugned the Protectorate policy of broad religious toleration, which was even broader in the implementation than in the letter. But, despite

that, Cromwell let it continue. It passed a mass of routine legislation, public and private, the sort of thing most people expected from a parliament. For Cromwell that was a decided step in the right direction towards normalcy. The constitutional implications of Nayler's case argued for revision of the Instrument, enhancing Parliament's role while releasing Cromwell further from the army, of which he was at once the leader and the led. The solution was to be kingship – a title and an office known, it was claimed, to tradition and the law. Oliver, probably truthfully, said that the title would be a mere 'feather in the cap', but in the event, having consulted Providence and the army, he rejected it. But he accepted the rest of the new constitution (*The Humble Petition and Advice*, May 1657), which included the re-creation of a second chamber, similar to but not the same as the House of Lords, to serve as 'a screen or balance' between Protector and Commons, and in June 1657 he was installed again in an impressive civilian ceremony.

That summer it looked as if Cromwell might yet sheath the Lord General's sword. But a price had to be paid. In a second session (January – February 1658) the Commonwealthsmen, smarting still from April 1653, were allowed back into the Commons where they deployed their notable parliamentary skills to bring the business of 'healing and settling' to a halt. The Protector was provoked into another abrupt dissolution. 'Let God be judge betwixt you and me!' Eight months later he was dead on his 'lucky day', 3 September, the anniversary of Dunbar and Worcester. Within eighteen more months Charles Stuart was back as Charles II – the Restoration.

The connection between these two events is remote. On Cromwell's death the royalists had expected to see a national rising. With the strong man gone, neutrals, moderates and the apathetic would be prepared to have the king over the water wafted home, but nothing of the sort occurred. Oliver's eldest son, Richard, his nominee, succeeded quietly. No Oliver, Richard was no fool either, and while in office performed well. When he saw that he could not keep together the warring advocates of what had once been a single 'Good Old Cause', though always, like 'the fundamental laws', undefined, he sensibly resigned, unwilling to plunge his country into bloodshed. For this survivor, who lived on, despite being a heavy smoker, into the reign of Anne, Voltaire had nothing but admiration. It was not in fact Richard, Oliver, or the royalists, who brought on the Restoration, which was not inevitable, but the sheer inability of its opponents to come together in the early months of 1660 to persuade General George Monck, intervening from Scotland, that there was another way.

Dryden had predicted that Oliver's 'ashes in a peaceful urn shall rest'. It was not to be. His bones were dug up, reviled and thrown symbolically for oblivion into an unmarked hole. But Cromwell was not forgotten then or later. There is uncertainty about just what his legacy was, though religious pluralism, fed by his toleration, was surely a part of it. He remains in popular and informed opinion a maker of England, the subject of an imaginative folklore, music-hall songs and vast historical literature. Neither a radical, nor a conservative, nor a moderate, but a unique blend of all three, he was not a type but an individual, not God's Englishman but one (we hope) of God's many Englishmen, and one who was more eloquent and revealing than most in his remarkable letters and speeches.

CHRISTOPHER WREN

1632–1723

WREN is often thought of as the greatest of English architects, but he was also much more than that. He came to the profession comparatively late in his career as a 'boy wonder', whose activities encompassed a variety of scientific fields, pure and applied. Although he did not publish much of this work – a trait shared with Isaac Newton – he seems throughout his long productive life never to have lost his taste for it and naturally his activity as an architect demanded that he drew a good deal on it. To rebuild London called for technological skills. To design a church that would stay up was as much a scientific and technical effort as an artistic one. Robert Hooke's praise of 'such a mechanical hand, so philosophical a mind' was entirely just.

Christopher Wren was born, like Newton a small and delicate child, at East Knoyle on 20 October 1632. Of mercantile stock, the family had significant ecclesiastical connections. An uncle was Mathew Wren, Bishop of Norwich, a keen adherent of Archbishop William Laud's campaign in the 1630s for unity through uniformity, and a staunch royalist who was lodged securely by Parliament in the Tower from 1643 to 1660. (He would give Christopher an early commission – a worthy piece of nepotism – for a new chapel at Pembroke, Cambridge, to commemorate the Restoration.) Christopher's father was Dean of Windsor, like many of his era a priest with wide interests, some shared with his son. He designed a few buildings himself and, fashionably, landscaped gardens. At Westminster School until 1646, the younger Wren distinguished himself by his aptitude for things mathematical – geometry and chronology. Like the young Newton – there are in fact a number of such parallels – Wren had a fascination for gadgetry. In the late 1640s he lived near Oxford, entering Wadham College in 1649, the first year of the Commonwealth. There he enjoyed the friendship of John Wilkins and Seth Ward, both later bishops, but also scientists and founder-members of the Royal Society. Wren had a wide acquaintance among virtuosi, dilettantes and men of science and affairs – an acquaintance that was deepened and extended over the years by correspondence, conversation and formal discussions.

In 1653, already characterized by the diarist John Evelyn as 'that miracle of youth', he became a Fellow of All Souls and in 1657 Professor of Astronomy at Gresham College, a private forerunner of the Royal Society. As an astronomer he formulated a conception of 'the galaxy as myriads of stars, every one as it were the firmament of another world'. His academic commitments encouraged an interest in technology and the practical applications of science – in telescopes, magnetism, and investigations of the problems of navigation, longitude in particular. Influenced by Bacon, he saw little distinction between thinking and doing and was aware that the apparently trivial might one day turn out to be significant. So, at Gresham College, he contemplated 'new ways of sailing', how to 'write in the dark', 'stay long under water' and 'perfect coaches for ease, strength and lightness'. Like Wilkins he investigated language and ciphers and, as a contemporary of the military revolution, 'inventions in fortifications', which among other things stimulated his appreciation of architecture.

With the Restoration Wren became Savillian Professor of Astronomy at Oxford, but continued to spend a good deal of his time in London, which was more lively than a university town dominated by clerics. Like Pepys and More, he was essentially a Londoner and love of the metropolis was no doubt one of the spurs to his concern for the great rebuilding after the Fire of 1666. It was natural for him to be involved in the foundation of the Royal Society, that copy, with some peculiar native traits, of the *Académie Française*, which was sponsored by Charles II, who had developed in exile a taste for things French, not all of them frivolous. The Society from the start showed itself aware of the likely social responsibilities of science, the necessity of facilitating 'useful inventions' for 'the ease, profit and health' of the nation and, indeed, of humanity, since most Fellows believed with Milton that God revealed himself first to his Englishmen. Like their contemporaries active in the fields of politics, the law and the constitution, they had, in seeking the welfare of the people, an eye to posterity, and none more than Christopher Wren, who throughout the long years of his Fellowship and Presidency (1680–82) was in-

satiable in his curiosity, presenting papers and reports in chemistry, microscopy, motion, anatomy, perspective, medicine, vivisection, optics, comets, the weather and agriculture.

Wren's move to architecture arose directly out of his other interests. It became as it were professional from 1663, although he had already acted as Surveyor-General to the King's Works from 1661. His first major commission was his uncle's chapel (1663–65). The Sheldonian Theatre at Oxford followed, so soon did he display a capability for both sacred and secular building, combining quantity with quality, though he was, of course, not without his failures. In designing and seeing a building through to completion he concerned himself with developments in building materials – the choice of stone, brick, wood, and plaster, whatever was most practical *and* pleasing to the sight. He was challenged too, by the problems of providing adequate acoustics. (Newton tried to check the speed of sound by experiments with the echo in the colonnade of Wren's marvellously idiosyncratic Library for Trinity, Cambridge, 1676–84.)

The Great Fire provided him with an enormous opportunity. Invited to prepare a scheme for an organized rebuilding, he was also put in charge of a team of architects for what might have been the greatest physical memorial to the reign of Charles II. His proposals were, of course, not the only ones. Almost everyone who fancied his own taste came up with a scheme, notably John Evelyn, who deplored the smog of the metropolis. None of them came to anything. The imagination of the citizens of London, individually or through their organizations, was limited by their regrettable, though understandable, desire to take up with the minimum of cost and delay the life and work of the City, which meant in practice putting their homes and municipal buildings swiftly and cheaply 'on their old grounds and foundations'. As so often private interests thwarted public concern. Not everyone could appreciate as Wren did that 'architecture has political uses, public buildings being the ornament of a country. It establishes a nation, draws people and commerce and makes the people love their native country.'

So it was that only a part of Wren's meticulous and systematic urban plan came to life – and that largely in discrete buildings which sprang up in an incongruous and unrelated environment. The citizens' impatience robbed posterity of what might have been Wren's supreme achievement, but at least it allowed him to devote more of his time to other projects. Over the next decades – he lived for an extraordinarily long time – he undertook diverse commissions at Windsor Castle, Westminster Abbey, Temple Bar, Greenwich, Chelsea (Nell Gwynn's hospital), Whitehall, The Customs House, Hampton Court and beyond.

Wren would build more that fifty London churches, the names of whose parishes are a veritable litany of the Church of England – St Benet Fink, St Mary-le-Bow, St Lawrence Jewry, St Stephen Walbrook, St Clement Danes, St Mary Allchurch, St Michael Royal, St Magnus, St Ann and St Agnes. But the major work must be the new St Paul's, with which he was involved from 1668 onwards, first of all in clearing away the old Cathedral, which he had been invited to repair before the Fire, and the rubble of its environs. By the early 1670s he had drawn up a grandiose design that had to be abandoned as far too costly to realize. His second, more modest scheme was accepted in 1675. Work soon started, but the project was

Sir Christopher Wren, with St Paul's Cathedral in the background, by John Closterman.

necessarily long-term and was modified in detail again and again. At one time he seems to have contemplated housing a huge telescope in the south-west tower. Increasingly the cathedral became characteristic of both its designer (who adored domes) and of the architectural style and religious tastes of a new era – the age of the Baroque and the Enlightenment.

There is a truth hidden in the clerihew:

> Sir Christopher Wren
> Went to dine with some men.
> He said, 'If anyone calls
> Tell them I'm designing St Paul's.'

He was a somewhat clubbable man who enjoyed the good things of life, though he could be detached and quizzical. He was pleased to be knighted (1673) and to have a portrait painted by Sir Godfrey Kneller. There is also an

expressive bust by Edward Pierce (*c*.1673). He valued conversation, chiefly about his intellectual and professional interests – 'petrification of bodies', 'plaisters', staining marble, cloth-printing, ghosts and spirits – but no doubt from time to time about lighter matters. He made and kept friends, but his tolerance and generosity were not boundless. He did not always get on well with other architects. Nicholas Hawksmoor, who, starting as a clerk, became an assistant and then, working on his own account, a genuine rival, did not long keep Wren's goodwill. On the other hand there was a bond of respect between him and Vanbrugh, possibly because the latter's talents for domestic as opposed to public building meant no direct competition. Wren did, in fact, design a few country houses, mostly modest, but many of those attributed to him were clearly by other hands, some of them actually antedating the Restoration.

Wren was a family man, married in 1661 to Faith Cogill, who came from his homeland. The union seems to have been a loving one which produced two sons. Faith died of smallpox in 1675. He remarried in 1677, rather higher up the social scale, Jane Fitzwilliam, daughter of Lord Lifford, by whom he quickly had a son and a daughter. After Jane's death in 1680 he was through with marriage, but the Wrens were a close-knit family as his nephew Christopher's great compilation *Parentalia* demonstrates. Other interests included public affairs. He had a brief parliamentary career, of a Tory inclination but not too partisan. He sat at first for Plympton, Devon. In the first two Parliaments after the Revolution he was elected

The interior of Wren's masterly Library at Trinity College, Cambridge.

for Windsor but was rejected by the Commons Committee on Disputed Elections. In 1701–2 he got in for Weymouth. His prime concern as an MP seems to have been getting support for financing the rebuilding of St Paul's. He had a few forays into commercial speculation, often connected with building, although his membership of the Council of the Hudson's Bay company would seem to have been more adventurous. He died quietly at home on 25 February 1723, sitting in his chair, nodding off after dinner. He was in his nineties – a remarkable tribute to the connection between unceasing activity and longevity. Naturally he was buried in St Paul's.

Christopher Wren is certainly the best-known of all English architects. He was perhaps fortunate to live at a time of great rebuilding, which was not only taking place in London after the Great Fire. It was also an age when there was great scope for his extraordinary range of additional skills and interests, notably through the Royal Society. Praise has never been universal. Even his masterpiece, St Paul's, has its detractors – too vast, too cold. Diverse opinion about him only emphasizes the complexity of his character (many aspects of which we can only guess at) and his achievement. Critics have suggested that the artist was inhibited by the scientist, too concerned with rules (particularly mathematical ones) and inclined to restrict his imagination, which he once said, though he can hardly have meant it, 'blinds the judgement'. Admirers argue that, in fact, Reason and Fancy made in him about as strong a union as is feasible in any human being.

Wren is reputed to have said that if you would see his monument you should look around. He presumably meant St Paul's. The

ABOVE *An eighteenth-century print of St Paul's. The zenith of Wren's achievements, it was finished in 1709.*

RIGHT *The interior of the domed St Stephen, Walbrook (1672–87), one of Wren's most original City churches.*

observer can make up his own mind about Wren's style, its nature and quality. He was a supreme self-taught architect, applying his knowledge from other fields in an idiosyncratic fashion and studying available illustrated treatises by leading foreign architects. He made only one trip abroad – to the area around Paris during a few months in 1665–6 – and positively declined to go south to Italy, on the grounds that what there was to see there was hardly worth the journey. This makes him sound more of a philistine than he was. Wren was capable of absorbing influences and particularly during his long, some think too long, reign as *the* royal architect, of giving them. Think of the list of his assistants and rivals – Hawksmoor, Vanbrugh and Gibbs. Yet it would be hard to identify a positive 'tribe of Wren'. He was too individual, too aloof, too 'different' for that.

SAMUEL PEPYS

1633–1703

THE YEAR 1659 saw the collapse of the Cromwellian Protectorate and the disintegration of the 'Good Old Cause' into disparate causes, bringing the country near to anarchy. On the last day of the year General George Monck, commander of a politically neutered army in Scotland, crossed the border into England at Coldstream to stabilize the situation, though just how was not clear. The next day a twenty-seven-year-old civil servant, sensing that 1660 would be a year to remember, sat down to start a diary that would record and comment idiosyncratically on both his private and professional life, alongside some of the news of the time. He began with a summary of the political situation, which he saw as very fluid, and of his own 'private condition', 'blessed be God ... in good health', 'living in Axe Yard, having my wife and servant Jane, and no more in family than us three. My wife, after the absence of her terms for seven weeks, gave me hopes of her being with child, but on the last day of the year she hath them again. . . .' That same day his wife burned her hand 'dressing the remains of a turkey'. He himself stayed 'at home all the afternoon, looking over [his] accounts'.

The tone of Pepys's *Diary* had been set. Written in a type of shorthand, perhaps simply for the diarist's own gratification and certainly not for publication within his own lifetime, it was surely intended for preservation. He kept it up religiously until 31 May 1669, when, fearing he was going blind, he gave up 'the keeping of [his] Journal' in his own hand, while contemplating for a while one dictated to amanuenses. That would have to be a very different sort of journal, since he could ask them to set down 'no more than was fit for them and all the world to know'. Although in the event his eyes did not give out, he was never a diarist again, apart from penning a few short pieces such as a 'journal' of his 1683 visit to Tangier. But over nine years he had filled six plump volumes, which went posthumously along with his splendid eclectic library – ranging from richly decorated manuscript maps to penny chapbooks – to Magdalene College, Cambridge, where it lay unnoticed until the *Diary* was transcribed and published in 1825, though bowdlerized throughout. Pepys's *Diary* was popular from the start, but although subsequent editions were fuller, none was complete. Not until 1977–83 was there what can fairly be called the definitive edition, in eleven volumes of text, commentary and annotations, edited by Robert Latham and William Matthews, though there will always be a demand for the 'Everyman Pepys' or a 'Shorter Pepys', abridged, but not, in these more permissive days, bowdlerized.

'Pepys' and 'Diary' have become synony-

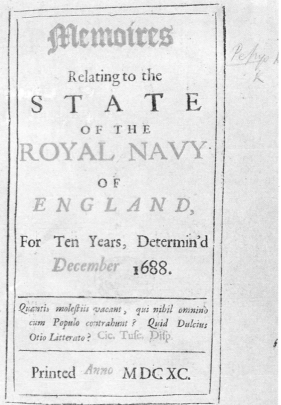

Title page of Samuel Pepys's Memoires of the Royal Navy, *published in 1690.*

mous, but there was more to him than that. When he started it he was already a man of affairs, a professional of proven quality, who, though supported by the patronage of Edward Montagu, would rise by his own talents. Even without the *Diary* he would have earned at least a footnote in the histories of his times. Born on 23 February 1633, just off Fleet Street, he was a Londoner all his life and would have agreed with Samuel Johnson that to be tired of

London was to be tired of life. The Pepyses had an East Anglian lineage with some connection with the Montagus of Hinchingbroke, Huntingdon, where Samuel had a little schooling before going on in the late 1640s to St Paul's. 'A good Roundhead', he saw Charles I executed in 1649, as he would recall on 30 January 1660. (The unforeseen nature of the Restoration is shown by his comment that day that 'General Monck doth resolve to stand to the [Rump] Parliament and nothing else.' Pepys himself spent the evening 'knocking up nails for [his] hats and cloaks in [his] chamber'.)

He entered Magdalene in 1651 and graduated in 1654, shortly after the inauguration of the Protectorate of Oliver Cromwell, of whose Council of State Edward Montagu, who gave Pepys his first job, was a member. Secretary to so considerable a naval person as Montagu was a good start for a bright young man on the make, enough to encourage him to marry in 1655 the fifteen-year-old daughter of a Huguenot merchant in the City, Elizabeth de Saint-Michel. The *Diary* tells us a good deal about her – her good looks, for instance, which were much admired by her husband and, to his satisfaction, by others. Though seen only through Pepys's eyes, she comes over as a decided personality in her own right. They did a lot together, often in bed, talking about this and that. But he also records his own in-

Pepys's wife Elizabeth, from an edition of his Diary *published in 1825.*

fidelities to her, actual or in fantasy. In 1662 he comments on the beauty of Charles II's mistress, the Lady Castlemaine, feeling some pity for her 'though I know well enough she is a whore'. Three years later he was dreaming of being in bed with her. Bed turns up frequently in the *Diary*, not always for sex, indeed, mostly for sleep and relaxation. Though essentially hard-working, Pepys was not a 'workaholic'. He liked to linger in bed in the mornings with or without his wife. We find him at home one Sunday doing his accounts in his nightgown.

In the hectic eighteen months or so between the death of Oliver Cromwell (3 September 1658) and the Restoration in May 1660, Pepys's progress continued to be tied up with Montagu's work with the navy, which throughout the interregnum was less of a political force and certainly less radical than the army. Loyal to the Cromwells while they lasted, Montagu began to drift towards royalism from the middle of 1659. Retiring to cultivate his garden at Hinchingbroke, he kept in touch with what was going on in the capital – 'the hub that turned the wheel of the commonwealth' – through Pepys. Perhaps it was this task that led Samuel to start the *Diary*, where a fair amount of directly political news and views is put down. When the Convention Parliament decided in April 1660 that 'the government is, and ought to be, by King, Lords and Commons', it sent Montagu to Holland to bring Charles Stuart home. Pepys went with him, seeing for the first time the affable monarch whom he would meet many more times therafter. Montagu won royal favour, becoming 'vice-admiral of the kingdom'. He did not forget his efficient young secretary. Pepys was soon appointed Clerk to the Acts of the Navy Board.

Over the next few years he worked his way steadily upward in naval administration, helped by patronage, certainly, but justifying himself by talent, energy and reliability. He came into contact with James, Duke of York, who had been born in the same year as himself and whom he had met at The Hague in 1660. They got on well together. Both were brisk, liking things to be yare, ship-shape and Bristol fashion. Samuel was a natural bureaucrat, in the best sense. Office gave him the chances, which he took, to use his initiative and those powers of flexible organization, which the *Diary* shows he brought to his private life, too. Indeed, without them he could hardly have combined business with pleasure in such a positive way. Business, never for him an evil or a bore, chimed well with the cultivation of his tastes for the theatre, music, books and art, still leaving him time and vitality for 'a great deal of merry discourse', interlarded with drinking, eating and strolling about town. No wonder, though, that he would on occasion fall asleep during 'the Lord's day' sermons. But he could stay awake often enough to have an opinion to record of a good many of them. Pepys was by no means indifferent to religion. He became very worried about his wife resolving to turn papist. In the *Diary* Sunday was always referred to as 'the Lord's day' – a hint of Puritan phraseology.

In the *Diary*, too, he looks back sometimes with respect and almost with nostalgia to his formative years during the interregnum. Although he quickly adapted himself to the atmosphere and ethos of the Restoration with its sharp reaction against all that had happened during 'the late troubles', he could not quite shake off the earlier experience. The *Diary* reveals a more than sneaking regard for Crom-well and many of those left over from the 1650s who were unable or unwilling to come to terms with the new regime. In February 1667, 'in good company' over dinner at The Sun in Leadenhall Street, 'there was much talk about Cromwell, all saying that he was a brave fellow and did owe his crown he got to himself as much as any man that ever got one.' Some months later he reports a conversation in which 'we run over many persons and things and see nothing done like men like to do well while the King minds his pleasures so much. We did bemoan it that nobody would or had authority enough with the King to tell him how all things go to wrack and will be lost.' Such passages help to explain the secret nature of the *Diary* more perhaps than the references to Pepys's (not very disturbing) sexual peccadilloes.

In the 1660s navy matters were never mere routine. War with the Dutch exposed flaws at all levels, on sea as on land. Corruption, speculation, waste and incompetence were rife. Pepys confronted all these ills with a patient optimism. He found no magic wand to wave them away but he put a sharp, trained mind to work. Painstaking, tactful but firm, he gradually forced through improvements in attitudes and practices, winning the co-operation and respect of superiors, colleagues and subordinates, though alienating some. Beyond the years of the *Diary*, the onset of eye troubles, the death of Elizabeth and other bereavements, the work went on. Promotion to the Secretaryship to the Admiralty Commission meant tougher assignments but wider scope, too, for professional skills and ingenuity. At the time of the Popish Plot (1678) his close association with the Duke of York brought a set-back. He was put in the Tower on some sort of suspicion but

A page from Pepys's Diary*, written in shorthand.*

was soon released. However, an embattled government, confronting the Exclusion Crisis (1679–81), with the Duke of York again the target, had to dispense for a while with Pepys's services, although he was not completely cut off from court. Charles II evidently enjoyed Pepys's company. At Newmarket in October 1680 he dictated to him a circumstantial account of his adventures after the 'Worcester Fight' (1651), his hiding in an oak tree at Boscobel and his miraculous escape to the continent. This narrative, preserved at Magdalene, Pepys took down in much the same shorthand as in the *Diary*. It was published in 1766 from a longhand transcript made under Pepys's own supervision and somewhat enhanced by the results of his own inquiries.

After a number of one-off jobs, such as his inspection tour at Tangier, Pepys went back to the navy as Secretary for Admiralty Affairs, shortly before Charles died (February 1685). During the brief years of James II he carried on working hard to bring in reforms. The Revolution of 1688–89 put him in a quandary. He found that his conscience would not let him break his earlier oath to a legitimate and anointed king, particularly one with whom he had worked upon such intimate terms towards a common objective. Unable to swear allegiance to William and Mary, he retired to private life. Much remained to be done for the improvement of the ships, commissariat and personnel of the fleet, but its performance in the wars to come against France showed that he had done enough to earn some part at least of Sir Arthur Bryant's accolade, 'the saviour of the navy'.

Though retired, Pepys could not be idle. Still emphatically a Londoner, he lived in the Strand, keeping in contact with the virtuosi of the Royal Society, where he had been elected to a Fellowship in 1666 and the Presidency in 1684–86. He spent a good deal of time and money on his library, which he would leave in trust to his nephew by marriage, John Jackson, who was required to pass it intact to Magdalene and who loyally did so in 1724. There – and not only through the preservation of the marvellous *Diary* – it has fulfilled Pepys's purpose of making a contribution 'for the benefit of posterity'. The marriage to Elizabeth had been childless and he did not venture into matrimony again, although he did have a long happy domestic relationship with his housekeeper, Mary Skynner, a great-grand-daughter of Lord Chief Justice Edward Coke. She was with him when on 26 May 1703 he died at the home of an old friend at Clapham. In 1983 a monument was erected to him, aptly in Seething Lane where his work for the navy in the first year of the *Diary* had begun.

Pepys has recently been characterized as 'a bourgeois soul', an abstraction as repellent as it is cryptic. He was, in fact, above all an individual, a recognizable human being, one of his times to be sure but with something to offer all ages. With no want of faults and foibles, revealed to us both consciously and unconsciously, but with many appealing features alongside the prejudices and unkindnesses so laconically set down, he makes it pleasurable and profitable to meet him at home or abroad in the streets, taverns and offices of his London. Any page of the *Diary*, taken at random, has its felicities. For example, in the account of the Great Fire of London in September 1666, he met the Lord Mayor 'in Canning Street, like a man spent, with a handkerchief about his neck', crying 'like a fainting woman, "Lord, what can I do? I am spent! People will not obey me. I have been pulling down houses. But the fire overtakes us faster than we can do it."' He went on 'that for himself he must go and refresh himself, having been up all night. So he left me, and I him, and walked home – seeing people almost all distracted and no manner of means used to quench the fire....'

We are left, historians and general readers alike, with but one regret about Pepys – that in 1669 he shut the window he had opened in 1660. But it is good to know that in the event he did not have to endure 'all the discomforts that [would] accompany ... being blind', a state for which in the last words of the *Diary*, after recording an hour or two in good company 'at the World's End, a drinking house by the park, and there merry; and so home late', he calmly asked 'the good God prepare me'. The pen was laid down – 'and so', no doubt, 'to bed!'

An elaborately decorated piece of calligraphy from Pepys's own collection.

ISAAC NEWTON

1642–1727

BY 1700 Isaac Newton was secure in his reputation as the greatest English scientist of his time – the culmination of 'the scientific revolution of the seventeenth century', associated in England with the influences of Gresham's College and the Royal Society and the names of Bacon, Harvey, Boyle, Ray, Halley, Hooke, Wilkins and many another. Newton surpassed them all in the breadth and depth of his accomplishments. Pure and applied mathematician, physicist, chemist, astronomer, he was also a practical man of affairs – Master of the Mint, President for more than twenty years of the Royal Society and regarded with awe as a polymath. Much of his work has, of course, been overtaken but it laid firm foundations. Not everything, indeed, perhaps little, of what he did was wholly original. Samuel Johnson with his usual perspicacity observed that 'he stood alone merely because he left the rest of mankind behind him, not because he deviated from the beaten track.' There is only a little truth in Pope's ecstatic couplet:

Nature and Nature's laws lay hid in night,
God said, 'Let Newton be!', and all was light.

no more than in the twentieth-century riposte:

It did not last. The Devil howling 'Ho!
Let Einstein be!', restored the status quo.

Newton portrayed himself as seeing further because he stood on the shoulders of the giants of the past, but braced himself to take the strain of his successors. No doubt most of his work on gravity, the calculus and the spectrum would have been done over the next few decades by others asking similar questions, but Newton got there first, the original if not the only begetter, much as Darwin did with the Theory of Evolution, though Wallace was already well advanced with his own.

Isaac Newton was born on Christmas Day 1662 at Woolsthorpe, near Grantham, the posthumous offspring of a fairly well-to-do yeoman, whose family had quietly risen from obscurity in the sixteenth century. (Isaac would later display a concern for his ancestry, acquiring a coat of arms to go with his knighthood in 1705.) He was a small, frail baby, perhaps premature, not expected to survive, but in fact he lived well into his eighties. He was short and stocky – in later years a little overweight. In old age he was still clear in his thoughts, even after a lifetime of unremitting activity. In the things of the mind he was a tireless traveller, although physically he never left England and never went further north than Lincolnshire or even as far west as Oxford.

His mother soon remarried a local cleric, Barnabas Smith. Through him young Isaac had access to a decent library, chiefly theological, a point of some significance in his intellectual development. At Grantham Grammar School he benefited from a standard classical education. An energetic, curious youth, skilled with his hands in making tools and devising gadgets, and observant of the natural environment, he was, however, not cut out by temperament or inclination for rural life. Already rather solitary and intolerant of distraction, he was adjudged by his family to be 'fit for nothing but the 'versity'.

So in July 1660, just after Charles II came back home, Isaac Newton arrived at Trinity, Cambridge, armed with a supply of ink, paper, candles and a chamber-pot, ready to work his way through college. He was soon filling notebook after notebook with his observations, calculations, deductions and experiments, intermingled with quotations culled from voracious reading. They reveal how early on he was taken into the fields with which his name is chiefly associated – dynamics, optics, fluids, astronomy, scientific instruments. Mathematics crops up in 1663, seemingly of its own accord – Newton was proud of being self-taught – but possibly due to the influence of the new Lucasian Professor of Mathematics, Isaac Barrow. Cambridge reinforced Newton's natural tendency to be solitary, marking him out for bachelordom and the avoidance of intimate friendships outside of professional interests. (Contemporaries commented on the coldness of his temperament.)

In 1664 he got a college scholarship and with it more time for research and reflection. He had already shown himself to be an original thinker, with an enviable capacity to pursue lines of thought rigorously, but at the same time he was intuitive and imaginative. At the age of twenty-six he would already have achieved much of his major mathematical work. In the mid-1660s, driven away from Cambridge by the plague, he returned for a while to Lincolnshire, but there was no going back to the rustic life. He took his work with him and continued to develop his propensity for identifying problems, which is well on the way to solving them. He could combine hard thinking with experimentation, which mostly seemed quite simple, but, infused by his genius, had dramatic results – as, for instance, in his use of a prism picked up at Stourbridge Fair in his work on optics.

The year 1667 was something of an *annus mirabilis* in which he did major work on fluxions (the differential calculus), gravity and optics. Little of it became immediately apparent. He was slow to publish, perhaps out of modesty, perhaps from an unwillingness to provoke controversy – although later he would conduct a long and bitter 'priority' dispute with Leibnitz over who first worked on flux-

Sir Isaac Newton, in a painting attributed to John Vanderbank, c. 1726.

ions. Perhaps he regarded preparing work for the press as mere drudgery. (That the great *Principia Mathematica* was eventually published in 1686–87 was almost entirely owing to the efforts of Edmund Halley.) In 1667, too, he became a Lucasian Professor. A Trinity Fellowship followed in 1669, then the Fellowship of the Royal Society in 1672. (He would be its President from 1705 to his death.) Time, fame and circumstance brought him somewhat out of the life of the recluse. London competed with Cambridge. In 1689 and again in 1701 he represented the University in Parliament. As Warden (1696) and soon Master (from 1699) of the Mint he showed himself practical and effective, a reformer at a time when the economic development of England emphasized monetary confidence. His reports on the Mint were regarded as particularly relevant. His posts at the Mint, incidentally, were well paid and, by living modestly, some would say stingily, and keeping careful accounts, he amassed a fortune.

For the last few decades of his life he was universally respected as a great scientist and a great Englishman, an ornament to his country and his times. Although contemporaries might not have understood just what it was that he had done, they glimpsed that it was significant. When he died, it was natural that his body should lie in state at Westminster Abbey.

Newton's view of the universe is of a vast mechanism set going by God, the first and most elaborate of clockmakers. (The metaphor is apt for the age which produced Thomas Tompion, creator of the most distinguished English timepieces.) The machinery ticked over according to laws fixed by the Creator, to whom the falling of a sparrow – or of an apple – was as of much concern as the movement of the planets. The latter moved in accordance with the music of the spheres, appreciation of which is part of the true worship of God. Aware of the force of his own intellect, Newton knew that the universe could proceed only with 'the counsel and dominion of an intelligent and powerful being' whose mind, like his peace, 'passes all understanding', but which God expected his creatures, men (Newton seems to have expressed no views on women), to seek to probe. Newton's universe has indeed been characterized as 'a cryptogram set by the Almighty', requiring hard thinking and experimentation (which is applied thought) to find a resolution. That, though ultimately impossible to uncover, must be attempted by man confidently deploying the reasoning powers with which an all-seeing but benevolent Father has endowed his children.

God allows for many Newtons. Until recently admirers have concentrated on Newton the scientist's scientist, whose outlook and fields of interest coincided with what was expected from a man of the age of Enlightenment. But the other Newtons – the theologian, the biblical chronologist and the alchemist – caused some embarrassment. This work, which even a cursory glance shows was extensive, profound and absorbing to its exponent, was charitably put down to a natural and forgivable relaxation on the part of an austere genius who took infinite pains in more important spheres. The intellectual climate of the late twentieth century, less certain than the nineteenth (except perhaps among some economists) about what is rational and what is not, has brought us to look again and more objectively at the beliefs and practices of our ancestors, which, especially in such areas as the occult, had been too readily dismissed as the activities of a 'lunatic fringe'. Just as Napier, the inventor of logarithms, regarded his interpretations of the book of *Revelation* as of equal value, Newton equated mechanics with theology, alchemy and optics. For him they were all of a piece, equally engrossing, equally respectable, equally deserving of his time and thought. Religion and alchemy were not hobbies for his lighter moments. He had few of those and is reputed to have laughed once and once only. Alchemy and religion were indeed central to his life and outlook. He therefore felt justified in reproving Halley, guilty as he saw it of superficial comment upon sacred matters, with the words 'I have studied these things. You have not.' For him one of the values of his scientific work was that it strengthened his religious beliefs. Much the same line was also taken by Boyle, the 'sceptical chymist'. Newton never published his alchemical work, not because he was ashamed of it, but because it dealt with matters so profound that he felt that premature disclosure might be dangerous. Newton was, perhaps, the first of modern scientists. He was also 'the last of the magicians'. One study of his alchemy concludes that 'Newton is the century's epitome; his great synthetic mind wove its multiple strands together to make a new tapestry.'

Integration is indeed the keynote of his life and labours, bringing together the work of the giants of the ancient world, the Renaissance and his own unique and inimitable qualities. This view is clinched by the catalogue of his library. There Boyle and the Classics jostle with tomes on sacred history, Bibles in umpteen languages, sermons, tracts, alchemical treatises, topography and records of travel. There is some 'imaginative' literature and plays, though no Shakespeare, some history and biography, only a couple of volumes of Bacon, but rather more Locke and works on trade and political economy. Among them all, typically, was a whole lot of notebooks into which he jotted down throughout a lifetime the quotations and the first thoughts that led him into his works of accomplished magnitude. Reading for him was not an end in itself, but a springboard into the great ocean of scholarship and discovery, where he swam as to the manner born.

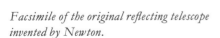

Facsimile of the original reflecting telescope invented by Newton.

129

ROBERT WALPOLE

1676–1745

THE CENTRAL fact of Sir Robert Walpole's career is his long tenure of political power during the 1720s and 1730s, within a period commonly characterized as 'the Whig Ascendancy'. Censured in 1739 by an eclectic opposition, including disgruntled Whigs, he said himself that his 'great and personal crime' had been his 'long continuance in office or . . . the long exclusion of those who now complain against [him]. They clamour for a change of measures but mean only change of ministers.' He is also credited with being 'the first Prime Minister', but such an office was not really feasible when the Kings, George I and George II, under whom he served, certainly ruled as well as reigned and when a party system, if born, was still in its infancy. The honour belongs less to Walpole, Samuel Johnson's 'fixed Star', than to his 'meteor', the Younger Pitt, and even he claimed to be merely *primus inter pares*.

Born on 26 August 1676, Robert Walpole was the third son, fifth of nineteen children of a father who was himself one of thirteen. Robert the elder was a hardworking, innovative farmer, well read, with a fine library. The family claimed to have been in Norfolk since at least the Conquest – Walpole was a village not far from Houghton, their seat since the twelfth century. For hundreds of years Walpoles, as their marriage alliances attest, looked solely for a local role, but by careful estate management they were set to extend their activities, including election to Parliament, under the early Stuarts. Young Robert went to Eton, thence to King's, Cambridge, to be called home in 1698, now heir through the deaths of elder brothers, to help an ailing father to run estates rich in corn and cattle. His father's death in 1700 could have meant an entirely rustic future. Instead, in 1701, having lavishly 'entertained' the electors, he became MP for Castle Rising, and within three days of the opening of Parliament was on a Commons committee. He enjoyed it. Making it his 'business' – a word he used with more respect than did Sir Thomas More – to pursue the interests (as he saw them) of Norfolk, he also set out in broader terms to become fully cognizant of that world of place-hunters, patriots, men of party and principle, which was Parliament and, beyond that, the court and the country of England of the later Stuarts. He learned fast, although he never seemed in a hurry 'because he always did [things] with method'. Hard-headed, unsentimental to the point of cynicism, he would play the system well, particularly in dealing with individuals and small groups, although throughout his career he was less happy with public opinion generally. But only at particular times was that an inhibition. Though the electorate was increasing through the growth of national wealth and population, politics was still very much the direct concern of a narrow élite – landed, financial and commercial interests – and of the Crown. It was a ministry's task to keep them all – groups and individuals – satisfied or at any rate content in some sort of working relationship. After a protracted apprenticeship Walpole mostly managed it. Hence his ultimate ascendancy.

During Anne's reign he mastered the financial conduct of his estates and, moving upward, of the various offices that came his way. Coarse, short and fat (gross, indeed, in his later years), he remained somewhat bucolic and seems in fact to have gone out his way to cultivate the image of one who would as soon scratch a pig's back as a politician's. But his brown eyes were watchful, hiding a working brain that thrived on technicalities, categorizing men and things, filing details away in a memory, which was readily drawn upon for information and 'know-how'. He became both a first-rate administrator and a subtle politician.

After being a member of a committee to advise the Lord High Admiral – Anne's amiable consort, George of Denmark – Walpole became in the latter stages of the War of the Spanish Succession Secretary-at-War and a member of the Council of the Admiralty, posts which brought contacts with leading politicians and in which he was able to build upon organization already undertaken by highly efficient administrators like William Blathwayt. Walpole was not an outright innovator. Always assiduous in his MP's duties, he took a leading part in the impeachment of the turbulent priest, Dr Henry Sacheverell, for a seditious sermon, and attacked his opinions on the Glorious Revolution as 'rubbage' and contrary to common sense. The performance

enhanced his reputation as an orator and debater. In the 1710 election he was thwarted in a bid to become a Norfolk knight of the shire but got in for King's Lynn, which he stuck to for the rest of his Commons career. With the Tories in power he was out of office during Anne's last years, but attracted attention by his vigorous defence of the financial honesty of 'the late administration', including, of course, his own. Already he was regarded as 'the master of figures of his time'. But he was voted guilty of 'corrupt practices' and confined for a while in the Tower. At about this time Swift sneered at his 'indifference to any principle' and his 'bold forward confidence'. Walpole would

Sir Robert Walpole, painted by Sir Godfrey Kneller, c. 1710–1715.

not have resented the second phrase, assured as he was that if there was a job to be done, he was the man to do it. He had no fixed plans for reform or constitutional change, but of course, over the four decades of his political life, change (as, for instance, in the development of the Cabinet) did come, though hardly because he positively willed it.

Walpole was a devoted Hanoverian and took office in the Whig ministry which, surprisingly with the dying Anne's blessing (July 1714), wrecked the grandiloquent Bolingbroke's scheme to subvert the succession. By September George of Hanover (great-grandson of James I's daughter, Elizabeth of Bohemia) was in London as George I, convinced of the unreliability of the Tories and ready to reward the Whigs, though not to put himself completely into their hands. As Paymaster, Walpole worked ably for the Crown, but was also in a position, which the extension of

The first lines of a broadside of 1730, aimed at Walpole (nicknamed Robin) and his monopoly of power.

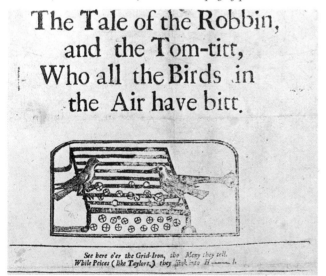

Houghton, its contents and its estates suggests he took, to help himself to wealth and influence. Not for the first time 'true self love and social [were] the same'. He used his growing power, too, to wipe out the Tories, whom he consistently associated with Jacobitism (support for the exiled Stuarts), inflating its threat to the security of the British Isles even after the failure of the 1715 revolt. Recent work suggests that his suspicions had some basis in reality. More overtly, within the apparent stability of the politics of the Whig Ascendancy there was continuing intrigue, with malcontent Whigs joining Tories, while among the ministers themselves personal and other rivalries for promotion and patronage, never enough to satisfy all claimants, meant that even the firmest political friendships could not be relied upon.

Walpole was still a long way from the seat of power. The high politics of the reigns of the first two Georges were too complicated to be readily summarized, even when concentrating on Walpole's rise. But two episodes deserve attention. One was the struggle over the Peerage Bill of 1719, which, by fixing the number of peers and curtailing the royal prerogative to make more, would have made the peerage something of a caste and destroyed the safety valve contained in the threat of mass creation of peerages in crises such as that of the Reform Bill of 1831–2 and the Parliament Bill of 1911. Walpole spoke against it with such force that its defeat focused attention on his genius. But it was overtaken by the bursting of the South Sea Bubble – a tale of financial euphoria, chicanery, ineptitude and luck (good and bad) – which has been taken as a turning point in Walpole's career and as an example of his consummate skills. The record shows, in fact, that Walpole was neither as far- nor as

clear-sighted in the furore as might be supposed, but that, having like the rest made
mistakes, he recognized them and swiftly
moved to extricate himself and (very important) the King and his entourage from the
consequences of their own greedy folly. Public
credit was restored as much by 'market forces'
as by Walpole's wizardry as Chancellor of the
Exchequer. It was the unforeseen death of the
Earl of Sunderland that clinched Walpole's
emergence as 'the first servant of the Crown'.
George I still looked on him with suspicion but
accepted that Walpole really was indispensable
in controlling the Commons, where he continued to build by patronage upon an almost
impregnable power base. Success bred success
but not over-confidence. Walpole was, indeed,
a prime exponent of politics as the art of the
possible, which consists not in accepting the
possible as constrained within fixed limits but
in calling for flexibility and thoughtful
enterprise.

Walpole's inclinations were always towards
domestic politics. His love of peace was genuine enough, and it was strengthened by his
particular concern with the economy, but was
also perhaps a reflection of a weaker grasp of
foreign affairs. This was a matter of some
significance since the two Georges were devoted to the interests of their Hanoverian
patrimony within a German and European
context. Since a – if not the – vital strand in the
rope that pulled men to power was royal
confidence and backing, Walpole had perforce
to take these things seriously and did so. It is a
tribute to his capacity that he was able to keep
out of military adventures as long as he did.

How did Walpole, having got into power in
the early 1720s, keep it until the late 1730s?
There are many reasons given different em-

phases by historians and biographers, but most
would agree that the top priority was his strong
relationship with two successive kings, George
I (to 1727) and George II for the next dozen
years or so. With George I he was on a less sure
footing. There was no personal warmth between them. George II was more trusting and
easy-going, especially as Walpole was favoured
by the Queen, Caroline, with whose opulent
body the King was so besotted that he was
inclined to be open to her political persuasive-
ness. But neither George I or George II could
be taken for granted by their ministers. Walpole appreciated that and took care to keep
them informed and involved, subtly moulding
'the decision-making process'. He talked to
and not at them (to George I in French in
which the King was fluent, while Walpole
evidently had at least a Churchillian smatter-
ing). He listened as well and got most of what
he wanted by persuading them, often correctly,
that that was what they – and the country –
wanted, too.

After the Crown came the court generally,
the ministry itself and Parliament. All called for
constant consideration; command was never
outright. The role of the Lords then (and since)
should not be underrated. Peers had a natural
influence. But it was the Commons, the representative House, which provided money,
'the sinews of government', and the fact that
only towards the end of his life did Walpole
take the peerage that would surely have been
his for the asking shows how seriously he took
the lower chamber. Walpole was not unim-
pressed by honours. He delighted in being a
Knight of the Bath and of the Garter, as much
of the decor at Houghton, well on the way to
becoming a great show-piece, reveals. But to
the Commons he devoted much of his time and

energy, by constant attendance, speaking in the debates, respecting the back-benchers and generally convincing them that here was a sound House of Commons man. The Septennial Act, though designed to ease the transition to the Hanoverians, also contributed to his standing in the Commons by limiting the frequency of elections to seven years. But it was patronage, at once a fuel and lubricant, which kept the administration and the parliamentary machine ticking over in both Houses (including the episcopal bench). Walpole sensed that it was not enough to buy sycophants; he must also have men capable of doing his jobs, few of which were out-and-out sinecures. The trouble was that there was not enough patronage to go round even that narrow élite. The numbers of disappointed – and therefore discontented – applicants grew. Within Walpole's own Whig party, which was never a monolith anyway, there were strains, including one of particular concern involving his old personal friend, Townshend, which culminated in the latter's exclusion by 1730 from the inner Cabinet, the small group of major office-holders with whom it was possible and essential to produce a unanimity of recommendations to put to the King. And those who fell from power – or were pushed away – did not always disappear but rather found a welcome haven in some opposition group.

The precariousness of Walpole's position was exposed in the furore over the Excise Bill of 1733. He extricated himself from that, but, growing older, he knew that sometime sooner or later his power must come to an end. He could maintain a unified control more or less of the British Isles. He could keep Britain out of the War of the Polish Succession (1733), but not out of the War of Jenkins' Ear (1739),

which was the product of a more than spontaneous expression of hysterical chauvinism. It was the effect of a concerted drive by a ragbag of unscrupulous opponents to get 'the great man' out of office. It was becoming clear that Walpole's removal alone could check the momentum towards breakdown. In time he saw it himself and offered his resignation to the King, symbolically underlining that it was the Crown and not Parliament or public opinion that made and unmade a minister. George II reluctantly accepted. Walpole at last took a peerage as first Earl of Orford. But he was still not devoid of interest or influence and still played something of 'the game behind the curtain', occasionally making a major speech in the Lords. He spent more time – and money – on Houghton, but could never be said to have retired there. Not till his death on 18 March 1745 did that brain cease to function incisively. Within the year the Jacobites, who he always said were a genuine danger, had made their bid for power. There may be some connection between the two events.

Amid all the high and low politics Walpole had had an active private life – two wives, a few mistresses, several children, among them the fastidious Horace of Strawberry Hill. He amassed a fortune and spent it on pursuits which bely the bluff philistine squire. Although he never visited Europe, there was a continental touch to Houghton. Coarse yet cultivated, crude yet subtle, he was an actor of immense range who wrote his own lines and competently directed the rest of a large cast, making up as he went along most of the plot and substance of a play that ran and ran.

A collection of broadsides and pamphlets issued at the time of the South Sea Bubble crisis (1720).

JOHN WESLEY

1703–1791

THE REVIVALIST John Wesley, the leader of Methodism, was the most influential Christian teacher and organizer in eighteenth-century England. He was born on 17 June 1703 in Epworth, Lincolnshire. His father Samuel was the Rector of Epworth, a scholarly, principled man, whose path to preferment was impeded by his politics and his obstinacy. His mother Susanna was a strong-minded and talented woman, who took an active interest in church work and the education of her many children. She was an exacting parent and John owed much of his early piety and academic success to her influence. At the age of eleven, he entered Charterhouse School, then in London, where he studied classics and, on his father's orders, ran around the green three times each morning. A promising scholar with a strong constitution, he left school with an exhibition at Christ Church, Oxford, where he graduated in 1724. As a young man he was sociable with temperate habits and literary leanings. But he does not appear to have given much thought to a career, and on the advice of his parents prepared himself for a life in the Church. Despite difficulties over certain Anglican doctrines, he was made a deacon in 1725 and began to preach in Oxfordshire soon after. The next year he was made a fellow of Lincoln College, which gave him financial independence but did not require him to reside permanently in Oxford.

As his father's curate (he was ordained in 1728) Wesley was often at Epworth, engaged in pastoral work and family matters. He read widely too, especially spiritual biographies and the works of High Church Anglicans. Much of what he read, however, made him unhappy with his own conduct. Above all, he became anxious to develop a practical Christianity, a theology tailored to the rigours and successions of daily life. When he returned to Oxford in 1729 as a college tutor, he joined the 'Holy Club', which was made up of a few young men, including his brother Charles, who were dubbed 'Methodists'. They were notable for their strict rules of religious observance. The regime admirably suited Wesley's disposition, for he was given to austerity and believed self-discipline essential to happiness. To cure himself of lying awake at night, for example, he rose at four. He soon took over the leadership of the society, and it grew to embrace larger numbers of undergraduates, fellows and townspeople. To the prayer meetings and Bible readings, the group added practical philanthropy in the form of prison and workhouse visiting, and set up a school for the children in the town. For Wesley the combination of religious devotion and charitable work was a godsend, which gave meaning to his college work. When his father asked him at the end of 1734 to succeed him at Epworth he refused, replying that Oxford offered him the best hope of usefulness and holiness.

A year later his father was dead and he was in Georgia undertaking missionary work as a chaplain for the Society for the Promotion of Christian Knowledge. The reasons for his departure from Oxford are obscure, but his father's death and disappointments in love probably contributed their part. Georgia offered him a wider field for his religious vocation, an opportunity to continue the evangelical work, not least among poor debtors, which had appealed to him in Oxford. Moreover, there were the Indians to be converted, a people he regarded as uncorrupted by civilization, 'fit to receive the Gospel in its simplicity'. Through his labours in Georgia he hoped to find the key to understanding unadorned Christianity and in so doing release himself from the terrors of self-examination. In the event, his work in Georgia lasted less than two years and was far from a success. It was marred by criticism of his punctiliousness in religious usage and by women, who either embarrassed or made a fool of him. (Wesley was a poor judge of women and his marriage in 1751 to the widow Molly Vazeille ended in separation and recrimination.) Nor did the Indians live up to his idealized picture of them. He returned to England in 1738 a wiser man, toughened by his experience, but more confused than ever about the state of his own soul. 'I went to America, to convert the Indians,' he wrote in his *Journal*, 'but oh, who shall convert me?'

It is not surprising that Wesley was in a state of personal crisis upon his return to England. Pressures from his parents, the strict religious regime at Oxford, his reading of the Bible and the churchmen had left him deeply introspec-

John Wesley by Nathaniel Hone, 1766.

tive. He longed for an end to his spiritual pilgrimage. Unsure of himself, he sought advice from the Moravian Brethren, in particular Peter Böhler, a learned Moravian missionary who visited Oxford. From Böhler he imbibed the doctrine of justification by faith, which was to become the single most important theme in his own teaching. 'Preach faith until you have it', argued Böhler, 'and then, because you have it, you will preach faith.' After much discussion and emotional turmoil, Wesley went through a 'conversion' experience in May 1738, at a meeting in Aldersgate Street, at which his 'heart strangely warmed'. At the end of it he felt an assurance that his sins were forgiven and that he had found peace in Christ at last. Doubts and depression lingered for some time, but gradually he found his equilibrium, and with it renewed purpose. After a trip to Germany in the summer of 1738 to visit the Moravians, with whom he would later disagree, he returned to London and soon struck

Wesley's Chapel in City Road, East London, with his statue in the foreground. Opened by Wesley in 1778, the chapel is considered the mother church of Methodism.

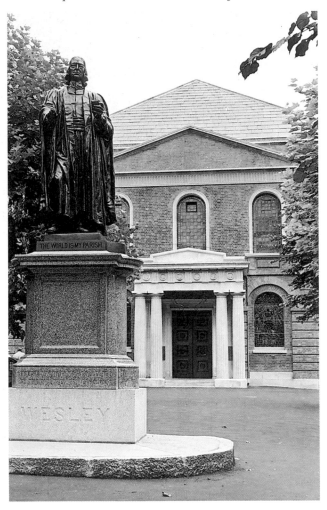

out on his own itinerant ministry. With it Methodism may be said to have been born.

Within ten years he created a movement which greatly altered the life of Britain and raised him to the level of a national figure. He worked indefatigably. Day in and day out, year after year, he travelled the country on horseback, preaching and organizing. He is said to have journeyed 4,500 miles a year, over 250,000 miles in his lifetime, and to have preached 40,000 sermons. The times were well suited to an itinerant ministry, for the industrial revolution was underway and the population was growing and unsettled. Cities were emerging out of villages, and where churches did not exist Wesley and his lay preachers would go directly to the people, often preaching to them in the open air. Though his missionaries, many of them artisans or small farmers, carried the faith throughout the country, he centred his work on the industrial heartland, in the triangle formed by London, Newcastle and Bristol. Here were countless souls neglected by the Church of England, in need of spiritual uplift or consolation. Some writers have argued that Wesley simply reconciled the working classes to intolerable conditions, leaving them with an ethic suited to the inhuman demands of industry. Wesley would, of course, reject this view. He did, indeed, consider man to be fallen and society corrupt, but for him religion was a sign of aspiration not despair.

Methodism was stamped through and through by Wesley's character. He was ascetic, exacting, genial, autocratic, invulnerable – a 'human gamecock', remarked Leslie Stephen. There was little of the gloom or glory of more imaginative men in him. He was unhappy with Calvinism, and mysticism seemed to him ridiculous. Though with little speculative insight, he had extraordinary practical gifts, especially in administration. A distinctive feature of Methodism was its highly centralized, efficient organization, which, subject to his authority, aimed to provide a lay order within the established Church. As a don and a classicist, he was in some ways at home in the prevailing intellectual climate. Yet his essential message was a reaction to the complacent, time-serving religious life of his day, a challenge to the formality and latitudinarianism of the Church. His faith, to use his words, was a 'religion of the heart'. Whether in his sermons or more informally, Wesley spoke to men plainly and directly, on their own terms and in their own language. What he had discovered in himself through his own conversion experience he wanted to share with others. He had the power that springs from personal witness, which aroused expectancy in his audiences and brought them into the fold. To his rationalist critics, however, this was just so much heat without light.

Wesley was essentially a conservative man. In theology he was heir to High Church traditions and insisted right up to his death that Methodists were true to the doctrines of the Church of England. There were divisions within Methodism in his lifetime, notably over his advocacy of the Arminian doctrine of free will; and there were growing demands for independence from the established Church. But as long as he lived, he sought to avoid sectarianism. In politics too he was conservative. A paternalist, he disliked democracy and republicanism, disapproved of the American cause in the War of Independence, and showed little enthusiasm for the reform of English institutions, though he was among the first to speak out against slavery. It is sometimes argued that Methodism, with its conservative moral and political code, cooled the passions of Englishmen and thus spared the nation a violent counterpart to the French Revolution. This argument seems unlikely, if only because there is little evidence to suggest that England was at the time inclined to revolution.

Until just before his death on 2 March 1791, Wesley kept up his demanding routine, travelling, preaching, reading prayers, taking Communion, writing his *Journal*. He had things to regret, not least his disastrous marriage and the growing rift with the established Church over his ordination of Methodist ministers. But he had much to be thankful for as well, most of all the 40,000 or so recruits to his faith, who he believed were on their way to salvation. (By the mid-nineteenth century their number had risen to 358,000.) Despite his great success in evangelizing, his ultimate importance is difficult to measure. He had initiated a revival which gave fresh vitality to both Anglicanism and Nonconformity, but even his most ardent champions could not claim that he had checked the growth of secularism. Yet he did reach humble people in distant corners of the kingdom who had hitherto been little touched by Christianity. He gave them a religious and social identity and a moral code which offered a key to respectability and self-respect. Moreover, he had enlivened the nation's social conscience. His emphasis on good works would bear fruit in innumerable Methodist charities which, along with other societies, moderated many of the worst effects of industrial change. In these and other ways, Wesley played a significant part in shaping nineteenth-century England, with its unique sense of national purpose and disciplined liberty.

ADAM SMITH

1723–1790

AUTHOR OF the *Wealth of Nations*, the bible of economic liberalism, Adam Smith was the founder of political economy as a distinct branch of knowledge. He was born at Kirkcaldy, Fife, on 5 June 1723. His father, who died before he was born, was Comptroller of Customs at Kirkcaldy; his mother came from a well-connected army family. He was deeply attached to his mother, an attachment that could only have been greater after his being carried off by gypsies as a child, though he was soon recovered. A delicate, abstracted boy, he attended the Burgh school of Kirkcaldy and at

Medallion of Adam Smith by James Tassie, 1787.

fourteen was sent to Glasgow University, where he came under the influence of the Scottish philosopher Francis Hutcheson. From Glasgow Smith went on to Balliol College, Oxford, where he led a somewhat isolated life. In the manner of the day, he sought to master the entire range of human knowledge, and by the time of his return to Scotland in 1746 he was well versed in Greek and in English literature. Back home he met the judge and author Lord Kames, and on his advice gave a course of lectures on English literature and eventually added further lectures on economics, in which he was critical of government interference in the affairs of business. In 1751 he was elected to the Chair of Logic at Glasgow University and the next year he became Professor of Moral Philosophy.

Smith was widely admired as a lecturer, and as his fame spread students came from far afield, including the continent. His reputation had more to do with his ideas than his delivery, for he was an artless speaker. Among his subjects were ethics, natural theology and political theory, and it is clear that the ideas associated with his writings often were generated in his lectures. But he was not simply a bookish man. Despite fits of absence of mind, for which he was remarkable, he was active in university business and served as Dean and Vice-Rector of Glasgow University. He was a keen participant in the club life of the day. In Edinburgh, where he often stayed with his friend the philosopher David Hume during the holidays, he helped to found the Select Society in 1754, in which the subjects under discussion ranged from agriculture to the fine arts. In Glasgow he joined the Literary Society and another club devoted to the discussion of commerce. In such societies he met the Scottish élite, not least its merchant class, who gave him insights into trade and industry. He, in turn, delivered papers on economics and converted Glasgow merchants to free trade.

In 1759 Smith's first major work appeared, a treatise on moral philosophy titled *Theory of Moral Sentiments*. It was well received by the critics and by David Hume, whose *Enquiry concerning the Principle of Morals* it resembled. In Smith's view morality was essentially a social phenomenon which arose from sympathy. Sympathy 'leads us to enter into the situations of other men' and thus resulted in approval or disapproval of their actions. It encouraged self-esteem and served as the basis for social stability. The *Theory of Moral Sentiments* became a classic of a certain type of ethical philosophy, in which human feelings are given paramount importance. It added greatly to Smith's already considerable reputation and helped to widen his circle of admirers and connections. He met Dr Johnson and had a famous altercation with him at a London publishers. More profitable was his association with Charles Townshend, soon to be Chancellor of the Exchequer. Townshend was stepfather of Henry Scott, Duke of Buccleuch, and he invited Smith to become tutor to the young man at double his university salary. Smith accepted, left for Paris with the Duke in 1764, and resigned his Professorship.

Smith remained on the continent for over two years. He toured southern France and visited Geneva to meet Voltaire, for whom he had the greatest admiration. He was introduced to Holbach, Turgot and other leading intellectuals and made the rounds of the Parisian salons, where he was much fêted in his own right. Among the 'Physiocrats', a group of social thinkers who sought to revive the national wealth of France through fostering agriculture, he found affinities and mental stimulation. But their influence on his economic doctrines is easy to overstate, for by the time he arrived in France he had already formulated his economic principles. If his intellectual debts were to anyone, they were to Hutcheson and Hume. In Paris he saw more of Hume and was said to have fallen in love with an English woman. A French marquise was said to have fallen in love with him. Both Smith and the marquise were disappointed. A reserved man with little emotional life apart from his devotion to his mother, he appears to have experienced little, if any, further romance in his life. His mother's death in 1784, at the age of ninety, appears to have been the greatest emotional blow of his life.

During his stay in France, Smith began to put together his thoughts for a book which was to become the *Wealth of Nations*. But when the Duke of Buccleuch's younger brother, who was also in his charge, was murdered in Paris in 1766, he returned to England. After an initial stay in London, he settled in Kirkcaldy with his mother and a female cousin, and over the next decade worked pretty consistently on his manuscript, travelling down to London for extended periods to read in the British Museum, deal with his publisher and enjoy the club life of the metropolis. He showed various parts of his manuscript to the London literati, including Benjamin Franklin, and after revisions he finally published the *Wealth of Nations* in 1776, the same year as Gibbon's *Decline and Fall of the Roman Empire*. Smith received £500

for the first edition and, as anticipated, it was a huge success and hailed as a masterpiece. Few books can have so quickly established a reputation with the public.

The *Wealth of Nations* was the first comprehensive treatment of the subject of political economy and was written in part to explain Brit-

Title page of the first edition of Wealth of Nations.

A N

I N Q U I R Y

INTO THE

Nature and Caufes

OF THE

WEALTH OF NATIONS.

By ADAM SMITH, LL. D. and F. R. S.

Formerly Profeffor of Moral Philofophy in the Univerfity of GLASGOW.

IN TWO VOLUMES.

VOL. I.

LONDON:

PRINTED FOR W. STRAHAN; AND T. CADELL, IN THE STRAND.

MDCCLXXVI.

ain's commercial pre-eminence. As an attack on the older mercantilist policy with its monopolistic and regulatory practices, its arguments were in tune with the views of the 'Physiocrats', but Smith did not share their belief that the essential source of wealth was land. For him the increase in wealth and productivity derived most notably from the division of labour and its growing specialization. In advanced countries like Britain price would be determined by wages, profit and rent. An advocate of freedom of commerce, he considered the ideal economic system to be autonomous, outside the sphere of government, subject to the working out of certain 'natural laws' of production and exchange. Highly individualistic, it was based on self-interest, the universal pursuit of which contributed to the wider public interest. In a famous phrase, borrowed from religious usage, the individual was guided by an 'invisible hand', which promoted an end unintended yet of universal benefit. An elaboration of these views by later British economists such as Ricardo was dubbed 'laissez-faire' by its opponents and made up the stock in trade of what is still called classical economics.

The elaboration of Smith's views began with Smith himself, for during his last years he spent much of his time revising and expanding his earlier work. Distracted by other things, he never produced another book after the *Wealth of Nations*. In 1777 he was appointed Commissioner of Customs at Kirkcaldy with an income of £600 a year, which made him well off. He fulfilled his duties, but as they were light he had time to read Greek in his extensive library and entertain his many friends, among them Edmund Burke and the chemist Joseph Black. On one famous occasion he was entertained by William Pitt, who asked him to be seated first, 'for we are all your scholars'. In 1787 he was elected Lord Rector of Glasgow, but his health was by now beginning to fail. His last lecture in Glasgow was characteristic of him and indicative of his obsession with financial probity. He told his students that he would repay part of their fees as he was unable to finish his academic duties. When the first student refused to accept it, Smith crammed the money into his pocket. He died on 27 July 1790, after settling his accounts and asking his friends to burn many of his manuscripts.

Adam Smith belonged to what he referred to as 'that unprosperous race of men commonly called men of letters'. It was his vast historical knowledge and literary flair that gave such distinction to his economic thought and raised ideas that were often part of the intellectual currency of the day into a brilliant synthesis. Smith lived in a stable society and did not preach revolution, yet his ideas had radical implications. They were corrosive of traditional institutions and can be seen at work in the extensive reform of British tax and fiscal administration that began under Pitt and continued under Peel. (Very interestingly, the Customs office in Kirkcaldy where both Smith and his father served was an institutional expression of the very regulatory system that Smith wished to see abandoned.) On the wider front, his defence of individual freedom and his belief in autonomous economic laws were challenges to unbridled state power and as such did much to enliven liberal capitalism. As to the study of economics, it has been argued, with some justice, that all political economy written in the last two hundred years is a series of footnotes to the *Wealth of Nations*. In this judgement, Smith is to political economy what Plato is to philosophy.

WILLIAM PITT THE YOUNGER

1759–1806

WILLIAM PITT was one of Britain's most distinguished Prime Ministers. A brilliant administrative reformer in peacetime, he guided the country through the long war with France without violent upheaval. Born at Hayes, Kent on 28 May 1759, he was the second son of William Pitt, the first Earl Chatham, and Hester Grenville. As a child he was precocious, though painfully shy, and by the age of seven he could write elegant Latin letters to his father, who took an active interest in his intellectual progress. Because of delicate health he was educated at home, but at fourteen entered Pembroke Hall, Cambridge, where he studied classical languages and mathematics. He graduated M.A. without an examination in 1776. Absorbed by politics, he often went to debates in Parliament during his Cambridge years and was present at his father's dying speech in the House of Lords in April 1778. Left with a small income after his father's death he was called to the bar in 1780, but in September of that year stood at the general election for the University of Cambridge, at which he came bottom of the poll. Through a university connection, however, he was returned to Parliament for the pocket borough of Appleby and took his seat in the House of Commons in January 1781. Ambitious and inscrutable, he sought to fulfil his father's expectations of him and to live up to his youthful visions of public service. He was twenty-one years old.

Upon entering Parliament Pitt attached himself to the party of Lord Shelburne, in opposition to Lord North's administration. His maiden speech, on economic reform, was a great success and made him a man to watch, all the more so as he supported peace with the American colonies and advocated parliamentary reform. Like his father before him he held independent views and saw himself above the political fray. When North's government collapsed he refused to accept a minor office in Lord Rockingham's administration. It was his tendency to be cautious and wait upon events, and when Rockingham died and Shelburne became Prime Minister his moment arrived. He was asked to become Chancellor of the Exchequer in 1782, at the age of twenty-three. When Shelburne was overthrown the following year by the coalition of Charles James Fox and Lord North, Pitt refused the Treasury, in spite of pressure to accept from George III. When the coalition, in turn, collapsed, the King appointed him Prime Minister, in December 1783. The Commons greeted the news with derisive laughter, fully expecting his quick departure, for he had little experience, few political friends, and awesome problems before him.

Pitt, now only twenty-four, had great difficulties in forming a government. But after the election of 1784 he had the country on his side, along with the King, who believed him to be the only man who could deliver him from his enemies. The defeat in the American War had left Britain deeply in debt and its prestige impaired. To stimulate trade and financial recovery he introduced sweeping reforms into a system of finance and administration which had become cumbersome and chaotic. He lowered duties on a wide range of commodities, passed new taxes, brought the East India Company under political control and generally promoted free trade. Less successful were his complex proposals for a 'sinking fund', which he hoped would pay off the

William Pitt the Younger, painted by Thomas Gainsborough in 1788.

national debt. Pitt was no democrat but he sought a reform of Parliament in 1785. He wished to eliminate many of the most corrupt boroughs and give, as he put it, 'fresh energy to representation'. But he was defeated on the issue and was never able to re-introduce it. Nor was he successful in his attempt to suppress the slave trade, a cause closely associated with his friend William Wilberforce. Peace was essential for the fulfilment of his domestic programme, and when his government was returned in 1790 he looked forward to further reform, not knowing that war would force its abandonment.

Domestic politics had tested his resolve, but foreign crises were to present him with trials of a different magnitude altogether. When the French Revolution broke out in 1789, Pitt regarded it with his natural reserve, but some sympathy. In the interests of peace his government maintained a cool neutrality. In the autumn of 1792, however, the situation changed. France had declared war on Austria and Prussia and now threatened Holland, to which Britain was bound by treaty. Despite reports of French agents stirring up revolutionary sentiments in England, Pitt still hoped to avoid war. But on 1 February 1793, shortly after the execution of Louis XVI, the French Republic declared war on Britain. At the outset Pitt decided to form a European coalition, though he expected the hostilities to be brief because of the state of French finances. In this opinion he was mistaken. The war persisted with calamitous consequences. Britain's own finances were strained to breaking point, her alliances fell into disarray and attempts at negotiating peace proved futile. Meanwhile, unrest in Ireland and at home left the country in a state of general alarm. Pitt remained remarkably calm through it all, though his health showed signs of the strain by 1798.

Pitt did not enter the war in an ideological spirit. Indeed, his management of it was essentially pragmatic. But like other members of the English establishment he worried about the spread of French doctrines, especially as evidence reached him of their influence on the English reform movement. He became fierce for moderation, and calls for parliamentary reform, to which he had been previously committed, he now dismissed as dangerous. As the Terror took hold in France, the English ruling class feared for its privilege and fell back on the remorseless force of law. Pitt's government suspended *Habeas Corpus* and passed a series of repressive acts restricting civil liberties. Prosecutions for treason and seditious libel came before the courts with results that were sometimes savage, especially in Scotland. When rebellion in Ireland broke out in 1798 further measures were taken to suppress secret societies and to regulate newspapers. In Pitt's defence it could be said that he believed that the fate of the nation was in the balance and that stern measures were needed against political agitators. Yet his suppression of dissent at home is difficult to justify. Perhaps, because of his aristocratic upbringing and temperament, the French Revolution had driven him into the arms of the reactionaries.

Politically, Pitt survived the enormous demands placed upon him by the French Revolution and the prolonged war, but his attempts to resolve the perennial problem of Ireland left him defeated. For years he had advocated Irish reform, and the rebellion in Ireland convinced

Pitt addressing the House of Commons, by Karl-Anton Hickel, 1793.

The DISSOLUTION, — or — The Alchymist producing an Ætherial Representation

him of the urgent need for a dramatic change in the constitutional relations between the two countries. In his view, Ireland needed not only a legislative union with Britain, but a union in which Catholics achieved political rights. Opposition to his policy was widespread and not confined to Ireland, where corrupt Protestant magnates were jealous of losing their political monopoly. George III, like many in England, accepted the union but was hostile to Catholic emancipation. After delicate negotiations and much bribery Pitt secured an act to bring about unification. But, disappointed that emancipation had not been included, he pressed for further reform. His relations with the King deteriorated, for George III, in a state of near derangement, declared himself the enemy of any man who proposed Catholic emancipation. In the circumstances Pitt felt unable to carry on his duties and resigned in March 1801. He had been Prime Minister for seventeen years.

Out of office Pitt relaxed somewhat, though he remained in communication with his successor Henry Addington. He advised him on the budget and other matters and approved of the Treaty of Amiens of 1802, which brought a much needed, if brief, respite from the war. He took the opportunity to try to reduce his enormous debts and do some farming. His mother's death in 1803 affected him deeply and his own health was failing. Afflicted by gout and alcoholism, he was unfit to endure further strains, yet he clung tenaciously to politics. With the collapse of Addington's ministry in 1804 he returned to office. His last administra-

A Gillray cartoon attacking Pitt's repressive policies, his dissolution of Parliament in 1796 and the building of a barracks without parliamentary sanction.

tion, which lasted less than two years, saw him inaugurate a more vigorous war policy and form the third coalition against France. He lived to see Nelson's bittersweet victory at Trafalgar, but the defeat of the allies at Austerlitz in December 1805, which shattered his coalition, dealt him a staggering blow. His health collapsed and he died on 23 January 1806, his last words being 'Oh, my country! how I leave my country.' The nation paid his debts, which amounted to £40,000, and voted a public funeral, which was carried out in Westminster Abbey.

Pitt is a controversial figure, who has not always been judged in the context of the norms and realities of his day. The quintessential practical politician, he often had to make difficult choices in unhappy circumstances. As a peace minister he was notable for reviving British commerce and prestige after the American War, for reshaping her imperial commitments, and for providing a structure of administrative and financial reform of lasting importance. But a career which showed such early promise as a reformer ended under the cloud of foreign war and unattractive domestic shadows. After 1793 his guiding principle, to which he sacrificed all else, was the defence of Britain. As a war minister he had his shortcomings, exacerbated by the genius of Napoleon. His coalitions were a failure and he distrusted his own judgement as a military strategist, yet his faith in British naval power resulted in victory at sea and the consequent deterioration of French trade. A man of remarkable self-discipline and resolve, he gave hope and confidence to his countrymen in calamitous times. He left behind no political party or political doctrine, no wife or children, and only a few friends to venerate his memory.

HANNAH MORE

1745–1833

HANNAH MORE, the writer and moral reformer, was arguably the most influential woman of her day, a celebrated 'Bluestocking' and leading light of the Evangelical revival. Born at Stapleton, Gloucestershire, on 2 February 1745, she was the fourth of five daughters of Jacob More, a schoolmaster of High Church views, and his wife Mary Grace, a fervent Nonconformist. Both parents wished to give their capable children an education that would prepare them for independent lives. Hannah, the most gifted, sailed through her lessons, which included French, Latin and mathematics, with astonishing ease. When her father discontinued her mathematics because she was better at it than the boys in his charge, she concentrated on history, languages and literature, for which she had a brilliant facility. When her eldest sister opened a school for girls in Bristol, she became a pupil there and later a governess. Charming and attractive, she delighted the children with her verses and dramas, some of which were later published. At twenty-three, she became engaged to a wealthy, though elderly, squire, William Turner. Though with the best intentions, the reluctant bridegroom was too shy to bring himself to the church, and after years of humiliation Hannah broke off the engagement and subsequently determined never to marry, despite other opportunities. Turner, who continued to admire her, settled a handsome annuity upon her, which she was eventually induced to accept. It gave her financial independence and the wherewithal to pursue her literary and philanthropic interests.

In 1774 Miss More travelled to London with her first play in her pocket, a loose translation of Metastasio's *Regulus* titled *The Inflexible Captive*. Though a humble provincial, she was taken up by the actor and impresario David Garrick, who, responding to her ingenuous flattery, introduced her to the literary establishment and arranged to have her play staged at the Bath Theatre Royal in 1775. This success was followed two years later by her much heralded *Percy*, which played to wildly enthusiastic audiences. Intensely patriotic, Miss More had hesitated to bring out the play when news reached London of the British surrender at the Battle of Saratoga. By now she was the darling of the literati, a friend of Burke, Reynolds and Dr Johnson, who, capping her gift for praise, called her the 'most powerful versificatrix in the English language'. Taken up by the Bluestockings, among them Mrs Elizabeth Montague, she became their poet and celebrated the learned ladies in her poem *Bas Bleu* ('Bluestocking') of 1786. But after Garrick's death in 1779 she gradually withdrew from the fashionable world which had embraced her and turned increasingly to religion.

A pious and practical woman, sensitive to 'the wickedness of London', she concluded that the stage and Christianity were incompatible. She displayed her rectitude by refusing to attend a performance of *Percy* when it reappeared in 1787, though there was a hint of inconsistency in permitting its revival.

Swept up by the Evangelical revival in the Church of England, Hannah More devoted the second half of her life to religion and practical philanthropy. Under the influence of the preaching of John Newton and her friendship with William Wilberforce, her writing took on greater sobriety and moral seriousness. She became increasingly sensitive to the prevailing corruption and irreligion of society and censured the middle classes for their complacency; in *Thoughts on the Importance of the Manners of the Great to General Society* (1788) and *An Estimate of the Religion of the Fashionable World* (1790), classics of Evangelical writing, she demonstrated the distinctions between 'vital' and superficial religion. By 'vital religion' she meant an intense biblical Christianity, urgent and emotional, which required, in her words, 'a turning of the whole mind to God'. Evangelicalism was narrow in its theology, but as a religion of social piety, which placed service above doctrine, it was wide in its sympathies. One of its greatest achievements was the campaign to abolish the slave trade, a cause most closely associated with Wilberforce. Hannah More joined the crusade with enthusiasm and between them they kept the movement alive during years of government inaction and the war with France. As Wilberforce's companion and through him an associate of the Clapham Sect, the 'Saints' as they were dubbed, she was drawn increasingly into the cause of moral reform. Through her writings and her

social connections she became the 'high priestess' of Evangelicalism.

With a longstanding interest in religious education, Hannah More turned her attention to the promotion of schools for the poor. In the summers she and her sisters lived in Cowslip Green, ten miles from Bristol, and a visit from Wilberforce in 1789 concentrated their minds on the depravity and ignorance of the inhabitants of nearby Cheddar. Hannah and her

Hannah More, 'the old bishop in petticoats', painted by H.W. Pickersgill in 1822.

sisters set up a Sunday School in the village and eventually added others in neighbouring parishes. The Mendip scheme was not the first of its kind, but it was the largest in its day, and before long included day-working schools and female benefit clubs which in return for subscriptions included insurance against sickness. Miss More's plan for instructing the labouring classes was strict and limited. Her aim was to promote useful citizenship and to her mind this was best achieved by infusing Christian principles. Thus the children were given a solid grounding in reading the Bible; writing was not taught, as it might educate the poor beyond their station. Such views were commonplace in the hierarchical world of the eighteenth century in which the poor were thought to have been allotted their lowly path by God. When criticism of Miss More's schools erupted in 1800, it was on the grounds that they propagated Methodist doctrines, not that they neglected opportunities to improve the material conditions of the children. The controversy surrounding the schools was a *cause célèbre* and persisted for three years, at the end of which Miss More, unused to criticism, complained that she had been 'battered, hacked, scalped, tomahawked'. She resolutely denied the accusation that she was a Methodist, though to many of her opponents her Evangelical enthusiasm came to the same thing. The controversy ended when a new Bishop of Bath and Wells came to her support.

As a pillar of the establishment, Hannah More was horrified at the prospect of French revolutionary doctrines spreading among the English lower orders. In response to a call on her services, she wrote a tract, *Village Politics*, in 1792. It was an answer to Thomas Paine's *The Rights of Man*, and was a sort of 'Burke for

Hannah More appears at the back (standing, second from the right) of this allegorical group portrait, The Nine Living Muses of Great Britain, *by Richard Samuel, 1779. Other Bluestockings included are Mrs Elizabeth Montague (seated, second from the right) and Mrs Elizabeth Carter (standing, far left).*

Beginners'. A grateful government distributed thousands of copies of this 'masterpiece' of counter-revolution around the country. Written for 'the most vulgar class of reader', it drummed home the message that politics were best left to one's superiors and that radicalism

and indecency were synonymous. Over the next few years she and her sisters poured out a stream of similar pamphlets, the *Cheap Repository Tracts*. Her object was to promote domestic peace and social cohesion and provide 'safe' books for the many adolescents who were being turned out by the charity schools, not least her own, with the ability to read. The style of the Tracts was unpretentious and full of contrived humour, a form of concrete writing that a labourer could grasp and enjoy without difficulty. Often they took the form of a brisk dialogue, where the solid, good-hearted citizen confuted the pretentious and misguided thinker through the inexorable logic born of experience and common sense. Two million copies of the Tracts were said to have been sold in a year, and well into the nineteeth century they made up a large part of the cottager's library. As a force for orthodoxy and social order in a time of national crisis they should not be underestimated.

As a didactic writer Hannah More had a huge following among the growing middle classes, many of whom were open to instruction on questions of manners and morals from a woman of unimpeachable social position. She was particularly anxious to reach those countless young ladies susceptible to lessons on religious propriety and 'decorous conduct'. Though she had denounced the evil influence of novels in her *Strictures on the Modern System of Female Education* (1799), she published one herself in 1808, *Coelebs in Search of a Wife*. Written for the subscribers to circulating libraries, it proved immensely popular with its readers (twelve editions in its first year), who readily imbibed Evangelical principles dressed up in the guise of fiction. Miss More was no friend of the 'Rights of Women'; indeed, she refused to read the writings of Mary Wollstonecraft. Yet she advocated a reform of womanly conduct that had tremendous repercussions for ladies severely constrained by social custom. Her ideal female was modest and unassuming, pious and self-sacrificing, 'to deeds of mercy ever prone'. When she wrote that 'the care of the poor is her profession', she offered her sex an opportunity for emancipation and social service that was compatible with conservatism and masculine prejudice. That women joined and ran charities in vastly increasing numbers in the early nineteenth century was in no small measure due to her influence.

In later life, from her home in Barley Wood, Somerset, which she shared with her sisters, Hannah More continued to write and promote her many charitable causes. Whether assisting neighbours or working for her much loved Bible and missionary societies, she was indefatigable. She still had time to carry on an extensive correspondence and to entertain an endless procession of guests, among them Elizabeth Fry and innumerable bishops, who came to pay their respects or beg a favour. In 1817, with the revival of radicalism following the end of the war with France, an appeal from the 'highest quarters' was made to her to supply 'antidotes to the spreading poison'. As the government included several of her friends, she agreed and launched a battery of tracts and songs aimed at the radical leadership, most notably William Cobbett. Compared to her anti-Jacobin pamphlets of the 1790s they were disappointing. Essentially a religious thinker, she was unable to distinguish between reform and revolution, and took the view that all political agitation was a breach of holy law. Cobbett, for his part, called her 'the old bishop in petticoats'. The following years were a burden to her. The last of her sisters, whom she had depended on for the management of the household, died in 1819, and poor health confined her to two upstairs rooms. Since she was kindly and easily imposed upon, her pampered servants multiplied and robbed her. In 1828 friends removed her to Clifton, where she died on 7 September 1833.

Hannah More's reputation has faded. The pieties and old-fashioned Toryism which she promoted are out of favour, her writings unread, and even her great services to philanthropy largely unrecognized today. Though a humanitarian, she never 'slipped into humanism', and her fixation with sin and individual redemption makes her distasteful to those for whom material and collective life is paramount. Few figures tell us so much about the differences between our age and hers. Highminded and austere, though not untouched by spiritual vanity, she was a telling critic of her society's pretensions and moral failings. She taught by example as well as by precept, and perhaps only Wilberforce could claim to have had a greater influence in reforming English manners and morals in the first half of the nineteenth century. Dwelling on man's depravity and God's mercy, she encouraged a greater sense of personal accountability and social responsibility among her countrymen. That Evangelicalism had a profound effect upon the national life is not in doubt. If the eighteenth century was noted for its brutality and aggressiveness, the nineteenth was remarkable for its piety and inhibitions. The gospel of service and the preoccupation with respectability and decorum which is so closely associated with the Victorians had its origins in the movement which Hannah More so brilliantly represented.

WILLIAM BLAKE

1757–1827

PAINTER, poet, visionary, William Blake was one of Britain's greatest engravers and the prophet of a 'New Age'. He was born at 28 Broad Street, Golden Square, London on 28 November 1757, the third child of a hosier James Blake and his wife Catherine. He was not sent to school, but was educated at home in a highly charged religious atmosphere. A dreamy child, he perplexed his parents with claims of having seen angels, prophets and God, who set him 'a-screaming'. His father encouraged his talent for draughtsmanship and sent him to a drawing school in the Strand at the age of ten, where he copied the works of his favorite artists, Raphael and Michelangelo. At twelve he began to write poetry, some of which was later published in the *Poetical Sketches* (1783). In 1772 he was formally apprenticed to the engraver James Basire, who was responsive to the boy's unusual sensitivity and gave him considerable freedom. Having served his apprenticeship, Blake became a student at the Royal Academy, but he was wholly unsuited to academic exercise and soon left, preferring to make a humble living as an engraver for London booksellers. He struck up friendships with the painter Thomas Stothard and the sculptor John Flaxman, who introduced him to a wider artistic and literary circle. In 1782 he married Catherine Boucher, the daughter of a market gardener. She was a patient, supportive and practical woman, an ideal wife for such an amiable eccentric. Although he enjoyed the company of children, he and Catherine had none of their own.

On the death of his father in 1784, Blake moved back to Broad Street, next door to his birthplace, and started a print-seller's business in partnership with a former fellow apprentice. But three years later the union dissolved and he moved to Poland Street. He had had some drawings exhibited at the Royal Academy and in 1789 he published, with his wife's assistance, a volume of illustrated poetry, *Songs of Innocence*. It was the first of his engraved, hand-coloured books, in which the interacting text and design stood out sharply. The form was ideally suited to his unique talent and straitened circumstances. Everything about the book, apart from the manufacture of the paper, was his or his wife's doing. Reminiscent of mediaeval illuminated manuscripts, the volume was rich in colour and Christian symbolism. His subject was the simple joy of childhood but underlying it was the theme of divine love and forgiveness. A few lines suggest the spirit and origin of the work:

> I pluck'd a hollow reed,
> And I made a rural pen,
> And I stain'd the water clear,
> And I wrote my happy songs
> Every child may joy to hear.

Blake published *Songs of Innocence* and another illuminated book, *Thel*, in the year of the French Revolution, an event which had a profound impact on him, as it did on most

William Blake, water-colour by John Linnell dated 1861, but originally painted from life in 1821.

English writers and artists. His books took on an increasingly revolutionary character. In *The Marriage of Heaven and Hell* (1790), a prose work influenced by the theological writings of Emanuel Swedenborg, and in the *Visions of the Daughters of Albion* (1793) and *America* (1793) he was in revolt against authority and conventional morality. In these years he was to be seen walking the streets wearing the red cap of liberty (until the Terror changed its symbolism). Through the bookseller, Joseph Johnson, who employed him as an engraver, he met many of the leading radicals of the day, including Joseph Priestley and Thomas Paine, whose political opinions, if not religious views, he shared. In 1794 he complemented the *Songs of Innocence* with the *Songs of Experience*. Together they captured 'the two contrary states of the human soul' and perhaps suggest Blake's own changing state of mind. Brightness gives way to foreboding. The innocent lamb of the earlier cycle, for example, is set off against the ferocious animal in 'Tyger! Tyger! burning bright', the most famous poem of the later cycle. Whatever these books tell us about Blake, they arguably contain the most perfect lyrical poetry he ever composed.

By the time of the publication of the *Songs of Experience* Blake had moved to Hercules Buildings, Lambeth, where he was to remain until 1800. By the mid-1790s he had become more mystical and in a series of illustrated prophetic books he carried forward his criticism of the prevailing moral code in mythological dress. Among them were the *Book of Urizen* (1794), the *Songs of Los* (1795), and the unfinished epic *Vala or the Four Zoas*. Difficult and often obscure, they were nonetheless rich in imaginative symbolism; some of his contemporaries thought them eccentric to the point of madness. Turning his attention to design he prepared 537 transparent water-colours for an edition of Edward Young's *Night Thoughts*, published in 1797. At about this time he was also producing frescoes, drawings and a book of water-colours for an edition of Thomas Gray's poems. Few artists can have been so frenetically busy and productive, yet his rewards during the years in Lambeth were disappointing. Neither his prophetic books nor his splendid illustrations for *Night Thoughts* made much impression; his former employers deserted him; and the hopes aroused in him by the French Revolution were dashed by the events in France and by political repression at home.

By the autumn of 1800 Blake was in need of a change of scene, and he accepted an invitation from the poet and amateur artist William Hayley to join him at Felpham in Sussex. The cottage provided by the sea was a haven to Blake for the next three years. Here he took on a wide variety of projects, including engravings for Hayley's *Life of Cowper* and tempera heads for his patron's library. It was in Felpham that he wrote and illustrated the poem *Jerusalem*, published in 1804, and began one of his greatest prophetic books, *Milton*, completed in 1808. Amongst his graphic work at this time there was the haunting *The Spirit of God moves upon the Face of the Waters*. Blake described his life at Felpham as 'three years' slumber on the Banks of the Ocean', but his life there was not without unpleasantness. Eventually his relations with his well-intentioned patron became unendurable and he decided to return to London whatever the cost to his finances. Just before he left, however, he was arraigned for sedition in a case brought by a soldier whom he had thrown out of his garden.

Title page of Songs of Innocence, *which Blake published with his wife's assistance in 1789.*

The charge that he had damned the King was a serious one, given the government's fears of a French invasion at the time, and Blake was perhaps fortunate to have been acquitted.

On his return to London in 1803, Blake and his wife lived at 17 South Molton Street, where today a plaque records his former residence. Despite his genius, perhaps because of it, he

ABOVE Glad Day *or* The Dance of Albion, *a line engraving finished in pen and water-colour,* c. *1795.*

was still little known. Unconcerned with money, he was often in need of it. As he wrote to Hayley, 'money flies from me ... profit never ventures upon my Threshold'. For most of his working life he was dependent on commissions from a few friends and patrons, such as Hayley and Thomas Butts. But, easily exploited and short of patronage, he was compelled to carry on as a journeyman engraver, which took so

RIGHT Beatrice addressing Dante from the Car, *pen and water-colour illustration for the* Divine Comedy.

P.g Canto 29 & 30

much of his time that he sometimes cursed his situation. In 1805 he received an attractive commission from the publisher Robert Cromek to produce illustrations for Robert Blair's *The Grave*. His designs were of great distinction, yet he was shoddily treated in the transaction. In 1808 he exhibited the fresco *Jacob's Dream* and *Christ in the Sepulchre guarded by Angels* at the Royal Academy. The following year he held a show of his works at his brother's shop in Broad Street, but it failed to bring public recognition. Charles Lamb admired the exhibition and years later said that 'nothing but madness had prevented [Blake] from being the sublimest painter of this or of any other country'. It was a not uncommon view of Blake during his lifetime.

Blake was never a man to seek fame or fortune but he gradually became better known as he grew older. Artists and the literati took a greater interest in his work. The poet Coleridge, having been lent a copy of *Songs of Innocence and Experience*, declared him a 'man of genius'. In 1818 Blake met the artist John Linnell, who introduced him to a group of painters, among them John Varley and later Samuel Palmer, who became devoted friends and disciples. Linnell also introduced Blake to patrons and connoisseurs, one of whom, Robert Thornton, commissioned him to do the woodcuts for the *Pastorals of Virgil* (1820), which rank among his most beautiful and poetic works. For Linnell himself Blake engraved the illustrations to the *Book of Job*, for which he received £150, the largest sum he ever made for a single project. His studies of Job's spiritual journey, which had long haunted him, were magnificently achieved, perhaps the most accomplished prints on a scriptural theme since Dürer. He was working

on another commission from Linnell, illustrations for Dante's *Divine Comedy*, when he died on 12 August 1827. One of his young disciples wrote: 'He died ... in a most glorious manner. He said he was going to that Country he had all his Life wished to see and expressed Himself Happy, hoping for Salvation through Jesus Christ.'

The range of Blake's art was remarkable, from poetry and prophecy to painting and printing. Whatever he touched was transformed by his imagination. Indeed, his favourite saying was that 'all things exist in the human imagination alone'. In this he was at home with the Romantic movement. More than any other British painter, with the possible exception of Turner, he had the capacity to interpret subjective inner vision. Yet the very intensity of his visionary material makes some of his work obscure, especially to those unfamiliar with biblical language and symbolism. Though he typically painted on a small scale, he had a striking ability to convey a sense of largeness of design. As his chief disciple Samuel Palmer remarked, he also had a unique way with colour, particularly fluctuating colour as in flame or fire, which gave life to his material. His essential theme, to which he returned again and again, was the spiritual nature of man; his essential aim was to free humanity from the deadening effects of systematic religion and conventional morality. But he offered no creed or political panacea, only spiritual struggle and faith in God's redemptive power. As he said of himself: 'I should be sorry if I had any earthly fame, for whatever natural glory a man has is so much detracted from his spiritual glory. I wish to do nothing for profit. I wish to live for art. I want nothing whatever. I am happy.'

HORATIO NELSON

1758–1805

HORATIO NELSON, the victor of Trafalgar, was Britain's greatest naval officer. Born in Norfolk on 29 September 1758, he was the son of Edmund Nelson, Rector of Burnham Thorpe, and his wife Catherine, who was related to the Walpoles. After a simple, though sound education at schools in Norfolk, he entered the navy at the age of twelve through the offices of his mother's brother, Captain Maurice Suckling. In the next several years he sailed to the East and West Indies, the Arctic and Gibraltar, learned practical lessons in seamanship and navigation and suffered the usual miseries associated with the life of midshipmen. (He never shook off his chronic seasickness.) In 1777, through his uncle's influence, he received his commission as second lieutenant of the frigate *Lowestoffe* and rapid promotion followed. Drawn to the study of tactics and eager for action, he gained invaluable experience, punctuated by bouts of ill-health, in the Caribbean, the Baltic and North America. After more than one disappointment in love he married the widow Frances Nisbet in 1787, while on duty in the West Indies as Captain of the *Boreas*. When the ship was ordered home and paid off in the same year, he and his wife moved to Bath and then to Burnham Thorpe where they lived with his father. Nelson remained in England for the next five years, frustrated by a government policy of naval retrenchment and by his own unsuccessful applications for another ship.

With the French Revolution and the deterioration of relations with France which followed, naval policy changed, and employment was found for officers who had a record of zealous service. In January 1793 Nelson was offered the command of a sixty-four-gun ship, the *Agamemnon*. He took up his appointment two days before the French declaration of war against England, which marked the beginning of the long struggle between the Royal Navy and the French navy and its allied fleets for command of the sea. The *Agamemnon* sailed for the Mediterranean with the fleet under Lord Hood, where it was ordered to Naples to bring up a convoy of Neapolitan troops. It was in Naples that Nelson first met Sir William Hamilton, the British Envoy, and his wife Emma, Lady Hamilton. The Mediterranean adventure was an opportunity for Nelson to show his brilliance. He made lightning raids on coastal shipping, blockaded Bastia and fought in the Corsican campaign, where he lost the sight of an eye. Transferred to the *Captain*, a seventy-four-gun ship, he was appointed Commodore. In February 1797, he showed conspicuous courage and 'famous indiscipline' in the decisive battle of Cape St Vincent against the Spanish fleet under Admiral Córdoba. It was a much needed victory, and Nelson, who deserved much of the credit, received the Order of the Bath.

Nelson's courage and unorthodoxy did not always end in dramatic victories, as his campaign of 1797 in the Canary Islands attests. A treasure ship from Manila had taken refuge in Tenerife and Nelson, now rear-admiral, attempted a daring night attack on Santa Cruz from his flagship the *Theseus*. His aim was to deprive the Spanish of much needed bullion and give his officers and men the spoils. In the event, the Spanish repulsed the attack and the British force was lucky to extricate itself without further losses. Nelson lost his right arm in the battle and had to return to England for a period of recuperation. But his fear that he would no longer be employed at sea was unfounded and he rejoined the fleet under Lord St Vincent at Cadiz in April 1798. His task was to track down and destroy the French fleet, which was known to be operating somewhere in the Mediterranean. He eventually found it in Aboukir Bay in August. The Battle of the Nile was an awesome victory, the greatest British naval success since the defeat of the Armada. At one blow, it made the British fleet supreme in the Mediterranean. As the news spread across Europe it revived the new coalition which England was building up against France. Nelson, again wounded, was showered with honours and gifts, and created a peer with a handsome pension.

Still suffering from his head wound, Nelson sailed into the Bay of Naples in the *Vanguard* in September 1798, to the frenzied enthusiasm of the population. There to greet him were Sir William Hamilton and his wife Emma, who celebrated his arrival with a party worthy of the Caesars and well suited to Nelson's love of display. As Lady Hamilton wrote, 'we are all be-Nelsoned'. A beguiling women, whose ageing husband made few demands on her, she became Nelson's constant companion, feeding his vanity by artful flattery. The infatuated Nelson, now forty, acted like a schoolboy having his first affair. Naples became his headquarters, but when the French marched on the Kingdom he and the English residents, including the Hamiltons loaded down with precious vases, embarked for Palermo. From there he conducted a blockade of Egypt and Malta and supervised convoys and the pacification of Southern Italy. But, coming increasingly under the spell of Lady Hamilton, he showed less and less enthusiasm for his duties. Criticism of his conduct mounted, and in May 1800 the Admiralty accepted his complaints of ill-health and gave him permission to return to England. He travelled overland with the Hamiltons, grandly fêted along the way, landing at Yarmouth in November. He joined his wife in London but after some weeks their relations soured. 'Sick of hearing of dear Lady Hamilton', she left him. Meanwhile, Lady Hamilton, amid great secrecy, gave birth to his child, Horatia, in January 1801.

Just before the birth of his daughter Horatia, Nelson was promoted to Vice-Admiral and joined the Channel Fleet. But bold action was needed in the Baltic and he was transferred to Sir Hyde Parker's command and hoisted his flag on board the *St George*. With the French victories at Marengo and Hohenlinden the European balance of power once again had shifted, and the Danes, Swedes and Russians had drawn closer together in a league of armed

Nelson successfully attacks a much larger Spanish launch in July 1797 during the blockade of Cadiz. Painting by Richard Westall.

neutrality. Eager to deliver a knock-out blow, Nelson wanted to send a detachment up the Baltic to destroy the Russian fleet, but Parker, a more cautious man, ordered that the Danish force at Copenhagen be eliminated first. Nelson entered Copenhagen harbour in April 1802, having moved his flag to the *Elephant*. The Danes put up a vigorous defence and the Commander-in-Chief sent a signal to discontinue the attack, but Nelson placed his telescope over his blind eye and refused to acknowledge it. Despite constant bombardment from shore batteries his squadron captured or destroyed all seventeen Danish ships. The savage battle ended in an armistice and the eventual dissolution of the northern league.

Lady Hamilton as Cassandra by George Romney.

Rewarded with a viscountcy, Nelson returned to England and was put in command of the squadron for home defence. But with the Peace of Amiens, which ended hostilities with France, he was able to relax and moved into a house in Merton, Surrey, with the Hamiltons.

The Peace of Amiens proved to be little more than a truce, which gave France an opportunity to regenerate her navy and extend her dominion over the shores of the Mediterranean. French intentions became obvious and the British government declared war in May 1803, before the French navy could complete its programme of ship-building. Nelson was appointed to the Mediterranean command in the flagship *Victory*, where he spent two years in difficult circumstances blockading the French fleet at Toulon. His wider object was to keep the French navy from the Straits of Dover, where it could give support to an army of invasion. In January 1805 Napoleon boldly decided to join the allied navies of France and Spain in an all-out effort to command the Channel. After initial difficulties, the French fleet at Toulon eluded Nelson's blockade and the 'long chase' began, through the Straits of Gibraltar, across the Atlantic and back again, to end, after much confusion and delay, off Cape Trafalgar. There, on 21 October 1805, Nelson and his fleet of twenty-seven ships met and defeated the combined naval forces of France and Spain, thirty-three ships of the line. Struck by a musket bullet, which shattered his spine, Nelson lived only long enough to learn of the triumph. His body, preserved in spirits, was returned to England in the *Victory* and buried in the crypt of St Paul's.

The Battle of Trafalgar was bittersweet, for the greatest British naval victory of all time was offset by the loss of the nation's most heralded and best loved officer. The universal sorrow at his death was a tribute to the man. The idealism and humanity, the courtesy and charm which made him the nation's darling also suggest the secret of his power over seamen. Such was his genius for leadership that his very appearance with the fleet could transform morale. He knew his men, their strengths and limitations, and painstakingly briefed his officers, imbuing them with his tactical ideas so that in battle they quickly responded to his intentions. The fleet under his command was disciplined and professional, yet flexible enough to take advantage of his tendency to bold, spontaneous action. Impetuous in battle, he felt any action was better than none. 'No captain can do very wrong if he places his ship alongside that of the enemy', he wrote in his famous memorandum before Trafalgar. The remark assumed a very high degree of practical seamanship from his men, indispensable if the greatest advantage was to be reaped from rapidly changing dispositions. Without numerical superiority and often less heavily armed than the enemy, the British navy under Nelson won the day by its calculated opportunism and by its superior training, seamanship and morale.

The war with France lasted for a decade after the death of Nelson, but the Battle of Trafalgar was a decisive turning point. The prolonged duel for supremacy at sea was over and Napoleon's dominion was restricted to the continent. The threatened invasion of Britain, which was abandoned two months before Trafalgar, would not be revived, and her colonies and trade routes were likewise secure. For over a hundred years her formidable and efficient navy, backed by tremendous resources, would guarantee maritime predominance. Among the galaxy of talented naval

Horatio Nelson by Lemanuel Francis Abbott, c. 1797.

officers who may be credited with bringing about Britain's naval mastery, Nelson stands supreme. No other officer had his unique combination of gifts, the flamboyant leadership or the tactical genius. His name is synonomous with the most glorious period of British naval history.

OVERLEAF *The explosion of the French flag-ship* L'Orient *during the Battle of the Nile, 1798, after burning for about an hour – an awesome moment in an awesome British victory. Painting by George Arnold.*

THOMAS TELFORD

1757–1834

FROM HUMBLE beginnings in the Scottish lowlands, Thomas Telford rose to become the father of British civil engineering. He was born at Glendinning in the Parish of Westerkirk in Eastern Dumfriesshire on 9 August 1757. His father, John Telford, a shepherd, died when he was an infant, and he and his mother moved to a small cottage in the Megget Valley where they eked out a living as occasional farm labourers. Responsive to the open air and the beauty of his physical surroundings, he grew up a cheerful, industrious and self-reliant boy. With financial support from his uncle, he attended the parish school at Westerkirk but acquired no more than a rudimentary education. Upon leaving school he was apprenticed to a stonemason in Langholm, a village in Eskdale, where the Duke of Buccleuch had in hand a programme of improvements on his estates. With a quick intelligence and great practical ability, Telford soon became an accomplished mason. At the same time he developed a passion for literature, especially poetry, which he retained throughout his life. Some of his own poems were later published, including *Eskdale*, which expressed his attachment to his native countryside. Robert Southey, who became his friend, remarked that poorer poems had won university prizes.

Telford left his beloved Eskdale in 1780 and walked to Edinburgh where he found further work as a mason. But his future, like that of so many Scots, was destined to take him south, and in 1782 he left for London on the long road through Carlisle. He soon found work on the new Somerset House, setting blocks of Portland stone on the south-west corner, which can be seen from Waterloo Bridge today. Though promoted to the rank of first-class mason, he was ambitious to move on to greater things. As he wrote to an old school friend, 'I am laying schemes of a pretty extensive kind if they succeed, for you know my disposition is not to be satisfied unless when plac'd in some conspicuous point of view.' In 1784 he had his first managerial post at Portsmouth Naval Dockyard, where he was to superintend the building of a new commissioner's house. Ever industrious, the time not spent on his duties he devoted to his verses and lessons in chemistry. When the work at the Naval Dockyard was completed a new and wider career opened before him in Shrewsbury, through the patronage of the MP William Pulteney, as Surveyor of Public Works for the County of Shropshire.

In Shrewsbury, now an architect, he renovated the Castle, rebuilt the High Street, constructed a new county gaol and infirmary, and, stimulated by his study of classical building, excavated the Roman city of Uriconium. His reputation in Shrewsbury was enhanced greatly when his prediction of the collapse of St

Chad's church, dismissed as nonsense by the churchwardens, came true. 'A very remarkable magnificent ruin', he commented dryly. He was not asked to rebuild it, but turned his knowledge of church architecture elsewhere, to Bridgnorth, where he designed the new church of St Mary Magdalene. But his most important work during this time in Shropshire was bridge-building. His first bridge was near Montford, which carried the Holyhead road across the Severn. The graceful Buildwas Bridge followed. Built in iron, it exceeded by thirty feet the span of the famous Coalbrookdale Bridge nearby, but was half its weight. No man knew better the qualities and capacities of cast iron or stone, and by 1796 Telford had built at least forty bridges in Shropshire in these materials. Increasingly he was turning away from architecture towards civil engineering. Very importantly, his bridge-building in Shropshire helped to form a strong team of contractors and associates who would assist him on later projects.

Always a man with various jobs in hand and schemes in mind, Telford took up a new appointment in 1793 as 'general agent, engineer and architect' to the Ellesmere Canal Company. The position changed his life, for as the greatest engineering project to date in Britain it put him in the national limelight. It also set him on course as an engineer rather than an architect, though in his contract he stipulated the right to carry on his architectural profession. Telford began a lifelong interest in canals with the Ellesmere project. His object was to facilitate the transport of iron and coal by connecting the Mersey, the Dee and the Severn. For the sum of £500 a year he was to draw and direct 'the making of bridges, aqueducts, locks, building reservoirs, wharfs

and other works in and about the canal'. The scheme did not result in the striking commercial success hoped for by its industrial promoters, but in engineering terms there were achievements of great originality, most notably the great aqueducts over the river Ceiriog at Chirk and the more famous 'stream in the sky' at Pont Cysyllte, opened in 1805. One historian of inland navigation put them 'among the boldest efforts of human invention in modern times'. Sir Walter Scott called Pont Cysyllte aqueduct 'the most impressive work of art that he had ever seen'. Telford's proudest boast was that in the ten years of its construction only one life was lost.

At the beginning of the nineteenth century Telford was active in a variety of projects in different parts of the country, most notably in Scotland where he carried out a survey of the

Thomas Telford with the Pont Cysyllte aqueduct in the background, from the title page of his autobiography.

economy and communications of the high-lands. Home again, he worked with patriotic fervour. The need for improvements in Scottish transportation had long been acknowledged. When Parliament finally authorized financial assistance in 1803, it was because of fears of further depopulation and the recruiting needs of the army and navy. Telford, who showed himself an able social economist, studied the causes of highland emigration and concluded that sheep had to give way to men if life was to be improved. Prosperity would only come, in his view, with better communications in the shape of roads, bridges, harbours and canals. Over a period of eighteen years he supervised the building of over 920 miles of new roads in Scotland, innumerable bridges, extensive harbour improvements, and the construction of the Caledonian Canal. With the possible exception of the Caledonian Canal, which was confounded by financial difficulties, the projects were not virtuoso feats of engineering. But the roads and bridges were remarkable value for money. Well constructed, they have only required significant alterations since the 1950s. All in all, Telford's programme of works in Scotland transformed the economy north of the border and may stand, according to his biographer, as 'the greatest achievement of his career'.

By now the leading engineer of his generation, with the possible exception of John Rennie, Telford was in great demand to advise and to supervise a large number of projects. His reputation had spread abroad after the completion of the Ellesmere Canal scheme and in 1808 he was asked by King Gustav Adolf of

The Menai Straits suspension bridge. Built in 1819–26, it is one of Telford's engineering triumphs.

Sweden to complete the construction of the Gotha Canal, which was to join the North Sea and the Baltic. Telford left for Sweden in the same year accompanied by two assistants, but commitments in Scotland and England were too pressing for him to commit himself to the project exclusively. Most of the credit for the Gotha Canal, finally completed in 1832, must go to Count von Platen, with whom Telford struck up a warm friendship. For his labours on the Canal, however, Telford was awarded a Swedish knighthood, an honour which he refused to have recognized in England. In 1815, still deeply involved in Scottish transport, he carried out a survey of the route from London to Holyhead. The carriageway he built over the next fifteen years, which drew on his Scottish experience, was of great quality, a road worthy of the Romans. To top it off there was the Menai Bridge, perhaps the engineering work for which he is best remembered today. It was a daring feat of iron suspension-bridge building, which influenced engineers around the world for decades.

Telford was seventy by the time of the completion of the Menai Bridge, but he went on to build, among other works, the bridges at Tewkesbury and the one over the Clyde at Glasgow; he designed St Katharine's Dock in London and carried out drainage schemes in the Fens. His life had been one of bustle and constant travel, being 'toss'd about like a Tennis Ball', he once wrote. As he grew older he longed to relax, to give himself more time for his many friends, his cultural interests and the activities of the society of engineers (later the Institute of Civil Engineers) which he had helped to found in 1818. He never married and for years used the Salopian coffee house in Charing Cross Road as his London head-quarters, where he entertained his associates and friends, including the poets Thomas Campbell and Robert Southey. 'A man more heartily to be liked', said Southey, '... I have never fallen in with.' Only late in life did he buy a house, in Abingdon Street, across from the Houses of Parliament. Here, in his last years, he began an autobiography and gradually slowed his hectic pace, troubled by the onset of deafness and the railway age.

At the age of seventy-four Telford took a trip from London to Stony Stratford by road steam carriage, fully believing it the most promising means of future transport. Along with some associates he was promoting a Steam Company just before his death, which planned to run a service of steam carriages between London and Birmingham. He had seen the use of steam locomotives on the railways but doubted their economic effectiveness because of their limited range of movement. But when railway mania swept the country soon after his death (he was buried in Westminster Abbey) his roads were emptied and his canals eclipsed. As the stock in George Stephenson and Isambard Brunel went up, his reputation suffered. His faith in road transport was a long time in being vindicated, and very few who travel his highways today have much idea of the man, once called the 'Colossus of Roads', who laid them. Perhaps another of Telford's punning nicknames, 'Pontifex Maximus', best suggests the source of his present reputation, for he was a bridge-builder of extraordinary talent. At Conway and over the Menai Straits, across the Dee, the Tay and the Spey in his native Scotland, he left bridges not only of triumphant engineering but of grace and beauty. The man who left the nation so many roads also put places on the map.

WILLIAM COBBETT

1763–1835

JOURNALIST, essayist, MP and farmer, William Cobbett was 'the poor man's friend', a leading political radical and an influential writer on domestic economy. He was born at Farnham, Surrey on 9 March 1763 of peasant origin. An industrious boy, he spent his time when not working in the fields studying, especially the classics of English literature. In 1783, after an unsuccessful attempt to join the navy, he went to London and found work as a clerk to an attorney. Soon bored, he enlisted in the army, rose to the rank of corporal and shipped off to Nova Scotia, where he spent the next eight years employed in keeping accounts. When his regiment returned to England in 1791, he received an honourable discharge, and the next year married Ann Reid, the daughter of a sergeant in the artillery. After an attempt to expose certain officers for corruption failed, he fled to France. Soon after, he sailed for America, taking with him, as he put it, his 'youth, a small family, a few useful literary talents, and that is all'. It was not enough to get him the place in a government office that he desired, but undaunted he settled down to teaching English to French refugees, translating and bookselling. Drawn into political controversy, he became a patriotic defender of British interests as a journalist and pamphleteer. He enjoyed great acclaim, or notoriety, not least for those works written under the pseudonym Peter Porcupine. When he returned to England in 1800 he was warmly received by the government party.

A mature political journalist by the time of his return, Cobbett was notable for his pungent use of plain English in works which effectively mingled autobiography and controversy. Settling in London, he allied himself with the anti-Jacobins and gave his support to the war effort against France. With tremendous enthusiasm, he started a newspaper and opened a bookshop in Pall Mall. He reprinted his American writings under the title *Porcupine's Works* (1801), began the *Political Register* (1802), which continued, with few interruptions, until his death, and published the *Parliamentary Debates* (1803), which T. C. Hansard eventually took over. Though patronized by the Tories, especially William Windham, a member of Pitt's cabinet, Cobbett displayed a wilful independence that was to mark the rest of his career, whichever side of the political fence he found himself on. In the early years of the nineteenth century he took positions which would embarrass many of his later devotees. In the *Political Register*, for example, he defended the slave trade, approved of bull-baiting as a pastime popular with the labouring population, and denounced the freedom of the press as a danger to national security, though he claimed that freedom for himself.

Gradually Cobbett's political opinions began to change, triggered by altered political conditions and by his growing interest in domestic issues, most importantly the state of public finance. He continued to express a good many Tory sentiments, but with a keen eye for corruption he began to denounce the stock-jobbers and *rentiers* who were being thrown up by the growth of the national debt. England was not the agrarian paradise that it had seemed to him in America but a nation racked by a parasitical commercial class. By 1808 he was firmly allied with the popular side in politics,

William Cobbett, c. *1805, by an unknown artist.*

had supported radical candidates at the hustings, and was making calls for parliamentary reform. In his conversion to radicalism the essential issue in his thinking was the condition of the labouring population, especially the agricultural labourer. As a countryman and a working farmer (he had moved to a large farm at Botley, Hampshire, in 1805) he stood for the England of traditional agriculture against the rising tide of commerce and manufacturing. For the rest of his life he remained the defender of the sturdy, independent yeoman, sharing his prejudices and jealous of his rights.

Cobbett's attacks on the government's conduct of the war with France and his vigorous campaign against political corruption came to a head in 1809. The government had been looking for a way of silencing him and found it in an article in the *Political Register*, in which he had criticized the use of German mercenaries in the suppression of an alleged mutiny of the militia in Ely. The Attorney-General filed an information for sedition and Cobbett was sentenced to two years in Newgate (1810–12) and fined £1,000. Prison was comfortable enough for those who could afford it, and Cobbett was able to carry on editing and writing for the *Political Register*. But the cost of maintaining two establishments, combined with the chaos in his business affairs, saw the ruin of his finances. Some of his finest writing came during these years, and the Luddite riots of 1811–13, in which there was widespread machine breaking, awakened his interest in the grievances of industrial workers. Out of prison he redoubled his efforts on behalf of reform. The end of the war in 1815 reinvigorated radicalism and encouraged Cobbett and other reformers to widen their campaign. To attract a working-class readership to the *Political Re-*

gister he reduced its price to twopence in 1816. Its circulation rose dramatically. The revival of radicalism in a time of depressed trade seemed especially dangerous to the establishment, and the government returned to a policy of repression. *Habeas Corpus* was suspended and, fearing for his safety, Cobbett sailed for America in 1817.

Cobbett settled on Long Island, where he remained for over two years, writing, farming and trying to keep up with events in England. He dispatched his copy for the *Political Register*, but at such a distance it lacked the freshness of his former articles. In America he published the *Grammar of the English Language*, which some believe to be his greatest work, and the highly individual *Year's Residence in the United States*, which was part farm almanac and part political tract. His last act in America was characteristic of him. Having pilloried the radical thinker Thomas Paine in the past, he now wished to make amends and disinterred his bones, with a view to enshrining them in a mausoleum in England. But when Cobbett returned with them in November 1819, no one wanted them and they remained in his possession until his death. They did, however, offer an irresistible opportunity to rhymesters and his political enemies. Even Byron, no opponent of reform, could not resist the fun:

> In digging up your bones, Tom Paine,
> Will Cobbett has done well:
> You'll visit him on earth again,
> He'll visit you in hell.

Cobbett was greeted enthusiastically upon his return by the most populist radicals (having savaged some prominent reformers in the *Political Register*). He was soon in the thick of the reform movement. He stood unsuccessfully

One of a series of satirical illustrations from Gillray's Life of William Cobbett, *published in 1809.*

for Coventry in 1821 and in that year led the popular cause in the Queen Caroline affair. The estranged wife of George IV was seen in the popular imagination as having been wronged by a prince who was deeply disliked. Cobbett's championship of her made him the darling of the working-class reformers. Deeply in debt, he had declared bankruptcy. To improve his finances he opened a seed-farm in Kensington and published a series of writings on domestic economy. Foremost among them was the *Cottage Economy*, the first part of which appeared in 1821. No one surpassed Cobbett in conveying practical information with such personality and flair and it was a tremendous success. Meanwhile, he wrote a set of moral tracts, *Cobbett's Sermons*, directed at the Evangelicals and what he saw as their hypocritical defence of the establishment in religious garb. In 1821 he set out on the first of his tours through the country. He published his day-to-day impressions in the *Political Register* and eventually brought them out under the title *Rural Rides* (1830). Written with great vigour, these observations of the land and its people, interwoven with politics and nostalgia for the rural past, are still read with pleasure.

Cobbett's last years were among the busiest of his life. The struggle for parliamentary reform was reaching its climax and, by now the leading journalist on the radical side, he pressed for a complete system of democratic representation. His many enemies, fearing his leadership of working-class radicals, wanted him removed; and in 1831 he was prosecuted for inciting labourers to arson and riot. A robust egotist, he defended himself with reckless confidence. The jury failed to reach a verdict and the case was dropped. In the event the Reform Bill fell far short of Cobbett's demands, but making the best of a bad job he supported it, treating it as simply the first instalment in reform. In the election following the passage of the Act, he was returned to Parliament for Oldham. Though he had lost none of his radicalism, he was by now an old man, and the long years in opposition were of little service to him in the House of Commons. He spoke often but with little impact, perhaps most memorably on the new Poor Law, which he saw as a threat to the traditional ways of life of the lower classes. Shortly before his election

to Parliament he had acquired a farm not far from his birthplace in Surrey, and it was there that he died on 18 June 1835, worn out by his labours, but full of hope for the future. He was buried in Farnham churchyard.

Cobbett's influence, though considerable, is difficult to assess. To the last he remained a romantic radical with strong Tory overtones. Close to the soil, he was a survivor of an older order, for whom industrial change was alien and unwelcome. Inconsistent and unoriginal, he had a limited vision, uninfluenced by abstract thought. Abuses and feeling, not ideas, moved him to anger and consequently action. His anti-intellectualism was, however, a great strength in awakening the labouring classes to their rights, for they could identify with a belligerent peasant of shrewd and independent judgement, who eloquently expressed their fears and aspirations. Through his popular political journalism he became the champion of a generation of labourers, especially those on the land, and the chief protagonist of the view that their economic improvement depended on parliamentary reform. As a journalist he played a leading part in the creation of a free press in England, the emergence of the signed editorial and the reporting of parliamentary debates. But for all his impact on the press, government and the labouring population, his contribution to the English language should not be forgotten. As a prose writer he was entirely professional, a master of polemic, with few equals in his evocation of the English countryside. It was on the land itself that his most noticeable influence was to be found, for gardens and farms on both sides of the Atlantic bore the fruit and showed the imprint of his enthusiasms as a farmer and as a writer on the domestic economy.

ARTHUR WELLESLEY
DUKE OF WELLINGTON

1769–1852

FIELD MARSHAL, Commander-in-Chief and Prime Minister, Arthur Wellesley, the first Duke of Wellington, was Britain's foremost soldier since the Duke of Marlborough and the most famous public figure of his generation. Born at Dangan Castle, County Meath, on 1 May 1769, he was the son of Garrett Wellesley, the first Earl of Mornington, and his wife Anne. Educated at a school in Chelsea and at Eton, he showed little aptitude for scholarship, and in 1784 his mother took him to Belgium where she entered him in a military academy. In 1787, through the influence of his elder brother Richard, he received a commission in the 73rd Highland regiment. For the next five years he was aide-de-camp to the Lord Lieutenant of Ireland, but there is no evidence that he did any regimental duty. Nonetheless, he picked up a knowledge of his profession and purchased the rank of major in the 33rd Foot, a Yorkshire regiment, in 1793. Having seen action in Holland against the French, he was ordered to India and landed at Calcutta in 1797.

When his brother Richard became Governor-General the next year, he was given important postings and rapid promotion. Both as a soldier and as a civil administrator he showed great ability and acquired a considerable reputation in the Maratha War of 1803–4.

His wide experience in India, not least in logistics, was to be the foundation of his future success as a soldier. But when he returned to England in 1805, Major-General, KB, he was not enthusiastically received. Britain was under threat of invasion from France and an Indian army officer, however capable, was treated rather like an admiral who had been sailing an inland lake.

Wellesley was elected to Parliament for Rye in 1806 and served as Chief Secretary for Ireland for two years (1807–9), but during this period he was also employed on active service. In 1807 he routed the Danes at Kiöge, for which he received the thanks of Parliament, and the next year, now a Lieutenant-General, was given command of the expeditionary force to be sent to the Peninsula to assist the Spanish resistance. Napoleon had turned to economic war after the disaster at Trafalgar and sought to shut out British goods from the continent by controlling the entire European coastline. As part of this policy he made his brother, Joseph, King of Spain and backed him with a large French army. Despite a considerably smaller force, Wellesley, created Viscount Wellington in 1809, sustained the Spanish resistance from his base in Portugal for five years. At Salamanca, Vitoria, the Nivelle and elsewhere he

The battlefield at Waterloo, June 1815, seen from the French side, with Napoleon on the right, and Wellington and his staff in the left background.

inflicted a series of defeats on the French which constituted Britain's most important military contribution to the downfall of Napoleon. From its inception through to its triumphant conclusion the plan of the Peninsular campaign was Wellington's. Promoted to Field-Marshal in 1813 he proved an audacious yet unwavering commander of rare shrewdness and versatility.

Wellington returned to England in 1814. Grandly received, he was created a duke and voted a large annuity. He took his seat in the House of Lords in June. Meanwhile, Napoleon had abdicated and had been exiled to Elba. Wellington was appointed ambassador at Paris but within a year succeeded his friend Castlereagh as chief of the British delegation at the

Congress of Vienna. After Napoleon escaped from Elba, landed in France and again proclaimed the Empire, Wellington was put in command of the British and Hanoverian forces, patched together a miscellaneous collection of troops and prepared for the defence of Belgium with his allies, the Prussians. The opposing forces met in June 1815 at Waterloo. Napoleon was narrowly defeated, later captured and again exiled. Much debate has surrounded the Battle of Waterloo and Wellington's role in it. To criticism of his generalship he replied: 'Damn them, I beat them, and if I was surprised, if I did place myself in so foolish a position, they were the greater fools for not knowing how to take advantage of my faults.' The victory was a critical one for the history of Europe. After it, Britain enjoyed nearly forty years free from hostilities on the continent. For Wellington it was the climax of his military career, and among the many honours and rewards heaped upon him he was created Prince of Waterloo by the King of the Netherlands and given a vast estate in Belgium.

Appointed to command the army of occupation after Waterloo, Wellington became an arbiter of European peace. He set up his headquarters at Cambrai, but preferring the life of a country squire he moved into a château some miles away, where he could entertain his officers and keep a pack of hounds for hunting. He acted as a referee for the settlement of claims against France and resisted attempts to reduce the size of the army of occupation. Meanwhile, he made trips back to England, as in 1817 when he was present at the opening of Waterloo Bridge. When his term as commander ended the following year, he returned to London and joined the government as Master-General of the Ordnance, with a seat in the cabinet. A Tory and a champion of aristocratic privilege, he was fierce in his dislike of democracy and the mob. 'Trust nothing to the enthusiasm of the people,' he once advised a colleague. One of his first responsibilities in his new office was the control of domestic unrest, which had been precipitated by the depression of trade after the end of the war and by the government's repressive legislation. Few men entering Westminster politics were as out of touch as Wellington. He had lived abroad for most of his adult life. The personification of stability, he was little suited to the reforming currents of post-war Britain. And, as a military man noted for his firmness, he was out of place in the give-and-take world of party politics.

Wellington recognized his own deficiencies for high political office, but like other generals in such circumstances he was taken up by a faction. Manoeuvred into its leadership, he reluctantly accepted office as Prime Minister in January 1828, following the collapse of Goderich's administration. His ignorance of the constitution was such that he believed that he could continue to hold the post of Commander-in-Chief, which he had recently assumed, with the Premiership. From the beginning his government was marked by dissension in the cabinet and controversy outside it. In foreign affairs he was disturbed by Russia's ascendancy over Turkey. At home, Catholic emancipation and the reform of Parliament demanded urgent attention. With Peel's help, he swept away Catholic civil disabilities. But as an extreme Tory and a Protestant from Ireland this was, as he later remarked, 'the most painful act' of his life. The extension of the franchise was anathema to him and his unequivocal opposition to it led to his resignation in 1830 and to a decline in Tory party fortunes. Wellington had failed to gauge public opinion or manage his party, and his reputation was at its nadir. In 1831, just after his wife's death, a mob attacked his London house and smashed many of its windows. He remained unperturbed and following a second similar incident he installed iron shutters.

Wellington's unpopularity, though extreme, did not long endure and he returned to politics in 1834 with the fall of Lord Grey's reform ministry. He served provisionally as Prime Minister until Peel returned from Italy and could form his own cabinet. Wellington was then shifted to the Foreign Office, but resigned a few months later with the collapse of the government. For the next several years he led the Conservative opposition in the House of

Wellington, painted by John Hoppner, 1806.

SIR ARTHUR WELLESLEY K.B

Lords and when Peel formed his second ministry in 1841 he took a seat in the cabinet but without portfolio. Now in his seventies, he was useful for his great reputation if not for his active participation. Nor was he finished as a military man. In 1842, for the second time, he became Commander-in-Chief. When the Chartists threatened London in 1848 he advised the cabinet on measures for their control. By now he held numerous other offices, among them Chancellor of Oxford University and Master of Trinity House. He took an active interest in Indian affairs, carried on a huge correspondence and was profuse, if undiscriminating, in his charities. A frequent visitor to the Great Exhibition in 1851, he stopped the show whenever he appeared. By the time of his death on 14 September 1852, 'the Duke' had become a legendary figure, basking in the afterglow of military exploits which shone all the brighter with the passing years.

It was said of Wellington by Lord Roberts that he was overrated as a man and underrated as a general. Certainly Wellington had his failings. His self-esteem made it difficult for him to admit a mistake and, although he usually kept his temper in check, his bluntness could made him appear ungracious. He was not without kindness and emotion in his relations with friends and mistresses but sympathy for others did not figure large in his make-up. His chief qualities were common sense, integrity, manliness and resolve; the appellation 'Iron Duke' which attached itself to him was not inappropriate. For the rank-and-file soldier he had little but contempt; 'the scum of the earth', he said of his troops at Waterloo. To him they were the military equivalent of the mob and needed to be restrained by harsh discipline and terror of brutal punishment. Reactionary in outlook, he opposed the abolition of flogging and most of the other proposals put forward by army reformers. In his view the army was best left alone and though he accepted a few minor changes, the use of technical advisers for example, he fought to keep it from falling into the hands of a civilian minister answerable to the House of Commons. His legacy as Commander-in-Chief was an army essentially the same as the one he led to victory at Waterloo, dominated by country gentlemen educated in the classics, many of whom had bought their commissions. The Crimea would point out its limitations.

Considerable controversy has surrounded Wellington's reputation as a general. The French, who dwell on his good fortune, are inclined to ignore or to disparage him. His admirers, on the other hand, pay tribute to his dash and coolness of judgement and see him as the modern Hannibal. Certainly his rapid grasp of varied types of warfare made him the greatest English general of his day and perhaps, after Marlborough, of all time. Whatever his rank in the military pantheon, his victories in India, the Peninsula and the Low Countries dramatically changed the course of events. What would have been the repercussions for Europe and the British Empire, or for the economy and institutions of England, had the Peninsular War or Waterloo been triumphs for Napoleon? In his political engagements Wellington was less fortunate and poorly equipped. After Castlereagh's death he had no guide through the minefield of party politics, and resolution could not serve where pliability was needed. Being public-spirited, he could not resist forays into politics, but more often than not they were damaging to his party and his personal prestige.

JOSEPH MALLORD WILLIAM TURNER

1775–1851

THE LANDSCAPE PAINTER Joseph Mallord William Turner is commonly held to be Britain's greatest artist. The complete professional, he was both a worthy successor to the tradition of European masters and a creative genius of great originality. Born in Maiden Lane, Covent Garden on St George's Day, 23 April 1775, he was the son of a barber, William Turner, and his wife Mary, née Marshall. His childhood was shaped by the lively atmosphere of the marketplace and the river, but was unsettled by his mother's recurrent bouts of insanity and the death of his younger sister, Mary Ann, when he was eleven. His relations with his mother, who died in Islington asylum in 1804, scarred him for life. Repressed and ridden with guilt, he found it difficult to form mature relationships. As a man, he was most relaxed with children, although he felt a lifelong, though rarely articulated, attachment to his father. As a boy, Turner sketched from nature, drawing on the London townscape and the countryside around Brentford where he had been a day boarder living with his uncle. His passion for the sea and ships probably dates from his time spent along the Thames around Twickenham, where he would eventually have a house. His professional career as an artist began very early, for his drawings could be bought in his father's shop for a shilling or two, and William Turner proudly announced in 1789 that 'my son is going to be a painter'.

Turner had an unconventional training as an artist. He attended various schools, including that run by Thomas Malton in Long Acre, where he studied perspective and architectural drawing, but his name is not intimately linked with any great master. Industry and moderation rather than formal education were the key to his success, as the artist Edward Dayes remarked. Entered as a student at the Royal Academy in 1789, he had his first picture, *Lambeth Palace*, exhibited in 1790. In the following years he became a regular exhibitor and in 1799 was elected an Associate of the Royal Academy, becoming a full member in 1802 and later Professor of Perspective. In 1790 Turner's sketching tours began, first to the west country and then to the remoter parts of England, Wales and Scotland. Sturdy and vigorous, he travelled twenty to twenty-five miles a day on foot, painstakingly gathering a vast range of material in his sketchbooks, to which he appended extensive notes. Although his sketches and water-colours of landscape and architecture in the early 1790s showed him to have a sharp eye for nature, he still worked in a traditional manner. His water-colours, for example, were similar in style to those of Dayes, whose influence on him was pronounced. There was little before 1796 to suggest the visionary painter of later years.

Rather, his work shows an apprentice struggling with his craft.

In the late 1790s Turner steadily advanced as a painter with a refined technique and enlarged vision. Stimulated by working with Thomas Girton and by a tour of the north of England in 1797, his painting took on greater breadth. He was now finding a larger audience for his work, and commissions from wealthy patrons became increasingly common. In drawing there were the skilful renderings of Salisbury Cathedral; in oil, the *Battle of the Nile*, which typified his growing interest in grand historical themes associated with the sea. He began French lessons, copied the water-colours of John Cozens, and read poetry, especially James Thomson, who challenged his aesthetic ideas. Like other British painters, he turned his attention to the European landscape traditions

Self-portrait by Turner, painted c.1798.

of Claude Lorrain and Nicholas Poussin, from whom he imbibed lessons in composition. It became his ambition to rival the landscapes of Claude. For this reason he left explicit instructions that after his death his works should be shown side by side with those of Claude, inviting a comparison that did not always do him a service. When Turner set off on the first of his European tours through Switzerland in 1802, his mind was full of Cozens and Claude. He returned with over 400 sketches, including *Devil's Bridge* and *Mer de Glace*, which Ruskin would later describe as 'quite stupendous'.

With the passing years Turner mastered his control of landscape and seascape and gradually freed himself from the influence of the old masters. In the haunting seascape *Calais Pier* he achieved the same symbolic power that he brought to his history paintings. The allegorical significance of his historical canvases reached a peak in the masterpiece of 1812, *Snowstorm: Hannibal and his Army crossing the Alps*. In other works, such as *Frosty Morning* and *Crossing the Brook*, he was creating a distinctive style of lyrical composition that owed less and less to other artists. Though a trial to him, his lectures at the Royal Academy helped him to refine his ideas; and, despite domestic crises and ill health, he continued to travel. His two trips to Italy in the 1820s were especially important in his development. They not only gave him fresh subject matter – the ruins of antiquity – but they revitalized his work. After Italy he achieved a greater unity of light and colour, which led to some of his greatest paintings. In the Venetian oils and the Parliament and Petworth pictures of the mid-1830s he brought his command of British and foreign influences into a personal, poetic synthesis.

Turner's last decade was difficult for him. Many of his closest associates died, his own health was failing and his paintings were often maligned by the critics; 'soapsuds and whitewash', remarked one of their number. He had perhaps lived overlong for his reputation, for the revolt and alienation which had underpinned the Romantic movement and which gave an edge to his own work had largely passed away. Still, there was a revival of interest in him after the publication of the first volume of Ruskin's *Modern Painters* (1843), which defended Turner against his detractors. And there were paintings in the 1840s which rank among his most brilliant, including *Snow Storm: Steam-Boat off a Harbour's Mouth; Goldau,*

a Swiss landscape; and *Rain, Steam and Speed.* The genesis of the latter illustrates an essential element in Turner's approach to art. On a train trip in a blinding rainstorm he was reported to have stuck his head out of the carriage window for several minutes, then returned to his seat and closed his eyes. Here was direct experience of nature recollected in and painted with emotion. His own ecstatic response to nature heightened its character in his work. Among his last finished pictures was *Angel in the Sun* (1846), which drew on Ruskin's insight that he was comparable to the Angel of the Sun in the Apocalypse. 'The Sun is God,' he was reported to have said on his death bed.

Turner's single-minded pursuit of artistic integrity left him with an enormous body of work but few social graces. Accounts of him in

Venice, *painted by Turner in 1833.*

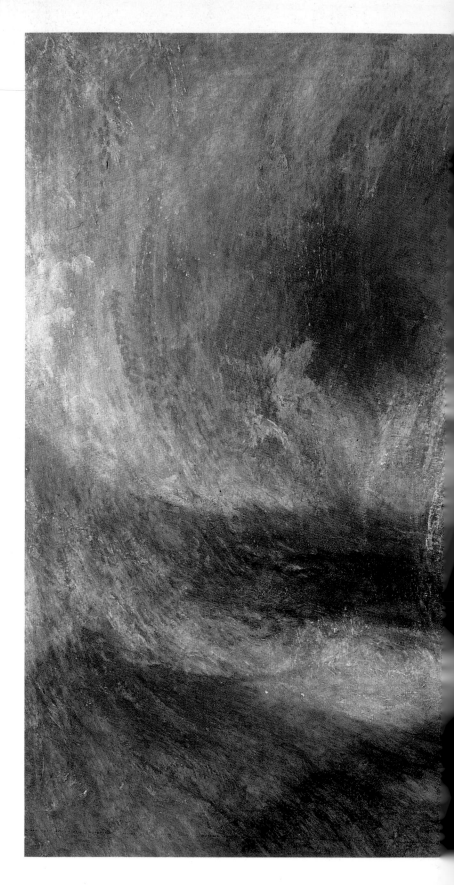

Snow Storm: Steam-Boat
off a Harbour's Mouth,
*exhibited in 1842. This was
painted from observations
Turner made when he had
himself lashed to the mast of a
steamboat while crossing from
Harwich in such a wild storm
that he had not expected to
survive.*

later life often commented on his rough manner, slovenly appearance and miserliness (he left an estate valued at £140,000 at his death). An unhappy love affair as a young man had encouraged his view of himself as unattractive and unlovable. Though suspicious of women, he eventually formed a liaison with the widow Sarah Danby, with whom he had two illegitimate daughters. Thinking of himself as a social oddity probably helped to free him from the deadening effects of convention and in particular of conventional art criticism. He was not immune to criticism. Indeed, it could reduce him to tears, but it never put him off his independent course. His sense of personal inadequacy, heightened by his difficult relations with his mother, gave a nervous tension and an adventurousness to his painting. He could be convivial among other artists but his greatest consolation was his work. As Dayes said of him: 'The man must be loved for his works; for his person is not striking, nor his conversation brilliant.' For Turner, art was not only a profession but a defence against the world.

Many scholars believe the key to understanding Turner's views on art and life is to be found in poetry, not least in his own poems, which he began to write in the 1790s. Few British painters, save William Blake, whose poems Turner apparently did not know, have been so influenced by poetry. So much so that it is impossible to isolate his poetic ideas from his artistic ones. Often his pictures had lines attached, from James Thomson and Milton among others. Sometimes Turner made up lines himself, often tinged with melancholy, and added them to the catalogue. Moreover, many of his landscapes derive from literary subjects or poems scanned for artistic inspiration. From poetry Turner found grand themes and specific ideas, and an aesthetic which moved him beyond naturalism and topography to the sublime and the romantic. The poetry in his paintings may be said to be seen in their intellectual power and dynamic intensity. As he had synthesized the best in European painting, he absorbed the poetry of his own country and his own imagination, reshaping it with paint and canvas. The apocalyptic *Slave Ship* (1839), for instance, which draws on Thomson's poem *The Seasons*, is a remarkable example of this transformation of literature into art, or 'airy visions', to use Constable's words, 'painted with tinted steam'. Here is a picture parable which for tragic grandeur no other British artist could match.

Turner's technique was ideally suited to searching out the poetic and emotional inner life of landscape. Beginning as a water-colourist, he was obsessed with the possibilities of coloured light. Inventive and quick to grasp essentials, he was notable with water-colour for his skill in removing colour by brushing, sponging, or scraping off drying paint with a knife. The broken texture and higher degree of brightness which he thus achieved represented a sharp break with the tradition of landscape water-colour as topographical painting. It has been argued that Turner felt most at home with water-colour, for the lighter medium suited his purposes better than the less easily manageable oils. Be that as it may, his water-colour work was much admired and widely imitated, by Palmer, Cotman, Bonington and Boys, among others. In oils, he was remarkable for his success in re-creating the clarity and airiness of his water-colours. Many of his mature oil paintings were pure experiments in colour, an attempt to recapture the Mediterranean light

Turner on Varnishing Day *by T.Fearnley, 1836.*
Turner was notorious for finishing his pictures on the
Academy walls before exhibitions opened.

and atmosphere. The result was landscape painting in oil of great boldness, refreshingly free from convention.

In achieving a harmony of light and colour, form and depth, few artists have been as effective with such economy of expression. With a few deft strokes Turner was capable of bringing a subject to a pitch of emotion and animation. In capturing grandeur and catastrophe, whether in landscape or seascape, he was unsurpassed, the 'virtuoso of the sublime'. Some critics saw only a chaotic haze in his later paintings, especially his vortical works which are so rich in symbolic tension and violence. But his very 'indistinctness' was the mark of a revolutionary sensibility which would profoundly influence other artists, not least the Impressionists, for decades to come.

ROBERT PEEL

1788–1850

THE MOST ABLE figure in Parliament for three decades, Robert Peel was an outstanding administrator and arguably Britain's greatest peacetime Prime Minister. Born on 5 February 1788 near Bury in Lancashire, he was the third child and eldest son of Robert Peel, a manufacturer and Tory MP, and his wife Ellen Yates. From the first his father wished him to become a statesman and gave him an education suited to this end. A sensitive and studious boy, he was sent to Harrow in 1801. Byron, who was a schoolfellow, remembered him as a considerable scholar and orator, for whom everyone at the school had the highest expectations. Four years later he entered Christ Church, Oxford, where he took a brilliant degree in classics and mathematics, without having to forgo his passion for shooting. His father procured a seat in Parliament for him in the Irish borough of Cashel and he entered the House of Commons in 1809, at the age of twenty-one. He gave his support to the Tory government and soon after his maiden speech, 'the best first speech since that of Mr Pitt', he accepted the post of Under-Secretary for War and the Colonies. When Lord Liverpool became Prime Minister in 1812, he became Chief Secretary for Ireland, where he successfully resisted calls for Catholic emancipation and maintained public order, assisted in this by the establishment of the peace preservation police, the 'Peelers'.

Although Peel relinquished the Irish Secretaryship in 1818, he continued to be immersed in public duties. As chairman of a committee of the House of Commons, he carried an act, 'Peel's Act', in 1819, which led to an important reform of the currency, returning the country to the gold standard. The following year he married Julia Floyd, the daughter of an Indian army officer. Though not political by inclination, she became Peel's closest confidante; the marriage brought him domestic happiness and seven children. About the time of his marriage, his political opinions began to change. Increasingly, he distrusted a rigid Toryism that was unresponsive to the needs and wishes of constituents. When he rejoined Lord Liverpool's cabinet as Home Secretary in 1822, he turned his attention to much needed reforms of the criminal law. In the next five years he mastered the intricacies of the subject and passed a series of Acts which amended and consolidated the criminal code. The result was a simplified and more merciful code, which was free of many of the unpopular capital offences. His measures did not go far enough for the leading humanitarian reformers, but Peel showed that he and his party were not insensitive to public opinion.

Peel resigned from the government in 1827 over the issue of Roman Catholic emancipation, which he and many of his fellow Tories opposed out of a mixture of support for Protestant landowners in Ireland and their anxiety about permitting Catholics to participate in legislation for Protestant institutions. Anxious to reunite his party, he joined the Duke of Wellington's cabinet a year later as Home Secretary and Leader of the House of Commons. As it transpired, his presence was essential to the government's survival. He continued to work on law reform and in 1829 he created a professional police force for London, which was eventually copied elsewhere. But with Ireland on the brink of open rebellion the issue of Catholic emancipation haunted him. For twenty years he had, with little foresight, opposed admitting Catholic subjects to civil equality. Now it was no longer a political issue but one of national security. Along with Wellington, Peel painfully accepted the need for reform. He offered his resignation, but Wellington persuaded him to remain in office and in 1829 he introduced, with consummate political skill, a bill which granted political rights to Catholics. It was the most difficult decision of his life, and it cost him and the Tory party dearly. It was one of the most notable examples of self-sacrifice on public record, although it failed to pacify Ireland.

When Wellington's government was defeated in 1830, Peel took his seat on the opposition bench. He had succeeded to a baronetcy and a fortune upon the death of his father and had also become member for Tamworth. Parliamentary reform was the great issue of the day and he vigorously but vainly opposed it. After the passage of the Reform Bill of 1832, he found himself the leader of a Tory party in disarray. But, always open to new impressions and reasoned argument, Peel was determined to reconstruct his party along fresh lines. He gave his support to Lord Grey's Whig government over various measures, including the emancipation of the slaves and the new Poor Law, and bided his time. When in 1834 the King dismissed Lord Melbourne and his ministers, Peel became Prime Minister. But, repeatedly defeated in the House of Commons by the Whig majority, he resigned four months later, having accomplished little beyond the establishment of the Ecclesiastical Commission. He returned to the opposition where for six years he struggled to lay the foundations of a conservative party open to new men and new ideas, a party whose principles he had sketched in his Tamworth Manifesto of 1834, committed to an acceptance of the reforms of 1832 and free from the unbending Toryism of the past.

Sir Robert Peel, engraved by C. Turner after Sir Thomas Lawrence.

In the late 1830s Peel's influence grew steadily and when in August 1841 he found himself in power, he headed a more disciplined party infused with confidence and a sense of national responsibility. The cabinet was remarkable for its talent and promise and contained seven past or future Prime Ministers, including both Gladstone and Disraeli. The essential aim of his administration was to promote the nation's economic growth while mitigating the damaging effects of industrial change. His first task was to implement financial reform. Through his budget of 1842 he initiated the first peacetime income tax and tariff reform, which greatly contributed to the country's financial stability. By reducing duties on a wide range of imports he encouraged trade and provided British consumers with cheaper goods. Other measures complemented his budgetary policy, most notably the Bank Charter Act of 1844, of which Peel was especially proud. It divided the functions of the Bank of England and took the first step towards giving it a monopoly of note issue. Peel's social policy aroused greater opposition and was more cautious. If it had not been for Lord Shaftesbury's influence over factory legislation it would have been less distinguished than it was. It is perhaps best described as muddling through.

Financial and social problems were amenable to reform, but the Irish question proved intractable, and led Peel to acts which eventually split his party and destroyed his government. His Irish policy has been variously described: neglectful when Ireland was tranquil, coercive when it was troubled by the campaign for the repeal of the Act of Union

RIGHT *The failure of the Irish potato crop in 1845 and the resultant famine and destitution often led to evictions, as depicted here. Peel's attempted solution – the repeal of the Corn Laws – brought about his resignation.*
BELOW *An early photograph of 'Peelers'.*

with Britain, and conciliatory when the campaign fell away in late 1843. But Peel's continuing worries over Ireland came to a head in the summer of 1845, with the crisis precipitated by the failure of the Irish potato crop. The government stepped in with a programme of public works, but more drastic measures were needed. In the interests of social stability and public order in Ireland, Peel decided to reverse his government's policy and repeal the Corn Laws, which restricted the introduction of much needed foreign grain. Thus in early 1846 he presented, in masterly fashion, a set of proposals for their elimination, along with plans for the abolition of duties on a range of manufactured goods. The bills passed the Commons to the delight of Free Traders but to the indignation of Tory protectionists. As in 1829 over Catholic emancipation, he had put necessity and the common good above his own party. Much maligned in Parliament, he resigned after a defeat in the House of Commons in June 1846.

Having split his party, Peel never returned to office after 1846. Fifty-eight when he resigned, he was now an elder statesman. His reputation was high in the country, where he was a hero not only to the middle classes but to a large section of the working classes as well. His popularity was a tribute to his success in reducing class divisions and vindicated his lifelong belief in aristocratic rule. His party, to which he was now indifferent, showed little sign of recovery and for some years after his death continued in abeyance. Peel, on the other hand, played a constructive role in Parliament in his last years as a pillar of free trade, but he refused to accept any higher honours. Never desirous of title or power for its own sake, he settled into repose, enjoyed his family and

circle of friends, optimistic about the nation's future. Though a man of legendary coolness, he could charm his companions with his good humour and vast storehouse of anecdote. His last speech in the House of Commons, on 28 June 1850, was a defence of diplomacy, which he described as 'a costly engine for maintaining peace'. The next day he was thrown from his horse while riding up Constitution Hill and died of his injuries three days later (2 July).

Few statesmen can match Peel's record of legislative achievement or his standard of political morality. His life was dominated by a sense of public duty and, though he revived and purified the Tory party, even it was sacrificed on the altar of responsible civil government. Reviled by some of his contemporaries for splitting the Tory party, he has been hailed since as a founding father of the modern Conservative Party. As a man he was selfless and wholly honourable. 'I never knew a man in whose truth and justice I had a more lively confidence', Wellington said of him. As a parliamentarian, in office or out, he was both courteous and formidable: strong in conviction, exact in detail, sensitive to the occasion, and bold in the expression of policy, even when he had come late to it. As a politician he had the gift of insight, if not originality. He bequeathed to the nation peace abroad and a series of commercial and financial reforms which contributed greatly to the prosperity of mid-Victorian Britain. For executive efficiency and honest government he served as a model for later Prime Ministers. While he is closely associated with the triumph of free trade, he is perhaps best remembered as a statesman who set the interest of the nation above that of class or party. More than any other public man of his day he raised the tone of British political life.

ALFRED TENNYSON

1809–1892

ALFRED TENNYSON was the quintessential Victorian, the most admired poet and man of letters of his day. He was born on 6 August 1809 at Somersby, Lincolnshire, the fourth of twelve children of the Rector of Somersby, George Tennyson, and his wife Elizabeth, herself the daughter of a churchman. At seven he was sent to live with his grandmother at Louth, a nearby town, where he attended the grammar school. But he was unhappy there and was withdrawn in 1820. He returned to a cultured home in which learning and poetry were encouraged. At the age of eight or so he had begun to write his own verse, and in the following years fell in love with the poetry of Pope, Byron and Scott. Precocious and somewhat ostentatious in his learning, he was often to be found in his father's library or in the fields declaiming his latest effusion. In 1827 he and his brother Charles published a book *Poems by two Brothers*, a juvenile work, part sentiment, part bluster, in imitation of Byron. The following year Alfred matriculated at Trinity College, Cambridge. There he pursued his poetic interests and developed a close friendship with Arthur Hallam, the son of a distinguished historian. In 1830 he published his *Poems, Chiefly Lyrical*. His life at Cambridge had been clouded by his father's ill health, and he returned to Somersby in 1831 without taking a degree, shortly before his father's death.

Tennyson remained at the rectory in Somersby, continued his studies and prepared a new volume of verse for publication. His sister Emily, to his delight, became engaged to his friend Hallam. *Poems* appeared at the end of 1832 (dated 1833) and although it contained some fine writing, including 'The Lady of Shalott' and 'A Dream of Fair Women', it was savaged by reviewers. The following year was one of the most fateful of his life, for Hallam died while on a European tour. Tennyson was inconsolable and lamented the tragedy for years afterwards. *The Two Voices* and the elegiac *In Memoriam*, though published later, were expressions of his sorrow. Despite it, he did not go into seclusion. From time to time he sought out the company and attention of friends. He visited Cambridge. In London he met Gladstone, Thackeray and Edward Fitzgerald. In 1836 he fell in love with the bridesmaid at his brother's wedding, Emily Sellwood, a moment captured in 'Oh happy bridesmaid, make a happy bride'. But because he feared his tendency to depression, which had afflicted his father, and perhaps because of his finances, their engagement lapsed.

Eighteen forty-two was something of a turning point for Tennyson, for during that year he brought out his long-awaited *Poems*, in two volumes. The first was a reissue of his verse from 1830 and 1833, much of it re-

Alfred Tennyson by Samuel Laurence, c. 1840.

written; volume two contained new material, including 'Locksley Hall', 'Morte d'Arthur', 'Ulysses' and 'Godiva', which showed the range of his poetic imagination and gift for melodic language, 'its silver ring' as one critic called it. But while the *Poems* were widely popular and added to his growing reputation, they did not relieve him of his financial worries, which had worsened when he invested most of his savings in a disastrous scheme to produce wood carvings by machinery. His hypochondria deepened and his friends, anxious on his behalf, persuaded the Prime Minister, Robert Peel, to grant him a Civil List Pension. At first Tennyson refused it, but ultimately accepted the £200 a year in 1845, an act which aroused no small degree of indignation among his critics. An acrimonious literary squabble broke out with the novelist Edward Bulwer-Lytton, which Tennyson soon regretted.

About the time of his feud with Bulwer-Lytton, Tennyson was at work on an elaborate new poem, *The Princess* (1847), which dealt with the timely issue of women's higher education. As a man of liberal sympathies and the brother of talented sisters, the reform of female education was to him desirable. Characteristically, he treated the subject as a parable set in the Middle Ages, an entertainment that did not require the reader to take on board his contemporary message. With this form, one of his biographers remarked, he hit upon a key to success: 'To sympathize with progress in theory, and at the same time to disprove it by caricature in practice.' *The Princess* was immediately popular with a public that wished to feel liberal without troubling overmuch to reform itself. *In Memoriam*, written over many years and published anonymously in 1850, also caught the public mood, but it was rather less successful with reviewers. It alienated some in the religious establishment, and one critic said that it must have been written by 'the widow of a military man'. A parable of man's soul in adversity, it begins in grief (for his friend Hallam) and moves through love to faith in human progress and immortality. (He could not bear the thought that life ended at death.) The poem improved his material prospects, thus finally permitting his marriage to Emily Sellwood, and contributed to his elevation to the office of Poet Laureate upon the death of Wordsworth in 1850. Tennyson was now a public institution.

After some difficulty in finding a house, the Tennysons settled in Chapel House, Montpelier Row, Twickenham. Their first child died, strangled at birth. A second child, Hallam, was born in August 1852. Soon after, Alfred wrote an 'Ode' on the death of Wellington, whom he greatly admired, in his capacity as Poet Laureate. In 1854 another son, Lionel, was born, by which time the Tennysons were living on the Isle of Wight, which suited Alfred's need for peace and quiet. The house, called Farringford, was to be their permanent home. There he worked on his dramatic poem *Maud*, the seed of which had appeared nearly twenty years earlier in 'Oh, that 'twere possible'. But the writing of *Maud* was interrupted in December 1854, when news of the Crimean battles appeared in *The Times*. His jingoism stirred, he wrote at a single sitting *The Charge of the Light Brigade*, an immensely popular poem which made him a revered Laureate. *Maud* came out in the following autumn. Full of melodrama and high-sounding phrases, parts of it, such as the stanza beginning 'Come into the garden, Maud', were of great melodic beauty. Tennyson, who craved approval, came out of seclusion to read the poem to friends.

By now Tennyson's prestige was such that his house was on the tourist map, and sightseers peered through his windows to get a look at him. He planted trees to give himself greater privacy. A picturesque figure in his black frock coat and his wide black hat, he made a striking impression when in public. Bertrand Russell, who knew him and thought him a humbug, said that Tennyson took care not to see you if you walked by him, so absorbed in poetic meditation was he. Despite his lack of social grace and need for retirement, he had many friends and entertained a host of prominent figures, including the Brownings, Matthew Arnold, John Ruskin and George Eliot. But the social rounds did not provide him with the poetic subjects that he required. His last major work, *Idylls of the King*, like *Maud* before it, drew on earlier ideas. Published in 1859 and added to in later years, it was an epic on the Arthurian legend, 'the drama of man coming into practical life', as he put it, 'and ruined by one sin'. That essential 'sin', in Tennyson's morality, was man's surrender to the seductiveness of woman, the triumph of the flesh in its continual battle with the spirit. Throughout his life, the reality of the spirit was uppermost in his writing.

Tennyson filled his last decades with extensive travel, visits to friends, reading and poetic labour. After the publication of *Enoch Arden* (1864), which sold 60,000 copies, he was dubbed 'the poet of the people'. There were also the additions to *Idylls of the King*, including 'The Holy Grail' and 'The Passing of Arthur' (1869). His anti-Catholic blank verse drama, *Queen Mary*, modelled on Shakespeare, was produced at the Lyceum in 1876, and *The Falcon* enjoyed a modest success at the St James' Theatre in 1879–80. Tennyson was often in London and saw much of Gladstone, who recommended him for a peerage, which he reluctantly accepted. Lionized, he met almost everyone of consequence. Meanwhile he kept up his scholarly and literary interests. He admired, for example, the novels of Jane Austen and Frazer's *Golden Bough*. The ballet, on the other hand, unsettled him, especially the girls in the chorus. Although his health became precarious late in life, he continued to enjoy his favourite pastime, yachting, and carry on his writing. Among his later works was the volume *Demeter and other Poems* (1889), which included the memorable 'Crossing the Bar'. He died on 6 October 1892 and was buried in Westminster Abbey.

Tennyson expected to be torn apart after his death by biographers, whom he compared to carrion vultures. Inevitably, as a tide of anti-Victorianism swept the intelligentsia, his reputation receded. One biographer went so far as to suggest that his 'idle high-mindedness' and 'false morality' contributed to the jingoism that resulted in the First World War. Others have reduced him to a frightened conformist and an 'unhappy mystic'. T.S. Eliot called him the 'saddest of English poets'; Auden called him the 'stupidest'. None of these judgements is fair to a many-sided master of lyric poetry, who displayed such craftsmanship and charm, learning and individuality. His identification with British values made him enormously popular; few distinguished writers have been so successful at reconciling popularity and art. Tennyson won this success at a price. He missed being one of the greatest English poets, perhaps because his life was too narrow and comfortable. His imagination depended overmuch for stimulation on suggestions from indulgent friends or readings from his library, and not from harsh experience, which so often forms the basis of supreme creative thought. But the value and permanence of his work is not in doubt. His writing remains relevant to those perennial human issues such as grief, religion and art, which he illuminated; and he will always be read for the range and richness of his imagery and the felicity of his language.

One of Gustave Doré's illustrations to Tennyson's Arthurian epic Idylls of the King.

CHARLES DICKENS

1812–1870

CHARLES DICKENS, Britain's greatest novelist and one of the world's greatest story-tellers, was also a committed social and political reformer who used his pen as a powerful weapon in the fight against injustice, poverty and oppression.

Dickens himself experienced at an early age the misery of poverty which he was later to write about with such passion and sensitivity in his novels. Born on 7 February 1812 in Portsmouth, he grew up under the shadow of the sizeable debts amassed by his extravagant father who was a clerk in the navy pay department. At the age of twelve he was forced to leave school and go to work in a London blacking factory – a grim experience which later found its way into his partly autobiographical novel *David Copperfield*. A few weeks later his father was arrested for debt and imprisoned with his wife and other children in the notorious Marshalsea Prison.

At fifteen the young Charles Dickens was able to find employment more suited to his intellectual abilities and his middle-class station when he went to work as a lawyer's clerk in Gray's Inn. It was there that he developed his contempt for the legal system with its endless red tape and delays which was to be displayed with such force in *Bleak House*.

A voracious reader since youth, Dickens took out a reader's ticket at the British Museum on his eighteenth birthday. Shortly afterwards he joined the reporting staff of *The Mirror of Parliament*, which carried verbatim reports of parliamentary debates. In 1835 he transferred to the *Morning Chronicle*, one of the leading London daily papers, where his journalistic talents won wide acclaim. Dickens wrote his first story for publication in 1833, dropping it through the letterbox of the *Monthly Magazine*. The editor liked it and asked for more stories, which were duly sent in under the pseudonym Boz; Dickens derived this from the nickname 'Moses' which he had given to one of his brothers.

In 1836 the aspiring young author was asked to write a story in twenty monthly parts to accompany a series of Cockney sporting prints already commissioned by the publishers. The result, *The Posthumous Papers of the Pickwick Club*, was a tremendous success: instead of the £400 which Dickens had expected to receive for his work, he made £2,000 and the publishers made £14,000.

For the rest of his career Dickens stuck to the pattern, which he had established with the Pickwick Papers, of producing his novels in monthly serial form. His next story, *Oliver Twist*, appeared in instalments throughout

Charles Dickens with his daughters, Mamie and Katey, at Gad's Hill Place in the mid-1860s.

1837 and 1838 and confirmed his reputation as one of the leading novelists of his day.

Many of the themes which loom large in Dickens's fiction reflect the experiences and interests of the author. The death of innocent youth, explored with such pathos in the passages on Little Nell in *The Old Curiosity Shop*, was a subject that came to haunt him after the death of his wife's sister, Mary, at the age of seventeen. For many years he dreamed vividly of the dead girl and frail adolescents held a particular fascination for him. In a more cheerful vein, Dickens's love of the theatre and passion for amateur dramatics found expression in his creation of Vincent Crummles and his touring company of players in *Nicholas Nickleby*.

The political and social radicalism which made Dickens a leading campaigner for such humanitarian reforms as the abolition of capital punishment and the ending of child labour in factories also found its way into his novels. Through characters like Oliver Twist and Joe, the crossing-sweeper in *Bleak House*, he brought home to his respectable middle-class readership the extent and horror of poverty in mid-Victorian London.

As well as being an active speaker at radical and reform meetings, Dickens was also a committed campaigning journalist. In 1846 he founded a new national daily paper, the *Daily News*, to be a crusading journal exposing the ills of the day and taking a Liberal line in politics. He gave his father a job as chief reporter on the paper and for several years was himself the editor. Later on the *Daily News* was merged with the *Daily Chronicle* to form the *News Chronicle*.

Four years after his venture into newspaper proprietorship, Dickens set up a weekly periodical, *Household Words*, which contained a mixture of short stories, serializations of novels and articles of a factual kind. This mix proved particularly popular with the Victorian reading public, who liked to be both informed and entertained, and attracted contributions from Wilkie Collins and Mrs Gaskell. It was in this periodical, which later changed its title to *All the Year Round*, that Dickens published the annual Christmas stories which followed his immensely popular tale *A Christmas Carol* and which did so much to establish the British Christmas traditions of turkey, plum pudding, mince pies, carol singing and stockings hung up to be filled with presents.

Although in his Christmas stories and in much of his other work Dickens idolized the pleasures of hearth and home and extolled the virtues of a happy family life, his own domestic circumstances were profoundly unhappy. He had married in 1836 Catherine Hogarth, daughter of the Scottish editor of the *Morning Chronicle*. Together they had ten children, one of whom died in infancy; Dickens found them a burden. His own wife he found increasingly unattractive and he had a series of Platonic love affairs with much younger women. Eventually in 1858 he and Catherine separated. They never divorced but in the 1860s, towards the end of his life, he took as his mistress Ellen Ternan, a strikingly drawn actress to whom he had first been attracted when she was in her teens.

Dickens's tempestuous married life and his pronounced radical views meant that he never won quite the same acceptance in polite social circles as his literary contemporaries William

Title page from a Danish edition of David Copperfield and Other Stories, *1888, showing Dickens and scenes from the novels.*

Title page of the 1842 edition of Barnaby Rudge *printed in Philadelphia. Dickens' pseudonym Boz was derived from his brother's nickname 'Moses'.*

Makepeace Thackeray and Alfred Tennyson. He did not meet Queen Victoria until shortly before his death in 1870 when he had a somewhat stiff audience during which she kept him standing for ninety minutes. But unlike many great writers, he achieved both fame and fortune during his life and did not have to wait for death to be recognized as a genius. He was able to send his eldest son to Eton and to install himself in Gad's Hill Place, a large mansion outside Rochester in Kent which he had often gazed on in wonder as a small boy.

As well as gaining a comfortable income from writing books, Dickens also made a small fortune from reading them aloud. Initially he conducted public readings for charity and it was while reading *A Christmas Carol* on behalf of the Great Ormond Street Children's Hospital that he conceived the idea of holding public readings of his work for profit. He went on a highly successful tour of the British Isles in 1858, filling public halls and theatres with audiences anxious to share with their creator such emotional scenes as Christmas Day at the Cratchits.

In 1868 Dickens took his readings across the Atlantic. He had been to America once, more than twenty years before, when he had railed against the evils of slavery. Now the Civil War had been fought and slavery abolished. Dickens performed to packed houses in Boston, New York and Washington, making more than £20,000 but ruining his voice and exhausting himself in the process.

When he returned to Britain he was a very sick man but he insisted, against doctor's advice, on throwing himself into another tour at home, including, for the first time, the reading of the bloodcurdling passage in *Oliver Twist* where Bill Sykes beats Nancy to death. His audiences shrieked and cried at the terrible events they heard while the author himself became weaker and weaker.

Dickens died on 9 June 1870 as he was working at Gad's Hill on his twenty-third novel, *The Mystery of Edwin Drood*. After a quiet private funeral, he was buried at Westminster Abbey, as befitted his position as the nation's favourite story-teller.

Dickens's legacy to the English-speaking world (and beyond, for his novels have been translated into many languages) is immense. He has given such marvellously expressive words as gamp, Scrooge and Micawberish to our language. He has created archetypal and universal figures like the perennially jovial and clubbable Mr Pickwick and the creeping and cringing Uriah Heep.

To read Dickens's books today is not just to encounter the social evils of Victorian England in a way which is much more vivid and affecting than that provided by any history book. It is also to enter into a rich and wonderful world of human characters who are timeless and universal in their appeal – some lovable, some detestable, some heroic, some tragic but all memorable and each in its larger than life way exhibiting some facet of that infinitely variable and infinitely interesting phenomenon, the human personality.

It is the set-piece scenes and the dramatic confrontations which stir us most today in television adaptations of Dickens's works just as they moved the thousands who read them in Victorian drawing rooms: the first meeting between Pip and Magwitch, the escaped convict, in *Great Expectations*; Miss Havisham sitting alone and half-crazed amidst the splendours of the wedding banquet that was never to be in the same novel; the evocation of the overpowering procrastination and inhumanity of the Court of Chancery which begins *Bleak House*; and, of course, that never-to-be-forgotten moment when Oliver Twist has the audacity to ask for a second helping during meal time at the workhouse.

Illustrated covers of the monthly parts of three of the novels and of Sketches by Boz. *Dickens produced much of his work in monthly serial form.*

In an age before radio, television and the cinema Dickens's novels won countless 'fans' because of the vividness of his imagination, the strength of his descriptive powers and the variety and originality of his characterization. Today, serialized on radio and television and turned into hit musicals and record-breaking films, they appeal for exactly the same reasons. Dickens was a master of the art of story-telling.

VICTORIA AND ALBERT
1819–1901, 1819–1861

FEW MONARCHS at any period of history and in any country have epitomized the spirit of the age in which they reigned better than Queen Victoria. Pious, high-minded, homely and dedicated to the improvement of the condition of all her subjects, she presided for sixty-four glorious years over a country at the height of its powers and over an empire which stretched across the globe.

The pure and blissful domestic life which Victoria shared with her beloved husband Prince Albert set an example which was followed throughout the land and established the cult of the home and the family which we associate with our Victorian forefathers. In her public life she showed a single-minded dedication to duty and won the affection of the people that has continued to be bestowed on the Royal Family to the present day.

Victoria was born on 19 May 1819, the daughter of Prince Edward, the Duke of Kent, who was the fourth son of King George III and his German wife Princess Victoria of Saxe-Coburg. The name of the new princess was not decided until the very moment of her christening. Her uncle, the Prince Regent, the future George IV, suggested that she be named Alexandrina after the Tsar of Russia. Her father preferred either Charlotte or Augusta. Eventually, with the baby waiting at the font in the Archbishop of Canterbury's arms, the two brothers resolved their argument by deciding to name her after her mother. The name Alexandrina did, in fact, remain her official first name until she had it removed after her coronation.

The young princess, who lost her father when she was just one, had a dull and lonely childhood. She was brought up by a strict German governess with whom she sat interminably repeating the words 'I will be good'. However, she enjoyed music, had a voracious appetite for reading and early showed herself to have a flair for mastering foreign languages.

In 1837 William IV died and Victoria found herself at the age of eighteen on the throne of Great Britain. 'I am very young', she wrote in a characteristic entry in her journal, 'and perhaps in many, though not in all things, inexperienced, but I am sure that very few have more real good will and more real desire to do what is fit and right than I have.' Those who came into contact with the young Queen were amazed at her poise and air of authority which belied her youth and her small stature – she was less than five feet tall. She was immensely helped in her early years on the throne by the fatherly advice of her first Prime Minister, Lord Melbourne, who schooled her in the duties and responsibilities of constitutional monarchy.

Queen Victoria early showed her forcefulness when in 1839 Melbourne was defeated in Parliament and Sir Robert Peel became Prime Minister. Peel insisted that he could only govern if certain members of the Royal Household were removed – in particular some of the ladies of the bedchamber who were married to his Whig opponents. The Queen stubbornly refused to accept his demands and a constitutional crisis ensued in which Peel was forced to step down and Melbourne resumed the Premiership once again. Victoria had proved that she was not to be pushed around by her ministers.

The year 1839 also witnessed a rather happier event at Court with the engagement of the Queen to Prince Albert of Saxe-Coburg. The marriage of these two cousins had been long planned by their uncle King Leopold of Belgium but no one had reckoned on how easily and swiftly it would come about once they themselves met. Albert arrived at Windsor Castle on 10 October, to find the Queen suffering from the after-effects of a meal of bad pork the night before and also upset because a madman had broken some windows in the castle. Five days later they were engaged and the marriage took place in February 1840.

Albert was the perfect partner for Victoria. Born on 26 August 1819, like her he had endured a lonely and unhappy childhood relieved by a fondness for music, reading and natural history. He come to Britain full of projects for reform and with a determination to make the Crown the patron-in-chief of arts and sciences. He himself was skilled in both areas, being an accomplished musician, a keen collector of paintings, a student of architecture and a knowledgeable agriculturalist with a particular interest in pig breeding.

Prince Albert became a very active member of the Royal Family, fully justifying the title of Prince Consort which Victoria bestowed on him. He was instrumental in designing the new royal homes at Osborne on the Isle of Wight and Balmoral in the Scottish Highlands. He presided over the competition to choose an architect for the new Houses of Parliament and took a particular interest in schemes to provide decent housing for the poor. His greatest achievement was undoubtedly the Great Exhibition held in the Crystal Palace in 1851, which was a showcase for the inventions and artefacts of the world and brought together his

Queen Victoria and Prince Albert, a studio portrait by Roger Fenton, c. 1860.

interest in art and science and his strong internationalism.

The Prince Consort regularly attended the audiences which ministers had with his wife and was instrumental in persuading her of the good points of Peel, who in 1841 became Prime Minister. The two were devoted to each other and to the nine children who were born between 1840 and 1857. Victoria was heart-broken when Albert died aged forty-two on 14 December 1861 – she had already suffered a nervous breakdown as a result of the death of her mother – and went into virtually perpetual mourning, withdrawing from all public engagements and remaining in quiet and melancholy seclusion at home.

She was coaxed out of this depressed state largely through the influence of one man, John Brown, the handsome, rugged Highlander who was the ghillie at Balmoral. In the winter of 1864 Brown came to Osborne House to look after the Queen's pony. She found him a reassuring and sympathetic companion and he stayed on to become 'The Queen's Highland Servant'. In the upright and dependable Brown, Victoria found an example of manliness which could at least soften, even if it could never compensate for, the loss of her dear husband.

For much of the 1860s and 1870s Victoria was preoccupied with the business of settling down and marrying off her various children. No one caused her more heartache and worry than Bertie, the wayward Prince of Wales whose womanizing boded ill for the future standing of the monarchy. In her public role she presided over a series of governments

Queen Victoria and her Indian servant photographed at Frogmore by Hills and Saunders, 1893.

which introduced major reforms into the life and institutions of the country. She was generally happy with the way that things were going and intervened little directly with the actions of her ministers.

There were, of course, some whom she liked better than others. During the 1850s she had found the gung-ho jingoism and gunboat diplomacy as well as the philandering of Lord Palmerston particularly distasteful. Victoria herself was not an advocate of wars and imperial expansion. She described the Crimean War as unsatisfactory and was never keen that Britain should embark on risky military adventures to prove its strength or extend its territory.

She did, however, believe strongly in defending the integrity of the British Empire as it stood and was not sympathetic to those who sought to break it up either by granting independence to its component parts or by letting others seize control. This was one of her many quarrels with William Ewart Gladstone who served four times as her Prime Minister between 1868 and 1894. Like Victoria, Gladstone was a deeply religious and high-minded individual but he struck her as arrogant, long-winded and pompous. She complained that he treated her like a public meeting. The Queen was particularly angry at Gladstone for what she took to be his dilatoriness in sending an expedition to relieve General Gordon, besieged in Khartoum in 1884. She was also unhappy about his desire to break up the integrity of the United Kingdom by giving Home Rule to Ireland.

Sir Edwin Landseer's conversation piece, Windsor Castle in Modern Times: Queen Victoria, Prince Albert and Victoria, Princess Royal, *1845.*

For Gladstone's great rival, Benjamin Disraeli, however, Victoria had nothing but affection and praise. He flattered and amused her, making her Empress of India and constantly praising her literary endeavours. The Tories' strong attachment to the monarchy and preservation of the institutions of the country also compared favourably with what she took to be the Liberals' Dangerous radicalism.

In 1887 celebrations were held throughout the land to celebrate Victoria's fifty years on the throne. The country rejoiced and celebrated a period of unprecedented peace and prosperity.

A rare photograph of Queen Victoria smiling.

The Queen herself was more subdued, noting in her journal on jubilee day: 'The day has come and I am alone . . . 50 years today since I came to the Throne! God has mercifully sustained me through many great trials and sorrows.'

In old age even more than in youth the Queen came to symbolize the dignity and respectability of the times in which she reigned. She also became increasingly a focus for the growing imperialist sentiment in Britain. This was particularly true during the Boer War which she saw as a struggle to avoid national humiliation and as an expression of 'high tone'. Curiously, for one who presided over the greatest empire that the modern world has seen, she travelled only very seldom beyond the borders of the British Isles and then only to the nearby countries of France, Switzerland and Germany.

Queen Victoria died on 19 January 1901 after a mercifully short illness and surrounded by her children and grandchildren. Her death was mourned as the passing not just of a much-loved monarch but of an epoch and a whole way of life. The twentieth century was to usher in a set of values and a position for Britain on the world stage very different from those which had existed during her long and benign reign.

Queen Victoria was loved and respected for her simplicity, her domesticity and her humanity. She was a child of her time in her earnest desire for improvement, her good manners and her tendency to prudishness. But she was also a romantic who loved nothing better than walks through the magnificent scenery of her beloved Scottish Highlands. Though her life was often clouded, she had an infectious zest for living which shines through the pages of her ever-readable journals.

BENJAMIN DISRAELI

1804–1881

AT FIRST SIGHT Benjamin Disraeli seems an unlikely figure to have been the most successful leader of the Conservative Party in the nineteenth century. Coming of Italian Jewish stock he stood completely outside the British political establishment. Yet, starting life as a wild radical and a romantic novelist, he was to become in middle age an arch-patriot, devoted to Queen Victoria and to the spread of the British Empire and the scourge of Liberals and Little Englanders.

Disraeli achieved his climb to the top of the greasy pole, as he put it, by a mixture of good luck, calculating opportunism and native brilliance and flair. More than any other individual he deserves credit for the creation of the modern Conservative Party – yet, ironically, he had been instrumental in the destruction of that party when it was led by his arch-rival, Sir Robert Peel. His oratorical skirmishes with Gladstone in the House of Commons set the pattern of adversarial two-party politics which was to remain unbroken for nearly a century.

Disraeli was born on 21 December 1804 in London where his father, Isaac, was a reasonably successful author. Unlike nearly every other future Premier before or since, he went neither to public school nor to Oxford or Cambridge. After an education carried out largely at home, and after qualifying at the Bar, he devoted himself to writing. His first novel,

Vivian Grey, about an ambitious and unscrupulous young man determined to succeed in life by his wits and temerity, was published in 1826 to a generally favourable reaction in the literary world.

There was undoubtedly an element of Vivian Grey in Disraeli himself. Increasingly attracted to the bright lights of London society, and keenly ambitious, he resolved in the early 1830s to enter politics with the idea of reaching the highest position open to a commoner in the land. The choice of party he made on pragmatic grounds. Believing Toryism to be a dying creed with the advent of parliamentary and other reforms, and having a dislike of the Whigs, he presented himself to the electors of High Wycombe in Buckinghamshire in 1832 as a Radical. After three defeats, however, he decided to change his allegiance to the Tories and it was under their banner that he entered the House of Commons as MP for Maidstone in 1837.

Disraeli's début in the chamber which he was later to dominate with his oratorical fireworks was unpropitious. His affected, florid style, enhanced by his foppish and dandified style of dress, did not endear itself to older MPs and his maiden speech was drowned in a cacophony of hisses, groans, hoots, catcalls and drumming of feet. It may well be that the rude reception spurred on the young man to work his way to the top of the political tree and to prove that an outsider could scale the heights of one of the most closed and impregnable strongholds.

Disraeli's political career was given a considerable boost in 1839 when he married Mary Anne Lewis, the widow of his fellow Tory victor at Maidstone in the 1837 election. Many people have assumed that he married Mary Anne, who was twelve years his senior, for her money. It is certainly true that his reckless and extravagant ways had got him deep into debt. But the couple seem to have been genuinely in love and their marriage was blissfully happy. Disraeli, who had been a notorious womanizer and indulged in more than one affair with married women, treated her more like a mistress than a wife and shortly before her death she told a friend that their life together had been 'one long scene of happiness, owing to his love and kindness'.

During the 1840s Disraeli emerged as the leading figure among a group of young Tories who idolized the chivalry and feudal values of the Middle Ages and defended Britain's ancient constitution against the assault of Whig and Radical reformers. The Young England movement, as this group of backward-looking romantics became known, set itself consciously against the harshness of mid-Victorian industrial society and in particular against the middle-class industrialists and mill owners who were becoming a dominant force in the land.

Disraeli wrote two powerful novels which expressed the philosophy of the Young England movement. *Coningsby* (1844) and *Sybil* (1845) deplore the divided condition of mid-Victorian Britain – indeed it is in the second of these two books that the memorable phrase 'The Two Nations' first appears to describe the different worlds of rich and poor. Although his novels and his participation in the Young England movement were motivated by a genuine concern about the plight of the working classes because of industrialization and urbanization, there is little doubt that Disraeli's main object in the 1840s was to undermine the position of the Conservative Party leader, Sir Robert Peel. Peel was all that Disraeli hated – a cold, middle-class intellectual from a family of industrialists who was prepared to change sacred British institutions. More to the point, perhaps, he had also refused the up-and-coming Jew a place in his government and for this he was never to be forgiven.

Disraeli was one of the main architects of the back-bench rebellion against Peel which followed the repeal of the Corn Laws in 1846 and which split the Tory Party down the middle. While most of the more talented and able Tories, including the young W.E. Gladstone, followed Peel, Disraeli remained with the protectionist rump of the party who refused to countenance what they saw as a sell-out of the traditional landed interest in favour of the dubious modern principle of free trade. It was in this dim and ultra-reactionary company that he was able to shine and rise up as leader.

Disraeli had to battle his way to the leadership of the protectionists in the House of Commons. He was still disliked and regarded as an outsider by most leading Conservatives despite the fact that in 1848 he became a country gentlemen like them by buying Hughenden Manor in Buckinghamshire. The Earl of Derby, who led the Tories from the Lords, was extremely unwilling to see Disraeli assume the position of leader in the Commons but eventually he was forced to accept the brilliant and pushy young man as his deputy.

Disraeli first saw office in 1852 when he became Chancellor of the Exchequer in Derby's government. The administration lasted less than a year, brought down by a budget over which Disraeli had failed to exercise any technical mastery and which was scathingly denounced from the opposition benches by Gladstone in a speech which marked the beginning of a duel that was to last for the next thirty years.

Although he was only to see office again for one very brief period in the next fourteen years, Disraeli used the long period when the Conservatives were in opposition to consolidate his position as leader of the party. Realizing that the Tories would never again become a permanent force in government unless they moved with the times and abandoned their more reactionary positions, he set about persuading his colleagues to drop protectionism and quietly swallow most of the reforms which he had earlier denounced Peel for introducing.

Recognizing that a fairly spectacular and daring political manoeuvre was needed to establish the Tories as a force to be reckoned with once again after their long period in the political wilderness following the split over the Corn Laws, Disraeli launched in 1867 one of the most remarkable coups ever in the history of British politics. The defeat of the Whigs in 1866, when some of their own supporters had joined with Tories to vote down a Reform Bill introduced by Gladstone, brought Lord Derby to power once again. Disraeli, once more in the post of Chancellor, decided to risk what he later called a leap in the dark and outflank the Whigs by introducing a Reform Bill more radical than theirs.

The short-term effect of the measure he introduced, which enfranchised many in the lower middle classes and the upper ranks of artisans and skilled workers, was to bring his arch-rival Gladstone to power at the head of the first Liberal (as distinct from Whig) government. But in the long run Disraeli's gamble paid off and showed that the Conservatives were a party prepared to move with the times and fit to govern the country.

Disraeli finally achieved the position on which he had set his heart in 1868 but it was only for a few months and he had to wait another six years until he was again Premier, this time for a long span. The government over which he presided from 1874 to 1880 was responsible for several important measures of social reform, including legislation to provide

Benjamin Disraeli by Sir Francis Grant, 1851, the year before he became Chancellor of the Exchequer.

better houses for working people, to regulate the conditions in which food and drugs were sold and to improve sanitation and public health. It was also firmly committed to the maintenance and expansion of the British Empire. Disraeli took Britain into wars in Afghanistan and against the Zulus. He purchased the shares in the Suez Canal that were to give Britain a major interest in Egypt for the next seventy years and he proclaimed Queen Victoria Empress of India.

Like many of his actions, the image created by this new title for the Queen was more important than the substance. Disraeli was devoted to Queen Victoria. He flattered her unceasingly and compared her to Spenser's Faery Queen. She responded with equal devotion to the man she described as 'my own, dear Dizzy' whom she found infinitely more congenial company than the solemn and disapproving Mr Gladstone.

Disraeli's time as leader of the Conservatives was marked by a transformation of the party's organization and electoral appeal and this was in many ways his most enduring contribution to British politics. Under Disraeli the Tories became the national party, able to appeal to all classes on a platform of patriotism, defence of the institutions of the country and concern for the social well-being of the people. They also became the most effective electoral machine in the country, with a network of paid agents and a plethora of convivial drinking clubs and social events at local level to attract members and money.

In 1876 Disraeli, by now in failing health, was elevated to the peerage and created the Earl of Beaconsfield. In 1878 he scored a major triumph in the diplomatic field when he dominated the gathering of European statesmen at the Congress of Berlin and gained for Britain possession of the island of Cyprus.

By the end of his six years as Prime Minister Disraeli had at last won the respect and even admiration of the political world which had for so long cold-shouldered him and which he had battled so hard to enter and to conquer. He had, indeed, become a venerable elder statesman, loved by his Queen and by many of the population. When he died a year later, on 19 April 1881, Gladstone, his long-time archrival, proposed that he should have a state funeral in Westminster Abbey. However, Disraeli's will gave instructions that he should be buried simply in the churchyard at Hughenden next to the remains of his 'late dear wife' who had died nine years earlier. A grief-stricken Queen Victoria sent a wreath made of primroses, his favourite flower, from the gardens of Osborne House.

Disraeli's name lives on in the Conservative Party – directly in the Primrose League which was set up in his memory two years after his death to uphold 'religion, the estates of the realm and the imperial ascendancy' and more generally as the originator of the 'One Nation' school of Toryism, classless and national in its appeal. In some ways it is ironical that someone who was a self-confessed and flagrant opportunist, schemer and loose liver should be so remembered and revered today. But if Disraeli was something of a rogue, he was a very charming and likeable one as Queen Victoria found, and his political career, though dominated by personal ambition, was also marked by a genuine concern for the good of his country and the welfare of its people.

Queen Victoria confers on Disraeli the title of Earl of Beaconsfield, Punch cartoon, 1876.

EMPRESS AND EARL;

OR, ONE GOOD TURN DESERVES ANOTHER.

LORD BEACONSFIELD. "*Thanks, your Majesty. I might have had it before!* Now *I think I have* EARNED *it!*"

ANTHONY ASHLEY-COOPER
EARL OF SHAFTESBURY
1801–1885

Anthony Ashley-Cooper, seventh Earl of Shaftesbury, was an aristocrat who cared deeply about the plight of the poor and working classes in Victorian society. A member of one of Britain's oldest established landed families, he led a life-long crusade against the suffering and oppression caused by industrialization, and despite the opposition of unscrupulous manufacturers he secured laws which protected those who worked in factories and mines.

His particular concern was for children and it is thanks to his untiring work that the evils of boy chimney-sweeps forced to climb up flues and girls made to drag cartloads of coal through badly ventilated mineshafts were banished from British life. Shaftesbury forsook what would almost certainly have been a glittering political career to devote himself to the unpopular and often thankless task of leading the movement to win basic rights for the many thousands of children whose labour helped to make Britain the leading industrial nation of the world.

Ashley-Cooper was born on 28 April 1801 and by his own account had an unhappy and lonely childhood. He appears not to have got on with his parents and exhibited from an early age the symptoms of what we nowadays call clinical depression which was to dog him throughout his adult life. The one person who provided him with warmth and love during these dismal early years was his parents' housekeeper, Maria Millis, a fervent Evangelical who was to have a major impact on his own religious beliefs.

Lord Ashley, as he was to be known for the first fifty years of his life, became himself a strong Evangelical. A loyal member of the Church of England, he clung strongly to the puritanical, Bible-based theology of the Evangelical revival which had swept through the Church in the eighteenth century, spreading a new 'vital' religion among its adherents in marked contrast to the easy-going liberalism which previously prevailed.

Throughout his life Ashley was to remain profoundly conscious of Evangelical notions of sin, judgement and personal salvation. He believed in the literal truth of the Bible and became a strong opponent both of those who took a modern, scientific approach to religion and to High Church Anglicans who sought to bring the Church of England nearer to Roman Catholicism and who stressed ritual and ceremony. To some extent his Evangelicalism was to make him a bigoted and stubborn opponent of other movements within the Church, but it was also to provide the driving force behind his personal crusade on behalf of the poor.

Ashley was first introduced to the reality of poverty when, as a boy at Harrow School, he saw a party of drunken men carrying a rough coffin which they suddenly let drop with much swearing and cursing. The sight of this pauper's funeral deeply affected the sensitive boy and he resolved to make the relief of such suffering his life's work.

In 1826 he was elected Tory MP for the pocket borough of Woodstock, which was in the gift of his grandfather, the Duke of Marlborough. He spent all but one of the next twenty-five years in the House of Commons, the majority of them as MP for the Dorset constituency in which the family seat was situated and where his father, the sixth Earl of Shaftesbury, was the leading local landowner.

Within a year of his election Ashley had plunged himself into a cause in which he was to remain interested for the rest of his life. He was appointed to the select committee on pauper lunatics and made his maiden speech urging better treatment for those locked up in mental asylums. In 1845 he piloted through Parliament important measures which ensured much better treatment for the mentally ill and provided safeguards against the unwarranted detention of patients.

Ashley took over the parliamentary leadership of the movement to secure better conditions for factory children in 1832 when Michael Sadler, another Evangelical MP who had previously led the campaign, lost his seat in the House of Commons. The main aim of the movement, which had much support from working people in the industrial regions of Britain but precious little among the industrialists and landowners in Parliament, was to

establish by law a maximum ten-hour day for young people working in factories. A ten-hour working day may seem long by our standards today but it represented a considerable improvement on the conditions then endured by most factory children, some of them as young as five, who often worked for up to sixteen hours. Ashley was appalled both by the hours worked by boys and girls in textile mills and coalmines and by the young age at which they were put to work, so he decided to lead the campaign for a ten-hour day, even though he

Anthony Ashley-Cooper, the seventh Earl of Shaftesbury, by John Collier, 1877.

realized that he was sacrificing all chance of political promotion.

The struggle was to be a long one, although he met with some early success. In 1833, largely thanks to his pressure, an Act was passed banning children under nine from working in textile mills and limiting those between nine and thirteen to nine hours' work a day and those between thirteen and eighteen to twelve hours. Four inspectors were appointed to enforce the new legislation. The measure fell seriously short of what Ashley wanted. The four inspectors proved wholly inadequate to enforce compliance by mill owners who managed to get round the Act by using a relay system which gave their young workers short breaks and still kept them at work for up to fourteen hours a day. It was not until 1847, when Ashley was briefly out of Parliament, that a Ten Hours Act was passed, but once again many mill owners found ways of evading its provisions.

Meanwhile Ashley turned his attention to other exploited groups of child workers. In 1840 he introduced the first of a series of measures which put an end to the practice of

Factory workers, especially young children, were the subject of Shaftesbury's reforms.

"Love conquered Fear."

BELOW *Children, known as 'trolley-boys', hauling coal. Shaftesbury's Bill of 1842 was designed to prevent this kind of abuse.*

employing small boys as chimney-sweeps' assistants and forcing them to climb up narrow and soot-filled flues. Once again unscrupulous employers ignored the legislation and it was not until 1875 when he secured the annual licensing of chimney-sweeps and put the enforcement of the law into the hands of the police that he finally ended the scandal which Charles Kingsley had so movingly exposed in his novel *The Water Babies*.

In 1842 Ashley put a stop to another abuse when he successfully introduced a Bill to end the employment of all females and of males under the age of thirteen in mines. In his researches he had been appalled to find that twelve-year-old girls were regularly used to carry a hundredweight of coal on their backs.

In 1851 Ashley's father died and he took his seat in the House of Lords as the seventh Earl of Shaftesbury. He continued in the Upper House the work which had occupied so much of his time in the Commons. The plight of factory children remained his prime concern. In 1862 he persuaded the government to set up a Children's Employment Commission which

revealed the extent to which child labour was still employed. As a result of the Commission's recommendations, legislation was passed in 1867 extending to all factories and workshops the restrictions on hours which had previously only applied to textile mills.

Finally in 1874, more than thirty years after he had first taken up the cause, Shaftesbury secured what he had long wanted – the reduction of the working day in all factories to ten hours and a prohibition on the employment of children until the age of ten in the case of part-timers and fourteen in the case of full-timers. A strengthening of the factory inspectorate made it more difficult for employers to ignore these regulations.

As well as being an active political campaigner, Shaftesbury was a committed philanthropist who devoted much of his time and his money to religious and charitable causes. He was particularly devoted to the Ragged School movement which sought to provide education for children in the poorest parts of cities. He was also much involved in efforts to give London a proper water supply and effective sewerage system.

Shaftesbury's Tory paternalism, which stressed the duty of those in the upper ranks of society to help those in the lower and the duty of the government to look after the weaker members of society, was one of the foundations on which the British Welfare State was to be built. He was far from being a socialist but he had a deep and abiding hatred of the uncaring and unbridled capitalism and thirst for profits which led employers to ignore the well-being of their workers. When he died on 1 October 1885, few people had done more to mitigate the less pleasant effects of the industrial Revolution.

WILLIAM GLADSTONE

1809–1898

WILLIAM EWART GLADSTONE is often seen today as a somewhat pompous and sanctimonious politician who made long and turgid speeches in Parliament about dry economic and constitutional subjects and give his name to a rather dreary kind of bag. He seems the very epitome of high Victorian seriousness – it is somehow appropriate that he is the only British Prime Minister to have an entry in the English Hymnal.

To his contemporaries, however, Gladstone was an altogether more interesting and attractive figure. He had a passion for singing and enjoyed nothing better than rendering 'The Camptown Races' in his rich deep voice. He was also an incurable romantic who courted his future wife in the ruins of the Colosseum at Rome by moonlight and who found his life-long inspiration in the poetry and art of the great classical civilization of Greece. Few men have ever had Gladstone's almost super-human reserves of physical and mental strength. He was Prime Minister at the age of eighty-five and until shortly before his death regularly burned off his excess energies in twenty-mile walks and tree-felling sessions at his estate in Hawarden in North Wales. He devoted the spare hours when he was not composing cheese-paring budgets or campaigning for Irish Home Rule to translating Homer, examining the Christian doctrine of eternal punishment and walking the streets of London in search of prostitutes to redeem.

His arch-enemy Disraeli described Gladstone as 'a sophisticated rhetorician inebriated with the exuberance of his own verbosity'. It is true that he was long-winded: his diary is longer than the Bible, his speeches in the House of Commons fill more than 15,000 columns of Hansard and his letters, bound in 750 volumes in the British Museum, form the largest single collection of papers left by any Englishman. But Gladstone was a superb orator, almost certainly the most accomplished Parliamentarian of the nineteenth century and an unrivalled speaker who could hold audiences spellbound for upwards of an hour in draughty halls around the country. He was the first leading British politician to take his message to the country at large and he was idolized in many working-class homes.

William Ewart Gladstone was born on 29 December 1809 in Liverpool where his father was a successful merchant. Although he was educated at Eton and Oxford, where he learned the art of debating and was a prominent figure in the Union, he never lost his northern roots. Equally, despite being aristocratic by temperament and an ardent High Church Anglican by

William Gladstone, Prime Minister four times between 1868 and 1894, by Sir John Everett Millais, 1885.

Gladstone's Home Rule Bill for Ireland proved unpopular with both Parliament and the electorate.

conviction, he was to find his greatest political supporters among the Nonconformist industrialists and artisans of the North, Scotland and Wales.

Gladstone was originally destined for a career in the Church and when he took up politics it was almost as a substitute religion. For him the political life was a matter of high moral principle – a series of crusades in which he battled for righteous causes like public economy, peace and the liberation of oppressed peoples. It was this strong moral stress that appealed to Nonconformists and gave him the natural constituency which he was to lead in the Liberal Party.

Elected to the House of Commons for a pocket borough at the age of twenty-three in 1832, Gladstone started his political career as an ardent Conservative, opposing the Great Reform Act of that year and the abolition of slavery a year later. Indeed, he was described by Lord Macaulay as 'the rising hope of the stern, unbending Tories'.

His conversion to liberalism was to be a gradual process over the next thirty years. It owed much to the influence of his great mentor, Sir Robert Peel, under whose Premiership he first attained cabinet rank as President of the Board of Trade in 1843. Like Peel, Gladstone was a convinced free-trader and, when the Conservative Party was split asunder over the abolition of the Corn Laws in 1846, he parted company from the protectionist bulk of the party and became one of the leading figures among the free-trading Peelites.

Gladstone served as Chancellor of the Exchequer in coalition and Whig Governments from 1852 to 1855 and 1858 to 1866. He rigorously pursued the policies of good housekeeping and balancing the budget and brought about sweeping reductions in public spending and taxation. Nothing in the way of waste escaped his eagle eye – he once even complained to his wife on a one-night visit to the Queen at Balmoral that he had been given clean sheets when he could easily have made do with soiled ones.

A visit to Italy in 1859, where he was profoundly moved by the plight of political prisoners, strengthened Gladstone's identification with the tide of liberal and reforming opinion which was sweeping through Britain as across the rest of Europe in the mid-nineteenth century. In the early 1860s he gradually emerged as the leader of the new

Liberal Party created out of a merger between the Peelites, the old Whig party and diverse radicals and single-issue pressure groups. He signalled his rejection of Toryism in a speech in 1864 when he came out unequivocally in favour of a further extension of the franchise. The following year Toryism rejected him when he was defeated in Oxford, the home of High Anglicanism and Conservatism and the seat which he had represented in Parliament for

In 1880 Gladstone succeeded Disraeli as Prime Minister, at the same time inheriting several foreign policy problems from his predecessor.

eighteen years. He hurried north to Lancashire where he told the electors, 'I come before you unmuzzled', and was returned with a triumphant majority.

In 1868 the Liberal Party won its first General Election victory and Gladstone became Prime Minister. He was to hold that office for a total of fourteen years – a record that no one has come near to equalling since. The great watchwords of Gladstonian Liberalism were peace, retrenchment and reform – policies which brought him into head-on collision with the Conservative leader Disraeli, with whom he regularly engaged in electrify-

PUNCH, OR THE LONDON CHARIVARI.—JUNE 19, 1880.

LABOUR AND REST.

Ex-Head Gardener (*retired from business*). "WELL, WILLIAM, YER DON'T SEEM TO BE MAKIN' MUCH PROGRESS—*DO YER!*"
New Head Gardener. "WHY NO, BENJAMIN; YOU LEFT THE PLACE IN SUCH A PRECIOUS MESS!!"

ing oratorical skirmishes on the floor of the House of Commons.

In domestic affairs, Gladstone was strongly committed to administrative and constitutional reform. His governments extended the franchise, ended the hold of aristocratic privilege on the armed services and Civil Service and extended important civil rights to Nonconformists and women. He was less committed to state action in the sphere of social welfare where he preferred the ground to be left to voluntary community initiatives, mutual aid and self-help.

The containment of public spending remained a key Gladstonian priority. It was his constant dream to abolish income tax, which he saw as a standing temptation to Governments to spend money which was not properly theirs – better by far, he believed, to let it fructify in the pockets of the people. In the event, he never quite succeeded in doing away with the tax although he did reduce it to fourpence in the pound.

In foreign affairs Gladstone was a strong opponent of the Conservatives' Imperialism and a believer in letting small nations determine their own destiny. It was the application of this principle which led him to take up the Irish cause, which he first espoused in the 1860s. In 1886 he became converted to the policy of Irish Home Rule and laboured hard but unsuccessfully to carry Irish independence through Parliament, splitting the Liberal Party in the process much as Peel had split the Conservatives over the Corn Laws in 1846.

In his later years, to the horror of Queen Victoria who had never liked him and who regarded him as dangerously close to being a Republican, Gladstone became increasingly radical. He castigated the House of Lords for rejecting Liberal measures, including Home Rule, and anticipated in his speeches some of the major social reforms like old-age pensions which were to be introduced by Liberals in the twentieth century. Yet he was not radical enough for younger elements in the party who blamed him for diminishing the Liberals' electoral appeal by pursuing the narrow cause of Irish Home Rule to the exclusion of domestic social issues of more concern to the increasingly working-class electorate.

Yet Gladstone cannot really be blamed for the decline of the Liberal Party which was so marked a feature of British politics in the early part of the twentieth century and which allowed Labour to emerge as the main political force on the Left. The Liberals had always been an uneasy coalition of diverse interest groups whom Gladstone had welded into a powerful reforming force by his own personal charisma and strength of character. When he finally relinquished the leadership in 1894, four years before he died (19 May 1898), the party was in reasonable shape although it took some time to adjust to life without the Grand Old Man at the helm and find a leader with even half his energy and ability.

In the force of his personality, the depth of his religious belief, the exuberance of his energy and the range of his interests and activities Gladstone stands out as a Titan in that extraordinarily talented generation who were the Victorians. His legacy to present-day Britain ranges from our narrowly restrictive pub-opening hours to the strength and variety of our daily newspapers which he invigorated by removing stamp and paper duties. He set a standard of rectitude in both public and private life which many later politicians have found difficult to follow.

WILLIAM MORRIS

1833–1896

WILLIAM MORRIS spent most of his life engaged in what he described as 'holy warfare' against the forces of capitalism. Yet without his own comfortable middle-class upbringing, and the £900 annual income that he inherited at the age of twenty-one, it is doubtful if he could ever have embarked on his hazardous career as designer, poet and revolutionary.

He certainly came of solid bourgeois stock. He was born on 24 March 1833 in Walthamstow, then a quiet village set on the edge of Epping Forest, the son of a discount broker in the City. It was in childhood walks and frolics in the forest that he developed the love of nature which was to dominate his art and his approach to life. Later, in his designs for wallpapers and tapestries he was to use again and again the forms of flower, leaf and bird that he remembered from his rambles as a boy.

Like so many English socialists, William Morris had a public school education although in his case it was cut short by a riot among the boys at Marlborough. He went on to Oxford where he was able to indulge his love of all things medieval and his taste for the High Churchmanship of John Henry Newman, John Keble and the other leading lights of the Oxford Movement.

While at Oxford, Morris joined an idealistic brotherhood set up by his greatest friend Edward Burne-Jones. Initially, the two youthful members of the brotherhood, which aimed to recapture the spirit of medieval chivalry, pledged themselves to go into the Church and work for the social and moral reformation of Victorian society which they saw as tainted by industrialism and materialism. But after a visit to the Gothic cathedrals of France, the two men decided to renounce their intention of taking Holy Orders and resolved instead to devote themselves to art.

In 1856 Morris had himself apprenticed to G. E. Street, the architect of the Law Courts in the Strand. He soon fell under the influence of the Pre-Raphaelite Brotherhood, a group of artists who centred around Burne-Jones and Dante Gabriel Rossetti and who sought to return to the artistic style of the Middle Ages before the academic and classical influences introduced by the Renaissance.

It was with fellow-members of the Pre-Raphaelites that Morris was involved in his first major artistic venture when he helped to design and paint the frescoes on the walls of the Debating Hall which had just been built for the Oxford Union. Shortly after completing this work he became infatuated with Jane Burden, the daughter of an Oxford stable-hand.

William Morris and Jane Burden were married in 1859. It was not destined to be a happy union. Morris found it easy to romanticize and idealize Jane, who had the perfect Pre-

Raphaelite features of a long pale face and black crinkly hair, in paintings and in verse, but impossible to treat her in real life as an ordinary working-class girl. She came to adopt the distant, melancholy role in which her husband and his friends cast her and was unable to cope with his fiery temper and untidy ways.

For his married home Morris had a large house built in the south London suburb of Bexleyheath. It was as a direct result of his efforts to decorate and furnish the Red House, as it was called, that he conceived the idea of going into business to design and manufacture furniture and works of art. In 1861 with other Pre-Raphaelites he set up a company that was to revolutionize design and taste in nineteenth-century Britain.

What was new about Morris's firm was his insistence that artists should involve themselves in the actual processes of production. He set himself against the prevailing trend of factory mass production and sought instead to revive the medieval ideal of craftsmanship. The firm produced stained glass, furniture, tiles, jewellery and, above all, the fabrics and wallpapers with which they were to make their name and which were soon adorning many of the most fashionable drawing rooms in Britain. In 1877 Morris & Co. opened showrooms in Oxford Street in the heart of London's West End.

Morris himself felt increasingly uneasy about the disparity between his ideal of reviving the democratic traditions of craftsmanship and the reality that his firm's products could only be bought by the very rich. 'I spend my life in ministering to the swinish luxury of the

William Morris, centre row, fifth from the right, with the Hammersmith Branch of the Socialist League, 1890.

The Orchard tapestry woven in 1890 by Morris & Co., adapted from a Morris design for a ceiling painting.

rich,' he complained in 1876. This led to a rejection of his early philosophy of art for art's sake and a much greater interest in social and economic affairs which was to turn him into one of Britain's first socialists.

Morris espoused socialism partly out of feelings of guilt when he compared his own comfortable life with that of the poor whom he saw out of the window of his house in Hammersmith (where he had moved in 1878). He was also strongly influenced by his conviction that good art could not come out of a society dedicated to profit where workers were

exploited and alienated from the pleasures of their labour.

By 1884 his copy of Marx's *Das Kapital* needed re-binding because of wear and tear and he was an active member of the Social Democratic Federation, which was the first socialist group in Britain. Within a year, Morris had broken away from the Federation because of its stress on parliamentary tactics and gradual reforms and formed his own Socialist League which was committed to the cause of revolutionary communism in Britain.

Morris was too much of an idealist and a purist to have any major influence on the course of British politics. He rejected those organizations and methods by which the

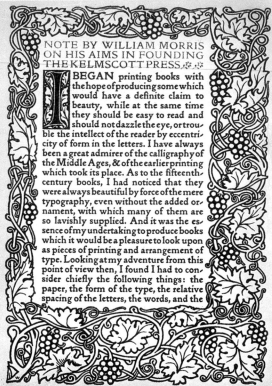

NOTE BY WILLIAM MORRIS ON HIS AIMS IN FOUNDING THE KELMSCOTT PRESS.

I BEGAN printing books with the hope of producing some which would have a definite claim to beauty, while at the same time they should be easy to read and should not dazzle the eye, or trouble the intellect of the reader by eccentricity of form in the letters. I have always been a great admirer of the calligraphy of the Middle Ages, & of the earlier printing which took its place. As to the fifteenth-century books, I had noticed that they were always beautiful by force of the mere typography, even without the added ornament, with which many of them are so lavishly supplied. And it was the essence of my undertaking to produce books which it would be a pleasure to look upon as pieces of printing and arrangement of type. Looking at my adventure from this point of view then, I found I had to consider chiefly the following things: the paper, the form of the type, the relative spacing of the letters, the words, and the

An early example of printing from the Kelmscott Press. The type is based on a fifteenth-century design.

Labour movement was being advanced, dismissing the reformist social democracy of the Fabians as 'gas and water socialism' and scorning the activities of the trade unions. Yet he built up a faithful body of young disciples, including W. B. Yeats, the Irish poet, who came regularly to the Sunday evening political meetings held in the coach house of his Hammersmith home.

Morris's greatest contribution to the development of socialism in Britain came from the series of poetry and prose romances which he wrote between 1885 and 1890. Set in the remote past or in the future they stressed the medieval values of community and kinship which he saw as infinitely preferable to the worship of individualism which characterized the nineteenth century. The greatest of these romances, *News From Nowhere*, serialized in *The Commonweal* magazine in 1890, ranks as one of the classic Utopian tracts in English literature. It portrays Britain in the twenty-first century as an ideal communist society which has ceased to worship production and become a craftsman's paradise. Work which is either inessential or unpleasant has ceased, having been taken over by machines, and England has returned to being one large garden with the Houses of Parliament being used for storing manure as there is no further need for politicians.

In 1891 Morris embarked on his last artistic project, the printing and binding of fine books. He set up the Kelmscott Press, which, like his house in Hammersmith, was named after the Oxfordshire village where he had had a manor house. Like the other artefacts with which he was associated, the books were very expensive but their popularity led other publishers to improve their typography and bindings and helped to produce a marked improvement in the standard of book production in Britain.

William Morris died on 3 October 1896 at the age of sixty-three. The family doctor declared that 'he died a victim to his enthusiasm for spreading the principles of socialism'. Another doctor remarked, 'The disease was simply being William Morris and having done more work than most ten men.' He was buried at a simple ceremony in Kelmscott churchyard.

Morris's influence lived on long after his death and extended to the many aspects of life in which he had been involved. He regarded himself first and foremost as a designer and it is in that sphere that his legacy has been greatest. Morris wallpapers and fabrics are still immensely popular today. His call for the revival of the medieval tradition of craftsmanship was one of the main influences behind the foundation of the Arts and Crafts movement at the end of the nineteenth century.

Morris has been seen as the father of the whole modern movement in design. He stressed simplicity and functionalism with his famous dictum, 'Have nothing in your house except what you know to be useful or believe to be beautiful.' He more than anyone else was responsible for sweeping away from Victorian drawing rooms the clutter of tasteless bric-a-brac and establishing the cleaner and simpler styles of furniture and decoration that have predominated in the twentieth century.

He was also in many ways the pioneer of the modern environmental movement. Deeply concerned with the preservation of Britain's architectural heritage, he set up in 1877 the Society for the Protection of Ancient Buildings, the first conservation society. He was one of the originators of the Garden City idea and an early advocate of town planning, clean air legislation and the control of industrial pollution.

In his own age Morris was regarded first and foremost as a poet. His poetic output was certainly vast, encompassing translations of the *Aeneid* and the *Odyssey*, versions of the Icelandic and Norse sagas, the long romances of his later years and many shorter works. Few of them are read today, but we can still salute William Morris the visionary, who looked beyond the mass production and class division of the world as it is towards a better world that might be created.

Woodcut signature from Beowulf, *1895. Morris used these in emulation of early printers.*

GILBERT AND SULLIVAN

1836–1911, 1842–1900

GILBERT AND SULLIVAN – the names go together like Rodgers and Hammerstein, Lerner and Loewe and Rice and Lloyd-Webber as one of the most famous and successful collaborations in the history of the theatre. Yet theirs was a very precarious partnership, constantly disturbed and interrupted by rows and quarrels.

It is, indeed, remarkable that Gilbert and Sullivan managed jointly to produce fourteen operas at all, let alone operas of such outstanding quality that they are still, except for one of which the music has been lost, regularly performed and enjoyed throughout the English-speaking world. Both librettist and composer basically regarded their comic operas on which they collaborated as a diversion from their real work. Gilbert saw himself as a serious dramatist and writer, Sullivan as an even more serious composer who should certainly not be wasting his time in producing comic burlesques with ridiculous plots. Yet it was together that the two men produced their best work. What they wrote on their own, by contrast, is now largely forgotten.

William Schwenck Gilbert was the older of the pair, being born in London on 18 November 1836. His father was a surgeon in the Royal Navy and a distant ancestor was Sir Humphrey Gilbert, the Elizabethan sailor and navigator. Gilbert was to put this seafaring blood to good use in his first full-length collaboration with Sullivan, *H.M.S. Pinafore*, which is set aboard a British man-of-war at the time of Nelson. Gilbert's first job was as a clerk in the Civil Service and he then practised for a while as a barrister, though not very successfully, before turning to full-time writing as a career. His particular talent lay in comic verse, and in 1869 he published a book entitled *The Bab Ballads*. Many of the characters and situations which were later to be fleshed out and incorporated in the Savoy Operas made their first appearance in that book.

Arthur Sullivan was born six years later than Gilbert on 13 May 1842, also in London. His father was a professional musician who played the clarinet in a theatre orchestra and was later to become a professor at the Military School of Music at Kneller Hall. Sullivan's mother was of Italian origin and had to struggle to provide for her family with the very limited means that her husband's music-making brought in to the household. Young Arthur soon showed himself to be a musician of some quality and at the age of twelve, in 1854, he was admitted as a chorister to the Chapel Royal, an élite choir which sang at important royal and state occasions. It was during this period that he first discovered the tradition of English choral music – a style which was greatly to influence much of his composing in later life.

After studying at the Royal Academy of Music, Sullivan won a scholarship to study at the Conservatory in Leipzig where he met Liszt and Schumann. He returned to Britain in 1861, the same year that Gilbert started to write comic verse, and had his first major work, a suite of music based on Shakespeare's play *The Tempest*, performed at the Crystal Palace. Sullivan's standing as a serious composer rose rapidly through the 1860s and at the end of that decade he was appointed a professor at the Royal Academy of Music. It was in 1869, too, that he first met the man with whom his name was to be inextricably linked for the next hundred years and more.

Gilbert and Sullivan were introduced by a composer called Frederic Clay during rehearsals for an operetta called *Ages Ago*, for which Clay had composed the music and Gilbert written the words. They met at the Royal Gallery of Illustration in Lower Regent Street where two years earlier a comic opera had been performed called *Cox and Box* with music by Sullivan and words by a librettist called F.C. Burnand.

History does not record what Gilbert and Sullivan said to each other during that first meeting in 1869 but it is unlikely that they touched on the subject of a possible collaboration. It was another two years before they were jointly commissioned by a theatrical impresario called John Hollingshead to produce a comic opera. The resulting work, entitled *Thespis*, enjoyed only a limited run in the West End and the two men went their separate ways again, Gilbert to write more plays, and Sullivan to compose church music, songs and ballads.

That the remarkable talents of the two men were to be brought together again four years later was due partly to accident and partly to the vision and imagination of Richard D'Oyly Carte, a theatrical manager who played the often demanding role of midwife for all the Gilbert and Sullivan operas. In 1875 D'Oyly Carte found himself at short notice in need of a one-act opera to complete the bill at his theatre in Soho. One story has it that Gilbert happened to walk into Carte's office at the time, another that the two men met in the street. However it came about, the meeting was fruitful. Gilbert already had the libretto of a one-act opera up his sleeve, a satire on the legal system which he had called *Trial by Jury*. D'Oyly Carte suggested that Sullivan would be the ideal person to set the new piece to music. Gilbert immediately went round to the composer's house and read him the libretto. Sullivan noted in his diary, 'I was screaming with laughter the whole time.' The opera was an instant success.

D'Oyly Carte was now determined to keep Gilbert and Sullivan together and establish an English school of light opera to rival the French *opéra comique* of Jacques Offenbach and the Viennese operettas of the Strauss family. He recruited four backers and set up in 1876 the English Comedy Opera Company with sufficient funds to enable composer and librettist to be paid in advance for their next collaboration.

For their first joint full-length work Gilbert resurrected the plot of a story he had written for a magazine, which centred on the effects of a magic love potion sold by a London firm of magicians to a local squire for distribution among his villagers. *The Sorcerer* opened in November 1877 at the Opera Comique Theatre just off the Strand which D'Oyly Carte had leased as the temporary first home for the new company.

Gilbert and Sullivan had their first big success with their next work, *H.M.S. Pinafore*, which ran for 571 performances. This introduced the world to the character of Sir Joseph Porter, the first Lord of the Admiralty who had never been to sea, a figure whom Gilbert based on W.H. Smith, the Conservative politician and founder of the High Street newsagents' business, who ran the navy in Disraeli's government from 1877 to 1880.

The next Gilbert and Sullivan opera, *The Pirates of Penzance*, had its premiere in New York rather than London. Gilbert and Sullivan went with D'Oyly Carte to the United States at the end of 1879 to present the authorized version of *H.M.S. Pinafore*, which in the absence of any international copyright arrangements had been produced in many pirate versions across the Atlantic. They also brought with them their new opera about the dastardly doings of Cornish pirates, major general's daughters and the doughty British policeman.

Gilbert next turned his sharp satirical eye on the Pre-Raphaelite and aesthetic movements which were gripping the world of art and letters in the 1870s and early 1880s. *Patience*

Sullivan (above) and Gilbert (right).

The Two Very Fanny Japs at the Savoy.

ABOVE *Sullivan and Gilbert depicted as the characters Ko-Ko and Pooh-Bah from* The Mikado, *which was first performed in 1885.*

ridicules the affectation and pretentiousness of the likes of Algernon Swinburne and Oscar Wilde. Indeed, D'Oyly Carte had the brilliant idea of sending Wilde on a lecture tour of the United States to promote the opera. Opening in April 1881, it moved in October to the brand new Savoy Theatre which D'Oyly Carte had just built on the south side of the Strand. He proudly announced to the audience that it was

SAVOY

R. D'OYLY CARTE

THE YEOMEN of the GUARD

Written by
W. S. GILBERT.

THEATRE

Proprietor & Manager

of The
MERRYMAN
& his
MAID.

Composed by
ARTHUR SULLIVAN

The programme designed by Alice Havers for the original production at the Savoy Theatre of The Yeomen of the Guard, *1888.*

the first theatre in Britain to be illuminated by electric light and to allay fears about the safety of this new invention he broke a light bulb to prove that no fire resulted.

The next two Savoy Operas, as Gilbert and Sullivan's collaborations now came to be known, *Iolanthe* and *Princess Ida*, poked fun at the House of Lords and women's education. Relations between the two men now took a turn for the worse with Sullivan demanding that for the next opera Gilbert abandon his ridiculous plots and topsy-turvy situations and produce a straightforward story and the librettist retorting angrily, 'I cannot consent to construct another plot for the next opera.'

Despite frantic efforts at mediation by D'Oyly Carte it looked very much by the summer of 1884 as though the partnership had come to an end. It was saved, however, by a dramatic accident. As Gilbert was pacing up and down in his study a large Japanese executioner's sword fell from its mounting on the wall and crashed on to the floor. This gave him the idea for what was destined to become the most popular of all the Savoy Operas, *The Mikado*, for which Sullivan wrote some of his most beautiful tunes. The Mikado's initial run at the Savoy Theatre, 672 performances, stretched over two years. It was followed in 1887 by *Ruddigore*, a send-up of Victorian melodrama, and the following year by *The Yeomen of the Guard*, Gilbert and Sullivan's most serious work and their nearest approach to grand opera.

In 1889 the partnership looked in jeopardy again. Sullivan let it be known that from henceforth he was only interested in grand opera and an acid exchange of letters with Gilbert ensued. Once more D'Oyly Carte had to use all his skills as a diplomat to get the two

men to bury the hatchet. This they eventually did and the result of their next collaboration, *The Gondoliers*, a satire on republicanism set on an imaginary island, was highly successful.

In 1890 Gilbert had another furious quarrel, this time with both Sullivan and D'Oyly Carte, about the cost of a new carpet for the Savoy Theatre. Relations between the triumvirate were never fully restored and the last two Savoy Operas, *Utopia Limited* and *The Grand Duke*, lacked the sparkle of the earlier works.

Sullivan died on 22 November 1900 and is commemorated by a statue in the Embankment Gardens in London. His music lives on, in the tune that he wrote for *Onward, Christian Soldiers*, in the ever-popular parlour ballad, *The Lost Chord*, and above all in the hundreds of melodies which he wrote for the Savoy Operas.

Gilbert survived as a rather crusty magistrate and country gentleman until he drowned on 29 May 1911 while trying to rescue a young woman who had got into difficulties in the lake at his home in Middlesex. His plays and comic articles lie largely forgotten but there can be few people who have not encountered the characters he created in his make-believe world of modern major generals, wandering minstrels and lord high executioners.

The Savoy Operas are essentially British, poking fun as they do at such hallowed national institutions as the House of Lords and the Royal Navy. They are also very much the products of their age: indeed, they can tell us as much about the Victorians as many a textbook. But there is also a quality of genius about their creators which makes them timeless in their appeal. It seems safe to predict that they will go on being performed in school halls and parish rooms around the country for many decades to come.

DAVID LLOYD GEORGE

1859–1947

DAVID LLOYD GEORGE is one of the most colourful and dynamic figures in British political history. His nickname 'The Welsh Wizard' perfectly sums up his mixture of Celtic charm, oratorical fervour and native cunning. His achievements were considerable: one of the architects of the Welfare State, he piloted Britain successfully through the First World War and played a major role in creating the Irish Free State. Yet he must also be held partly accountable for splitting the Liberal Party and dooming it to a long period of opposition.

Born in a remote North Wales village on 17 January 1863, Lloyd George lost his parents at an early age and was brought up by an uncle who was a strict Baptist. He first developed his oratorical powers at Bible classes and temperance meetings and, although in later life he was to depart from its strict standards of morality, he remained deeply imbued throughout adulthood with the vigour and passionate radicalism of Welsh Nonconformity.

Lloyd George was the first British cabinet minister to be born in poverty. He retained from his childhood vivid memories of the exploitation of Welsh small farmers by English landlords. As a young solicitor in Caernarfon he rose to political fame championing the cause of land reform, Welsh nationalism and temperance, and fiercely denouncing English landlords and the English Church.

In 1890 he was elected Liberal MP for Caernarfon, the constituency which he was to represent for the next fifty-five years. Winning the contest against the local squire, he proudly announced, 'The day of the cottage-bred man has at last dawned.' He soon emerged as one of the most outstanding young Radicals on the Liberal benches and when the party came to power in December 1905 he was given the important post of President of the Board of Trade. Here he showed his superb talents as a negotiator, bringing together the two sides of industry in several major disputes and persuading them to settle matters by arbitration.

In 1908 on the accession of H.H. Asquith to the Premiership, Lloyd George succeeded him at the Treasury. As Chancellor he introduced the radical and controversial 'People's Budget' which sought a significant redistribution of wealth in Britain by taxing the rich to pay for old-age pensions and other benefits for the poor. Lloyd George described it as a war budget 'for raising money to wage implacable war against poverty and squalidness', and it certainly aroused the bitter hostility of the upper classes and the House of Lords.

Lloyd George relished taking on the peers and in a famous speech in the hall of a public house in Limehouse in July 1909 he tore into the privileges of the aristocracy in a way which some observers felt was more reminiscent of a revolutionary socialist than a liberal. After two indecisive elections in 1910 the Lords eventually gave way, the People's Budget was passed and the Parliament Act put an end to the Upper House's ability to frustrate the will of the Commons in respect of all measures dealing with finance.

Working in close harmony with his friend Winston Churchill, Lloyd George went on to set up national schemes for health and unemployment insurance and a network of labour exchanges to help the unemployed obtain work. He also established a Development Fund to provide substantial investment in public works. The two men were to fall out, however, on the question of Britain's response to the substantial rearmament programme in Germany in the early 1910s. As Secretary for the Admiralty, Churchill favoured a major programme of battleship construction which Lloyd George opposed both on grounds of economy and because of his natural pacifist leanings.

Lloyd George was extremely reluctant to see Britain become involved in the war that loomed with Germany but, once the neutrality of Belgium had been violated and Britain's participation in the conflict became inevitable, he bent all his determination to winning the war and winning it quickly. As minister of munitions in Asquith's 1915 coalition government, he streamlined the production and procurement of armaments and galvanized industry into action to speed the war effort.

The death of Kitchener in July 1916 brought Lloyd George to the key position of Secretary of State for War. From this position he launched a devastating attack on Asquith, the Prime Minister, whom he accused of being indecisive and unfit to lead the country through one of the greatest crises in its history. There was some truth in his criticisms but there was also something rather unseemly about the way he himself ousted Asquith at the end of the year in a spectacular coup engineered with the help of Churchill, the Conservative leader Bonar Law and the press magnate Lord Northcliffe.

Asquith never forgave Lloyd George for what he saw as an act of treachery, nor did many Liberals. However, there was no doubt that with Lloyd George at the head of the War Cabinet from the end of 1916 the Allied fortunes turned and Germany's military might began to crumble. Lloyd George directed Britain's war effort in a dictatorial but highly efficient manner. He brooked no opposition and clashed violently with General Haig whom he accused of sacrificing thousands of men to the dubious tactics of trench warfare rather than exploiting the advantages of tanks. Lloyd George unified the Allied command structure under France's Marshal Foch and set up the convoy system to protect the vital supply lines across the Atlantic. He deserves no small part of the credit for securing victory against Germany in the First World War.

In the election that followed the ending of the war in 1918 Lloyd George fought at the head of a coalition of Liberals and Conservatives. The result was a triumph for the coalition but it also showed a deep split in the Liberal Party with Asquithian Liberals having stood in many constituencies against pro-Lloyd George candidates.

Lloyd George remained Prime Minister until 1922. He led the British delegation at the

Lloyd George by Augustus John, 1916. Toothache may account for his rather formidable expression.

Arran. September. 1913.

Churchill, Asquith and Lloyd George (second from the right) on the Isle of Arran, 1913.

international peace conference at Versailles where he advocated a policy of moderation and conciliation towards Germany and opposed the French call for heavy reparations and punishments. Had his view prevailed, some of the feelings of resentment which Hitler was to capitalize on in the 1930s might have been avoided.

Lloyd George's other great achievement in the early 1920s was to settle the thorny problem of Ireland by persuading all parties in that troubled country to agree to a partition, with the South becoming a free and independent nation and the Protestant counties of Ulster remaining in the United Kingdom. It needed all his skill as a negotiator to persuade the Sinn Feiners to agree to this compromise solution but eventually it was accepted.

Lloyd George's own political position in the 1920s was a curious one. He had no party base, having effectively cut himself off from the Liberals, and to raise money for his political machine he indulged in a number of dubious practices including, so his opponents maintained, the trading of peerages for cash. He tried seriously to create a new centre or national party in British politics, building on the strength and popularity of the war-time coalition. But in 1922 the Conservatives let it be known that they would be fighting the next election on their own and the coalition, and Lloyd George's Premiership, came to an end.

From 1922 until 1945 Lloyd George played a rather curious role as a somewhat raffish and maverick elder statesman. Reunited with Asquith in 1923 through their common opposition to the Conservatives' new-found protectionism, he became leader of the Liberal party in 1926 but never saw office again. His main contribution to politics was in promoting the ideas of bright young thinkers like the economist John Maynard Keynes who argued for a major programme of public works to give jobs to the unemployed.

The stream of books and pamphlets produced by Lloyd George's 'think tank' in the 1920s played an important part in setting out the expansionist and social democratic direction which successive Conservative and Labour governments were to take for much of the next fifty years. He himself in 1934 tried unsuccessfully to launch a British version of President Roosevelt's New Deal which had brought high employment and prosperity to

Lloyd George streamlined the production of armaments to speed the war effort as minister of munitions in Asquith's 1915 coalition government.

DELIVERING THE GOODS.

[April 21, 1915.]

Lloyd George at the front.

the United States by the application of Keynesian ideas.

In 1936, aged seventy-three, Lloyd George met Adolf Hitler at Berchtesgarten. The German leader gave him a signed photograph inscribed 'to the man who won the war'. For his part he described the German dictator as 'a born leader of men. A magnetic, dynamic personality with a single-minded purpose, a resolute will and a dauntless heart.'

The words could easily have been applied to himself. Lloyd George's guiding aim in life was to get things done and he did not, perhaps, mind over-much if he trod on a few toes or cut a few corners on the way. His talents were perfectly suited to the demands of wartime leadership. In peace he never quite found a role. He died on 1 January 1945 a few months after accepting a peerage largely for the benefit of Frances Stevenson, his mistress for many years and latterly his wife, to whom he was devoted in an almost childlike way.

JAMES RAMSAY MACDONALD

1886–1937

THE LABOUR PARTY's first Prime Minister was born in genuinely humble circumstances in a two-roomed 'but and ben' in the Scottish fishing village of Lossiemouth on 12 October 1886. He was the illegitimate son of Anne Ramsay, a farm servant, and John MacDonald, a ploughman. Throughout his life MacDonald remained deeply embarrassed by the fact of his illegitimacy. He was educated at the local board school where he became a pupil teacher. In 1885 he worked briefly in Bristol helping to organize a Church boys' club. It was while in Bristol that he first became attracted to socialist politics and it was there that he joined the local branch of the Social Democratic Federation. The SDF gave him his first experience of street corner political evangelism but its Marxist ideology was not to his taste. A year later he became a member of the Fabian Society and it was here that he came into contact with the ideas of progressive and radical reformers which were to guide him for much of his political career.

The membership of the SDF and the Fabians were predominantly middle-class. (The mainstay of the SDF was a stockbroker, H.M. Hyndman.) That fact alone went far to explain why both groups had such difficulty in attracting a mass following among the working classes. Many trade unionists in the 1890s were deeply suspicious of middle-class political groups, however well intentioned, who offered them socialism as a panacea for all their troubles. One labour organization which did not have this problem was the Independent Labour Party, established in 1893 by a Scottish miner and trade union leader, Keir Hardie. Although the ILP called itself a socialist party its political programme laid far more emphasis on the need for immediate and piecemeal reforms rather than on the total transformation of society. MacDonald joined the ILP in 1894 and fought Southampton as one of the Party's candidates in 1895, although he only polled 886 votes.

A year later MacDonald's personal life was transformed by his marriage to Margaret Gladstone. Margaret was the daughter of a distinguished scientist and their marriage brought MacDonald both financial security – hitherto he had been scraping a living as a journalist – and great happiness. She gave him the warmth and family life he had never enjoyed during his own childhood. Margaret also took an active part in her husband's political career. MacDonald was an aloof and sensitive man but Margaret had a gift for close friendship and was able to make their home in Lincoln's Inn Fields the centre of both their family and political life. The couple had six children but their life together was all too brief. In 1912 Margaret contracted blood poisoning and died.

MacDonald was left desolate and, although he enjoyed the friendship of a number of intelligent women in later life, none of them ever remotely filled the gap in his life left by Margaret's death.

MacDonald had first begun to make a real impact on the Labour movement in 1899 when, together with Hardie, he drafted a resolution calling upon the Trades Union Congress to convene a conference to draw up plans to secure the return of more working-class representatives of labour to Parliament. In 1900 their work gave birth to the Labour Representation Committee, the direct forerunner of the Labour Party. As no one else appeared to want the job, MacDonald became its first secretary. Until he relinquished the post in 1912 he worked tirelessly travelling all over the country organizing the new Party. In deference to the very strong tradition of co-operation with the Liberal Party to which many trade unionists still adhered, the new Party was committed to co-operation with any other parties willing to further the aims of labour. MacDonald gave expression to this willingness to co-operate with the Liberals in 1903 when he negotiated an electoral pact with the Liberal chief whip, Herbert Gladstone, the son of the former Liberal Prime Minister. Thanks largely to the Gladstone-MacDonald Pact Labour was able to establish itself as a parliamentary party, winning 29 seats in the 1906 general election.

Ramsay Macdonald.

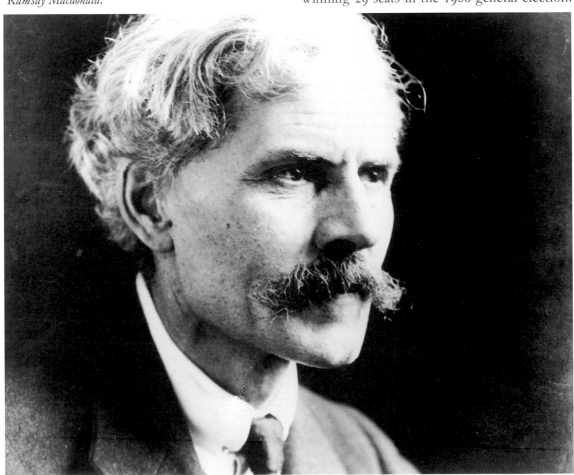

MacDonald himself was elected for Leicester and in 1912 he also became Party chairman.

On 4 August 1914 Britain declared war on the Kaiser's Germany. A day later MacDonald resigned from the chairmanship of the Party. The majority of trade unionists and Party members supported the government's decision. MacDonald was never a pacifist but he believed that the war was unnecessary and could be ended immediately by negotiation. His stand made him deeply unpopular. During the war his public meetings were regularly broken up by rowdy patriotic crowds and he was subjected to scurrilous abuse by the gutter press. The most spiteful attack on him was made by Horatio Bottomley's weekly paper *John Bull*. In September 1915 it printed a facsimile copy of MacDonald's birth certificate, thus revealing to the public the fact of his illegitimacy. MacDonald bore this smear campaign with courage but it resulted in him losing his seat in the general election of 1918.

He returned to Parliament as MP for the Aberavon division of Glamorganshire in November 1922. By then Labour's electoral prospects had been transformed. The war had left the Liberal Party divided and it was withering away in many constituencies. By contrast Labour's local organization was rapidly gaining in strength. In the 1923 election Labour won 191 seats and, although the Party did not have a majority, MacDonald was able with the tacit support of the Liberals to form the first Labour government. MacDonald was intent on giving the lie to the accusation that Labour were not fit to govern. But in trying to do this he sometimes went to ludicrous lengths. He insisted, for example, that Ministers who attended court functions at Buckingham Palace should wear court dress, something they could

obtain for £30 from 'Messrs Moss Bros', according to the King's private secretary. The government survived in office for less than a year but that was long enough to demonstrate Labour's weaknesses as a governing party. Apologists for the Party claimed that without a clear majority the government could not pass any really radical legislation to overcome the problem which dominated the lives of the first two Labour governments, unemployment. But, in fact, although MacDonald and his chancellor, Philip Snowden, spoke about the need to create a socialist society, they had little idea about how to go about it. Their economic ideas did not really go beyond those which had been pursued by the progressive wing of the Liberal Party before 1914.

The intellectual lacuna at the heart of MacDonald's socialism was even more cruelly revealed after he became Prime Minister for a second time in 1929. For the first two years of his government he immersed himself in foreign affairs. In October 1929 he became the first British Prime Minister to visit Washington and in 1930 he scored a modest success at the naval disarmament conference in London by persuading the United States and the Japanese to sign an agreement limiting their warship construction programmes until the end of 1936. But domestic problems would not go away. By the summer of 1931 the economy was in the depths of the 'Slump', unemployment had exceeded two million and the only solution MacDonald and Snowden could prescribe was the strictly orthodox remedy of a balanced budget and ensuring that Britain remained on the gold standard. The final crisis came in August 1931. Balancing the budget and keeping Britain on the gold standard required sharp reductions in government expenditure, includ-

ing a 10 per cent cut in unemployment benefits.
The TUC and the majority of cabinet ministers
balked at that last point. The unemployed had
been victimized enough by being thrown out
of work. It was unfair to victimize them
further. But MacDonald refused to be dictated
to by the unions. He believed that they were
only a sectional pressure group representing
their members' interests but that the Labour
Party should seek to represent the whole
nation. 'If we yield now to the TUC we shall
never to be able to call our bodies or our souls
or intelligences our own,' he wrote in his diary
on 22 August.

He did not yield, although it would have
been better for his reputation if he had done.
Instead he was repudiated by the Labour Party
and between 1931 and 1935 he became Prime
Minister of the Conservative-dominated National Government. He thus became the target
for the scorn of his erstwhile Labour colleagues
and, as he grew older and his powers grew
weaker, an increasing embarrassment for his
new followers. In the general election of 1931,
which confirmed the National Government in
office, Labour was reduced to a mere rump of
52 seats. MacDonald, standing as a National
Labour candidate, retained his seat at Seaham
in County Durham which he had first won in
1929. In 1935 he resigned from the Premiership
and took the sinecure office of Lord President
of the Council. When, shortly after, Stanley
Baldwin, the new Prime Minister, decided to
hold an election, MacDonald was humiliat-
ingly defeated at Seaham by the Labour candidate Emanuel Shinwell. The government only
contrived to secure his return to the Commons
through the back door device of a by-election
for the Scottish Universities seat. MacDonald,
now an increasingly sad and pathetic figure,

*Ramsay MacDonald, J.H.Thomas, Arthur Henderson
and J.R.Clynes, leading figures in the first Labour*

government, formed in 1923, visit Buckingham Palace in January 1924.

was thus able to linger on as Lord President for another seventeen months. He died on 9 November 1937 and was buried beside his wife at Lossiemouth.

After 1931 MacDonald passed into the Labour Party's demonology as a traitor to his class who placed his own career before the needs of his Party. He does not deserve this reputation. If he had been anxious only to carve out a brilliant career for himself he would not have joined the infant Labour movement in the 1890s, nor would he have worked tirelessly to create the Party's constituency organization before 1914. An unprincipled man would not have risked his entire career by taking the deeply unpopular anti-war position that he adopted between 1914 and 1918. MacDonald was not a turncoat. He was an idealist who tried to make the Labour Party a truly national party and not simply the political arm of the trade union movement. No Labour Prime Minister has ever enjoyed an entirely harmonious relationship with the trade union wing of his movement. In MacDonald's defence it can be said that in trying to develop this relationship he did not have the experiences of any predecessors to guide him. His concept of socialism was evolutionary, not revolutionary. He can justifiably be criticized for failing to realize that, as Labour was wedded to Parliamentary democracy, then a Labour government required a legislative programme of specific reform measures if it was going to make a success of government. But his Party believed that a socialist society could be built using the profits of capitalism. In 1931 capitalism was not making a profit. As the Party's leader and one of its most prominent ideologues MacDonald must bear his fair share of responsibility for the débâcle which followed.

JOHN MAYNARD KEYNES

1883–1946

UNTIL THE 1970s it was widely believed that Keynes had 'solved' the problem of unemployment. His *General Theory of Employment, Interest and Money*, published in 1936, had provided the framework for economic policies in the 1950s and 1960s, when unemployment was below 3 per cent of the labour force and when the annual increase in prices was usually below 5 per cent. However, the experience of inflation, combined with rising unemployment, in the 1970s raised doubts about the applicability of Keynes's theories to a society in which the bargaining power of trade unionists was much greater than it had been in the 1930s. After the Conservatives won the 1979 election, Keynesian economists found that government looked elsewhere for advice.

Keynes himself believed that the world was ruled by little else than the ideas of economists and political philosophers. However, he also believed that few people over twenty-five or thirty years of age were influenced by new theories, so that civil servants and politicians were always likely to be out of date. His own career as an economist-statesman was devoted to persuading people to accept new ideas. His *General Theory* was an attempt to make economists re-examine their basic assumptions. He wrote innumerable polemical articles in newspapers, to influence public opinion, even while he was being consulted by the very politicians

and civil servants whom he criticized. In both world wars he was called to service in the Treasury, and in 1942 he was raised to the peerage as Baron Keynes of Tilton.

Born on 5 June 1883, the son of a Cambridge don, Keynes had a rigorously intellectual upbringing, and shone as a scholar at Eton and at King's College, Cambridge. He was a member of the Apostles, the University's most intellectual society, and he was for a long time more interested in philosophy than economics. He was also devoted to the arts throughout his life, and his closest friends included members of the Bloomsbury Group, such as Lytton Strachey. Although a homosexual, Keynes married a famous Russian ballerina, Lydia Lopokova, in 1925. In his later years Keynes was well able to patronize the arts, for he made a considerable fortune as a speculator, using the profits from his publications.

Keynes came second in the Civil Service examination in 1906. Curiously, his examiners judged his worst papers to be in mathematics (in which he had graduated with first-class honours) and economics. He served briefly in the India Office before returning to Cambridge in 1909 to teach economics, a subject in which his formal training was limited to one term's postgraduate work. Keynes learnt on the job and from 1912 to within a year of his death he was editor of the *Economic Journal*, the profession's most prestigious journal. As early as 1913, when he was a member of the Royal Commission on Indian Finance and Currency, he impressed Whitehall with his grasp of complex monetary issues.

Keynes was consulted by the Treasury during the financial crisis at the outbreak of the First World War and he became a temporary civil servant in that department at the beginning of 1915. Two years later he was head of the division dealing with external finance, which meant that he was responsible for 40 per cent of war expenditure. In 1919 he was the Treasury's principal representative at the Paris peace conference. Keynes was convinced that the reparations clauses of the Versailles Treaty would damage European recovery. He resigned from the Treasury and published his arguments in *The Economic Consequences of the Peace* (1919), a book which persuaded many that the Treaty was unjust. Although some people in authority were offended by his action, the Treasury continued to consult him as it struggled to control the inflationary boom of 1919–20, and Keynes's advice showed that he was no less convinced than his former colleagues that inflation was a threat to the capitalist system.

Keynes's real break with the Treasury came over the decision to return to the gold standard in 1925 at the pre-war parity of $4.86. In his *Tract on Monetary Reform* (1923) he had argued that while the gold standard would stabilize exchange rates, it would not guarantee stability in the value of money (and in this he was right, for world prices fell dramatically in the post-1929 slump). Keynes wanted the currency to be managed so as to stabilize domestic prices. He criticized the chosen exchange rate on the grounds that it was too high for British exports and that it would require high interest rates to maintain it (and would thereby reduce investment and employment). Winston Churchill, the Chancellor of the Exchequer responsible for the decision to return to gold, was impressed by Keynes's arguments, but, lacking any real understanding of finance, Churchill felt he had to accept the advice of his officials. Ironically, Churchill's leading official adviser was Sir Otto Niemeyer, who had beaten Keynes into second place in the Civil Service examination in 1906 and who had therefore gone to the Treasury instead of Keynes. Economic historians still debate the extent to which unemployment in the 1920s was caused by the return to the gold standard, but undoubtedly export industries were placed in great difficulties and Churchill came to regard the decision as the greatest mistake of his life.

From 1924 Keynes supported proposals to create employment through public expenditure on roads, housing and other forms of public investment. He contributed to the Liberal Party's 'Yellow Book', *Britain's Industrial Future* (1928), and, with Hubert Henderson, wrote a famous pamphlet, *Can Lloyd George Do It?*, in support of the Liberal leader's public works programme of 1929. Keynes's first major work of economics, *A Treatise on Money* (1930), tried to show how not all savings found their way into capital outlay (as orthodox economics then taught). Keynes was disappointed by economists' reception of his book, and went on to write his *General Theory* during the worst years of the Depression. The *General Theory*, too, was controversial when it appeared in 1936, but its analytical framework came to be accepted by the younger generation of economists in the 1940s. The essential points of Keynes's arguments were that total expendi-

ture in the community should always be sufficient to provide full employment (although not so high as to force up prices) and that the best way to achieve this was for the government to control the level of investment. Governments, Keynes believed, should be prepared to borrow to whatever was the required level of public expenditure necessary to ensure full employment, even if this entailed budget deficits. This last point was contrary to the financial orthodoxy of the day, which required governments to balance current expenditure with revenue.

Even while working out his theories,

LEFT *Maynard Keynes by Duncan Grant, 1908.*
BELOW *Duncan Grant and Maynard Keynes,* c. *1911.*

Keynes kept up a steady stream of practical advice. He was a member of the Macmillan Committee on Finance and Industry (1929–31) and joined Ramsay Macdonald's Economic Advisory Council in 1930. As a member of the Council's Committee on Economic Information he came into close contact with leading Treasury officials, and forced them to think about the theoretical basis of their policies. Keynes was also an active propagandist, and his pamphlet *The Means to Prosperity* (1933), which was originally published as articles in *The Times*, made his ideas accessible to the intelligent layman.

In 1937 Keynes fell seriously ill with heart trouble and he was still a sick man when war broke out. Even so, he applied the concepts of the *General Theory* to the problems of war finance, and his pamphlet *How to Pay for the War* (1940) showed how the inflation of the previous war could be avoided. In 1940 Keynes was invited to return to the Treasury as an adviser, and the budget of 1941 was the first to incorporate his ideas, dealing as it did with the total income and expenditure of the community and not just the central government's accounts. Keynes carried a heavy burden in negotiations with the Americans, leading to the Bretton Woods Agreement of 1944, which set up the arrangements for the post-war international monetary system, and the Anglo-American Financial Agreement of 1945, which arranged terms for American credit to tide Britain over the period of post-war reconstruction. The terms of the latter were much less generous than Keynes had hoped for, and the convertibility crisis of 1947 was to show that Keynes's critics were right when they said that Britain would be unable to carry out the Agreement. The strain told on Keynes and almost certainly hastened his death, from a heart attack, on 21 April 1946.

Meanwhile Keynes's ideas had been incorporated into the Churchill coalition's White Paper on *Employment Policy* (1944). Keynes himself played only a limited role in drafting the White Paper, but some passages showed how younger economists in government service had accepted his theories. Other passages, however, showed that the Treasury was still reluctant to accept the idea of deficit finance, and full acceptance by Whitehall of Keynesian economics was only to come after Keynes's death.

The apparent success of post-war employment policy ensured that at first historians of the inter-war period would accept Keynes's version of what could have been done to reduce unemployment during the slump. Since the 1970s, however, some economic historians have expressed doubts as to whether Keynes's ideas would have been as effective as he had claimed, and the Keynesian interpretation of history is now as much a matter of controversy as is Keynesian economics. It is too early to assess Keynes's importance to English history, but there can be no doubt that he was the most brilliant economist of his age and that his ideas dominated both economics and the interpretation of inter-war history for a generation after his death.

Maynard Keynes with his wife, Lydia Lopokova, in their home in Gordon Square, Bloomsbury, in 1940.

VIRGINIA WOOLF

1882–1941

VIRGINIA WOOLF'S reputation rests on the novels and essays she published in her lifetime as well as on the fact that she was a founder of the Bloomsbury Group of artists, writers and intellectuals. Her reputation has been consolidated by the posthumous publication of five volumes of letters and six volumes of diaries which make hers possibly the best documented literary life of the century. The Bloomsbury Group included artists and critics like Clive Bell and Roger Fry as well as intellectuals like the economist Maynard Keynes. Their free thinking and outspoken views set the stage for much of the social change which marked the post-war era in Britain.

Born Adeline Virginia Stephen on 25 January 1882, the daughter of Julia Duckworth and Sir Leslie Stephen, philosopher, critic and editor of the *Dictionary of National Biography*, Woolf's early years were marred by the death of her mother in 1895 and of her father in 1904. She was the subject of continuing sexual interference from her half-brothers George and Gerald Duckworth, events which affected her deeply and which emerge in various of her fictional and autobiographical novels. In 1906 her favourite brother Thoby died of typhoid after a misdiagnosis. She first attempted suicide prior to her marriage to Leonard Woolf in 1912. Within a year of

marriage to Woolf she made a second, more serious attempt, by swallowing a potentially fatal dose of veronal.

Woolf's first novel, *The Voyage Out*, was published in 1915. On the surface it is a fairly conventional novel about a motherless young woman who is taken by a favourite aunt on a sea voyage. The heroine, Rachel Vinrace, is abruptly embraced and kissed by a Conservative MP. The event affects her so that she is unable to feel; she dissociates herself from her body and identifies with waves and birds on the sea. She falls in love with a Cambridge graduate, but develops a mysterious fever. Woolf describes vivid hallucinations which refer directly to her own early experiences. Rachel eventually dies. While the novel adopts a seemingly conventional narrative form, it indicates the subjective preoccupations which the author would translate into a form uniquely her own in later works.

Woolf's next novel, *Night and Day* (1919), also follows a traditional form and was among her least distinguished works. Through her heroine, Katharine Hilbery, she explores social aspects of relations between the sexes. In 1919 Virginia and Leonard Woolf founded the Hogarth Press – at first a box of type and a small printing press in their house at Richmond – partly as 'therapy' for Virginia. Her short stories *Kew Gardens* (1919) and *Monday or*

Tuesday (1921) were published by the Hogarth Press, as was T.S. Eliot's *Poems*. The press proved a great success. Virginia and Leonard no longer had to negotiate for publication of their books; and, in financial terms, it was highly profitable.

Woolf moved closer to her mature style with her third novel, *Jacob's Room*. In part an attempt to exorcise her brother Thoby's ghost by his imaginative re-creation, the novel marked a further stage in Woolf's progress towards describing the interior, subjective life of her characters.

Throughout her life, Woolf was a prolific reviewer and essayist, mainly writing unsigned reviews for the *Times Literary Supplement*. Her first apologia for a subjective approach to characterization rather than the traditional descriptive approach of writers like John Galsworthy, Arnold Bennett and H.G. Wells – *Mr Bennett and Mrs Brown* – was published in 1924. In 1925 her first collection of essays, *The Common Reader: First Series*, appeared. The second volume came out in 1932. Numerous volumes of essays were published posthumously. Woolf's piercing and entertaining brand of criticism was written against the highbrow approach of academics. She never allowed herself to become bogged down in footnotes and bibliographies, although she probably read more assiduously in pursuit of a short essay than many of her academic contemporaries.

In 1925 Woolf published *Mrs Dalloway*, a short novel describing the events of a single day in the life of the wife of a Conservative MP, her old lover and a 'madman' – Septimus Warren Smith. This work marked the beginning of her maturity as a novelist. She contrasts the interior worlds of men like Richard Dallo-way, whose concern is for the objective world of war, commerce and politics, with the subjective lives of women like his wife, who spends the day preparing for a party where many of the characters are brought together at the end. In portraying Septimus Smith, Woolf describes her own experience of being diagnosed as mad, and of being treated by doctors who are unable to imagine her point of view and the source of her anxieties.

To The Lighthouse (1927) is a powerful novel which, like *Jacob's Room*, attempts to exorcize personal ghosts. In this instance it is the ghosts of her parents. Woolf's achievement here is to take autobiographical material and transform it through her art to create an aesthetic work of the highest order. Through the character of the painter Lily Briscoe, Woolf asserts her belief that art is the unifying principle of life, just as Mrs Ramsay – based on Woolf's mother – proves a unifying social force among the disparate guests who are gathered at a summer house.

At the time she was writing *Mrs Dalloway*, Woolf developed a close relationship with Vita Sackville-West, wife of the diplomat and writer Harold Nicolson. In love with her lineage and with her estate at Knole as much as with the woman herself, Woolf celebrated their relationship in the exuberant and fantastic *Orlando* (1928). This affectionate tribute covers four centuries, and sees the main character change from male to female. Leonard Woolf, perhaps understandably, dismissed this and a later work in a similar vein, *Flush* (1933), as mere caprice. But *Flush*, an account of Elizabeth Barrett Browning's dog and her relation-

Virginia Stephen, later Woolf, photographed by G.C. Beresford in 1902.

The MOMENT
and other essays

Virginia Woolf

ship with Robert Browning, is full of references to Virginia's own experience of illness, of being forced, of being denied her rights. Read with sufficient attention, it is as disturbing as it is amusing.

Woolf twice turned her hand to proselytizing essays. The first, *A Room of One's Own* (1929), was based on lectures given to a women's college at Cambridge. A bold and well-argued examination of the position of the woman writer, the essay argues that 'A woman must have money and a room of her own if she is to write fiction.' Woolf concludes, 'Lock up your libraries if you like; but there is no gate, no lock, no bolt that you can set upon the freedom of my mind.' It is a work which occupies an important place in the history of feminism in the twentieth century. Her second political work was *Three Guineas* (1938), written in response to three separate requests for donations: from societies devoted to preventing war, women's education and obtaining employment for professional women. Written on the eve of the Second World War, it is a powerful indictment of attitudes which Woolf perceived as lying at the root of injustice and aggression: 'the dangerous and uncertain theories of psychologists and biologists' and 'the priesthood of medicine, of science, of the church'. She argued that one did not have to look to Germany or Italy for demonstrations of gross abuses of personal freedom: the worm of fascism could be found in many aspects of English life. Not surprisingly, the book met with a hostile reception.

In 1931 Woolf published what many critics believe to be her most accomplished novel, *The*

Jacket illustration by Vanessa Bell, Virginia Woolf's sister. The Moment was published in 1947.

Waves. Tracing the progress of six friends from school to middle age, Woolf achieves a depth of characterization rare in the genre, relying wholly on descriptions of interior life and relationships rather than external events. Her penultimate novel, *The Years*, was less successful in artistic terms, but her most popular novel in her lifetime. In a return to the semi-traditional form of her first two novels, she borrows the convention of the family saga to analyse the oppressive nature of Victorian patriarchy. Her last novel, *Between The Acts*, reiterates her essential themes against a background of history – of the race as well as of England. She reaffirms her enduring view that art is the central unifying force in life, and concludes with a village pageant in which the actors turn to face the audience with looking glasses.

Woolf made one partially successful foray into biography with *Roger Fry*, a life of the painter and art critic who had been her sister Vanessa's lover for a time and who was a central figure in the Bloomsbury Group. Her belief that biography should portray essential kernels of personality rather than a list of good deeds was one she put into practice in her fictional works with great success. But *Roger Fry* failed to capture the man, and the discipline of writing from factual sources proved not to be congenial.

Woolf's novels, like those of James Joyce and the poetry of T.S. Eliot, marked a definite break with the Victorian world view. *To The Lighthouse* and *The Waves* stand out as among the most important novels of the century. Yet many critics are reluctant to place her in the first division of novelists – alongside Henry James, for instance. This stems, in part, from the difficulty of her work. Her language and

her style are directed against an objective or scientific world view in which character can be approached by analytical means; in this respect, she is somewhat un-English in her approach, and is more likely to be appreciated by fans of Proust rather than John Galsworthy.

As a maker of history, Virginia Woolf was a modernist; but she incorporated and modified tradition rather than discarded it. For Woolf, history was personal. Her novels are exercises in personal history, undertaken for the same reasons that historians pick up their pens: to illuminate dark corners, to understand, to make sense of, to put the record straight.

RIGHT *Virginia and Leonard Woolf, 1912.*
BELOW *Virginia Woolf at Knole in 1928.*

WINSTON CHURCHILL

1874–1965

WINSTON SPENCER CHURCHILL was the out-standing statesman of modern British history. Though a few historians may cavil at this verdict, both the British public and world opinion correctly award the palm to Churchill. Undoubtedly Churchill's 'finest hour' was his period as Prime Minister during the Second World War. His leadership from Britain's 'darkest hour' in 1940 to 'victory in Europe' in 1945 made him a national hero and a major figure in the world. Yet this period was only a crowded chapter in Churchill's remarkably long and varied career. He was an MP from 1900 to 1964 and a government minister for nearly thirty years. He held, at different times, nine cabinet posts including the Chancellorship of the Exchequer and three Secretaryships of State. He was First Lord of the Admiralty at the outbreak of both World Wars and Prime Minister for the second time from 1951 to 1955. Nevertheless the importance of Churchill's ministerial career should not be overstressed, for there were long periods when he was out of office because he was out of favour with either his party or the electorate. But whether Churchill was in or out of office he was always a prominent figure in British politics and often in international politics as well. He played an important role in most political controversies from the Tariff Reform debate of 1903 to the Suez crisis of 1956.

Churchill's prominence in political life owed a great deal to familial inheritance. He was born on 30 November 1874 into a family who had occupied a first rank position in England for two centuries. When Churchill became MP he merely followed in the footsteps of five generations of his immediate Churchill ancestors. Both his grandfather, the seventh Duke of Marlborough, and his father, Lord Randolph Churchill, were Tory cabinet ministers. Indeed Lord Randolph had briefly been leader of the Conservatives in the House of Commons.

When Lord Randoph died prematurely in 1895, his twenty-one-year-old son vowed to pursue his aims and vindicate his memory. As a young politician Winston cultivated his father's friends and consciously adopted his father's politics. Winston's biography of Lord Randolph gave him both an insight into recent political history and much needed cash and publicity. Although Winston's career soon outstripped that of Lord Randolph, he always remained loyal to his father's political ideology, enshrined in phrases such as 'Tory democracy' and 'Trust the people'. Winston also derived financial profit and political inspiration from his study of his most famous forebear, John Churchill, first Duke of Marlborough. Winston's biography of Marlborough was written in the early 1930s at a time when he was increasingly concerned with the reviving

power and aggression of Germany. Winston portrayed Marlborough as a man who utilized both his military and his diplomatic skills to maintain an alliance which removed the threat to the liberty of other European states posed by the then dominant military power. Thus Winston's study of Marlborough provided him with a model for his own role in the Second World War.

Churchill's prominence in public life also owed much to his personal character and qualities. Although he was neither good-looking nor academically brilliant, he was naturally gregarious, garrulous, self-confident and egotistical. He possessed a dynamic and magnetic personality which it was difficult to ignore. Lord D'Abernon noted in 1930 that 'even in those circles least favourable to him... men and women are led by an obscure but irresistible instinct to discuss Winston.' By the time he was an adult Winston was convinced that he would become Prime Minister and when he reached his goal in 1940 he felt that he was 'walking with destiny'. During the Second World War, Churchill's sense of mission, combined with his exceptional powers of resilience and stamina, enabled him to persevere despite a succession of military disasters and personal illnesses. His powers of recovery from illness were still notable during his second Premiership. At the same time there was a melancholy and introspective strain in Churchill's temperament. He was often moody and sometimes depressed, particularly when he was out of office and in poor health as during part of the 1930s and in his final years.

Throughout his active life, Churchill applied

Winston Churchill with the Prince of Wales at the House of Commons in 1919.

great energy and industry to his public and private pursuits. He dealt quickly and thoroughly with matters to hand and expected his hard-worked subordinates to do likewise. His war-time minutes characteristically demanded 'Action This Day'. Churchill was an inveterate traveller and preferred to deal with problems on the spot. When he was young he travelled extensively on four continents and during the two World Wars he made many visits (some of them arduous and dangerous) to the main theatres of events. But Churchill's energy and industry were best reflected in his countless speeches and writing. He wrote his own speeches and always took great pains with their preparation and delivery. They illustrate the essential consistency of his outlook on most issues despite changing circumstances. Churchill's resonant voice and skill as a phrase-maker made him an exceptional orator. In his famous wartime broadcasts he generated patriotic emotion and endeavour while also appealing to the moral conscience of the world.

Churchill was a wonderful writer as well as a memorable talker. His personal papers are an archive of unparalleled size and importance and include many brilliant examples of his powers of premeditation, presentation and prescience. Churchill wrote well partly because he was a professional writer. For many years he supplemented his otherwise limited income by writing articles for the press on a great variety of political and other topics. These articles formed the basis for many of his twenty-seven books, although the latter also included a novel and some independent historical studies. Readable and entertaining, as well as informative and educative, they reflect the breadth of his interests and experiences and the way in which his career was intertwined with the history of

Churchill as Chancellor of the Exchequer on Budget Day, 1929, with his wife, daughter and son Randolph.

Britain. No other Premier (not even Disraeli) has made a comparable contribution to English literature, and what other world statesman has received the Nobel prize for literature? Moreover Churchill's largely self-taught skill as a landscape painter was also remarkable and was recognized when he was made an honorary Royal Academician Extraordinary.

Winston's success as a public and private man reflected the support he received from his wife and other female members of his family. His American mother, Jennie Jerome, encouraged and assisted his political career for a quarter of a century after his father's death. His paternal aunt, Cornelia Guest, used some of the wealth of her ironmaster husband to help Winston establish himself as a Liberal MP in the early 1900s. Churchill's conversion to Liberalism was further encouraged by his marriage to Clementine Hozier in 1908. Although she was an impecunious aristocratic cadet, Clemmie brought Winston assets money cannot buy: a loving family, loyalty and constant concern for his welfare. Clemmie also helped Winston in his constituency campaigning: no light task given the length of Churchill's parliamentary career. Their only son Randolph had an unsuccessful career as a politician, but two of their daughters, Mary and Diana, married future Conservative Cabinet ministers: Christopher Soames and Duncan Sandys. Thus the Churchill women helped to create, consolidate and perpetuate Churchill's political career.

Churchill's career in British politics was handicapped by his changes of party allegiance. He began as a Tory but soon fell out with the

Conservatives. He became a Liberal in 1904 and continued on till 1924. In that year he again became a Conservative and remained one until his death. The changing policy of the Conservative party prompted Churchill's changes of allegiance in 1904 and 1924. Nevertheless many Conservatives distrusted Churchill as a renegade and opportunist until 1940. Churchill was even more vehemently disliked by Socialists during the inter-war years. Churchill disliked class confrontation and 'big government' and he opposed the 1926 General Strike on constitutional grounds. Yet Churchill had a social conscience and sponsored numerous welfare reforms. Churchill was a Liberal-minded conservative (with a small 'c') who sought to blend tradition with reform. He put patriotism before party and country before class. Consequently he actively supported Lloyd George's coalition government during and after the First World War and was an ideal leader of the all-party coalition government formed in 1940. During the war Churchill enjoyed largely good relations with his Labour colleagues, but this ceased when Labour withdrew from the coalition in 1945. But thereafter Churchill still appealed, with some success, to Liberal voters. Throughout his career he was a passionate supporter of parliamentary government in general and of the House of Commons in particular. Churchill's reverence for Parliament was matched only by his reverence for the monarchy: the living symbol of Britain and the British Empire. Churchill enjoyed good relations with every sovereign from Edward VII on, but his imprudent support for Edward VIII's desire to marry Mrs Simpson in 1936 temporarily weakened his parliamentary position.

Throughout his career Churchill was closely involved with military and strategic affairs. In the 1890s he was a Sandhurst cadet and then an army subaltern and war correspondent. Before he became an MP he had seen more fighting than most generals. As First Lord of the Admiralty he ensured that 'the fleet was ready' at the outbreak of the war with Germany in 1914. He initiated the Gallipoli campaign of 1915 – although the reputation for its subsequent failure gained at this time was to dog his later career. In 1916 he was briefly a commander on the Western Front and in 1917–18, as minister of munitions, he developed links with America and France which were to prove useful in the next war. In 1919 and 1920 Churchill was Secretary for War and Air and responsible for sensitive military operations in Ireland, Russia and the Middle East. In the 1920s Churchill published *The World Crisis*, a notable history of the First World War which blended his memoirs with a broad survey of events. While out of office in the 1930s, Churchill persistently drew attention to the danger which the re-armament of Nazi Germany posed to Britain and Europe. When war broke out in 1939, Churchill returned to his old post at the Admiralty before becoming Premier and Minister of Defence. In this latter role Churchill was responsible for the operations of all three armed services – a task for which he was uniquely qualified. He forged close relations not only with the British service chiefs but also with the Allied military leaders such as Eisenhower and De Gaulle. He thus fostered successful military co-operation be-

ABOVE RIGHT *Churchill with General Montgomery, visiting the battlefront in Normandy in June, 1944.*
RIGHT *Churchill with Roosevelt and Stalin during the conference at Livadiya Palace, Yalta, February 1945.*

tween the Allies. After the war, Churchill wrote *The Second World War*, which remains the classic personal account of that conflict.

During his second Premiership Churchill encouraged the development of regional security organizations, notably NATO. He was always quick to appreciate the significance of new military technology. He played an important role in the development of the tank, the Royal Air Force, radar and the nuclear bomb. Although Churchill profited – both politically and financially – from the study of warfare, he was always revolted by its brutality. In 1909 he told his wife that, 'Much as war attracts me and fascinates my mind with its tremendous situations – I feel more deeply every year ... what vile and wicked folly and barbarism it all is.' The mass slaughter of two world wars increased Churchill's conviction on this point and he spent more of his career trying to prevent war than actively pursuing it. He always preferred 'Jaw, jaw,' to 'war, war'.

Churchill acquired an unparalleled experience of international affairs during his long career. Although he was never Foreign Secretary, he had great influence on British foreign policy and on Britain's standing in the world. His basic outlook on the world changed remarkably little after he reached manhood. He loved his country and served its interests abroad but he also respected the power and patriotism of other nations. He believed that Britain should continue to maintain its historic role: maintaining the balance of power in Europe. To further this end he favoured good relations with France and Russia so long as Germany was paramount and good relationships with France and Germany when Russia appeared a greater threat. Churchill did not believe that ideological differences were neces-

sarily a bar to good relations. He sought Soviet help against Nazi Germany despite his dislike for communism. After the war it was the *military* power of the Soviet Union which prompted Churchill to foster a new western alliance. But he sought détente, not 'cold war' with Russia and spent his second Premiership trying to arrange a summit conference. 'Half-American but all British', Churchill appreciated that the United States could play a vital role in helping Britain and preserving the balance of power. He welcomed and encouraged American assistance against Germany in two wars and in checking Russia after 1945. He also appreciated American support for British interests in the Far East. But Churchill's fondness for America also reflected his awareness that Britain and America shared a common heritage, a common ideology and a common language. Churchill profited personally and politically from his American connections but he also taught Europeans to appreciate the value of American goodwill.

Churchill's belief in the British Empire seems somewhat anachronistic today. But many, if not all the aspects of Churchill's imperial policy stood the test of time. He never thought the British Empire should be isolated economically, militarily or politically – from the wider world. For years he was a convinced free trader and opponent of imperial preference. He played an important part in giving both South Africa and Southern Ireland internal autonomy and dominion status in the Empire. But Churchill opposed granting India and the whole of Ireland unitary autonomy because he did not believe that they were united communities. The partition of Ireland in 1921 and of India in 1947 was, as Churchill realized, a manifestation of deep-rooted communal differences which could not be disguised by any constitutional artifice. But Churchill underestimated the ability of the Hindu community in India to create a tolerant, stable, progressive and democratic regime.

Churchill's view of the world was inevitably historic, and thus Conservative and often reactionary. He assessed the worth and weight of separate states according to their role in the history of the world over the last century or so. Thus states like Russia mattered in a way that Poland and India (as a separate unit) did not. But Churchill recognized that patriotism was a powerful force in all communities however small. He acknowledged that the smaller countries of the world could collectively play an important part in preserving international order. In the inter-war years Churchill strongly supported the League of Nations as a forum where all the states of the world could play a part, although he regretted that the League lacked the machinery to take effective military action against aggression. In this respect Churchill hoped that the United Nations would be an improvement. Despite its limited success, he regarded the UN as the best hope for maintaining world peace.

Churchill's political outlook was more complex and more individual than is generally assumed. Though Churchill championed common causes such as patriotism and democracy, he invested them with a distinctly Churchillian character. This was less because he was an egotist than because he had a genuinely individual approach to statesmanship. As Churchill once observed, 'I have mostly acted in politics as I felt I wanted to act.' Churchill's independent cast of mind was encouraged by its 'three-dimensional' nature: his preoccupation with the present was fully matched by his preoccupation with the past and the future. He thus had the rare ability to place current events in a wider perspective. His sense of history helped him to make history, and his prescience about the future was rooted in his study of the past.

Churchill's influence on the internal development of Britain was less marked than that which Roosevelt exercised in America or Stalin in Russia. But Churchill was a maker of English history primarily because he was a maker of world history. He was the only statesman in any country who played a major role in both world wars and he was one of the chief architects of the modern world. Thus Churchill's place in history is assured. His death on 24 January 1965 was followed by a state funeral at which almost the whole world paid tribute. But he was also, despite his faults, a great man in a personal sense as well. There was certainly enough glamour and incident, triumph and tragedy in Churchill's career to make him a hero in a romantic sense. He also displayed heroic qualities of magnanimity, goodwill and humanity, which heightened the moral sense of the world at a time when it most needed it.

Winston Churchill with his dog, leaving Downing Street for his house, Chartwell in Kent, 1953.

CHRONOLOGY

BC **43** Roman conquest begins

AD **61** Boudicca's revolt

122 Hadrian's Wall begun

367 Invasion of Picts and Scots

409 End of Roman rule in Britain

563 Columbus arrives at Iona

597 Arrival of St Augustine's mission in Kent

664 Synod of Whitby

731 Bede completes his *Ecclesiastical History*

871 Wessex attacked by the Danes; Alfred becomes King of Wessex

878 Alfred defeats the Danes at Edington; Guthrum, their leader, is baptized

899–939 Reconquest of Danelaw by Kings of Wessex

1014 Battle of Clontarf: victory over the Danes

1066 Duke William of Normandy defeats and kills King Harold of England at Hastings; William is consecrated king; foundation of Anglo-Norman empire

1086 Domesday survey

1087 Accession of William II Rufus

1100 Accession of Henry I

1135 Accession of Stephen

1139–53 Civil war in England

1154 Accession of Henry II

1170 Murder of Thomas Becket at Canterbury

1173–4 Rebellion against Henry II; William 'the Lion' (King of Scotland) invades the north

1189 Accession of Richard I

1190 Richard I on crusade to the Holy Land

1199 Accession of John

1215 Magna Carta; civil war in England

1264–5 Barons' war against Henry III: Simon de Montfort killed

1272 Accession of Edward I

1277–83 Edward I annexes Wales

1296–1336 Anglo-Scottish wars

1306 Rebellion of Robert Bruce

1307 Accession of Edward II

1314 Scottish victory at Bannockburn

1315–16 Great famine

1321–2 Civil war in England

1327 Accession of Edward III

1337 The Hundred Years War begins

1347 English capture Calais

1348 First occurrence of plague in England

1377 Accession of Richard II

1381 The Peasants' Revolt

1390s Geoffrey Chaucer writes *The Canterbury Tales*

1399 Deposition of Richard II; accession of Henry IV

1413 Accession of Henry V

1415 English victory at Agincourt

1422 Accession of Henry VI

1455–87 The Wars of the Roses; Henry VI and Edward IV alternate on the throne

1477 William Caxton's first printed book in England

1483 Accession, deposition and death of Edward V; accession of Richard III; rebellion of Henry, Duke of Buckingham

1485 Death of Richard III at Bosworth; accession of Henry VII

1509 Accession of Henry VIII

1512 War with France and Scotland

1513 Battle of Flodden: English victory over Scotland

1527 Beginning of Henry VIII's divorce crisis

1529 Fall of Wolsey: Sir Thomas More succeeds as Lord Chancellor

1534 Act of Supremacy

1536 Dissolution of the Monasteries; union of England and Wales

1547 Succession of Edward VI

1549 First Book of Common Prayer

1553 Accession of Mary

1554 Wyatt's rebellion

1554–58 Brief Catholic restoration

1558 Accession of Elizabeth I

1577–80 Drake's circumnavigation of the world

1587 Execution of Mary Stuart

1588 Defeat of the Spanish Armada

c.1589–*c*.1613 Shakespeare writes his plays

1603 Accession of James VI of Scotland as James I

1605 Gunpowder Plot

1607 Settlement of Virginia

1609 Rebellion of the Northern Earls in Ireland; beginnings of the Planting of Ulster by Scots and English Protestants

1611 Publication of Authorized Version of the Bible

1620 Pilgrim Fathers inaugurate religious migration to New England

1625 Accession of Charles I

1629 Charles I dissolves Parliament

1637–40 Breakdown of Charles's government of Scotland

1640 Long Parliament summoned

1642–48 Civil Wars in England

1649 Trial and execution of Charles I: England a republic

1649–53 Government by sovereign single-chamber assembly, the 'Rump' Parliament thoroughly purged of royalists and moderates

1649–52 Oliver Cromwell conquers Ireland and Scotland

1653 Cromwell becomes Lord Protector

1658 Cromwell dies and is succeeded by his son Richard

1659 Richard overthrown by the army; Rump restored but displeases many in the army

1660 Restoration of the monarchy under Charles II

1665 Great Plague (final major outbreak)

1666 Great Fire of London

1667 Publication of Milton's *Paradise Lost*

1678 Publication of Bunyan's *Pilgrim's Progress*, part I

1685 Accession of James II; failure of rebellion by Charles II's protestant bastard, the Duke of Monmouth

1687 Publication of Newton's *Principia Mathematica*

1688 William of Orange invades: James II flees; accession of William III (of Orange) and Mary

1690 Battle of the Boyne: William III defeats Irish and French army

1694 Bank of England founded

1702 Accession of Queen Anne

1707 Union of England and Scotland

1714 Accession of George I

1715 Jacobite rebellion fails

1716 Septennial Act sets the maximum duration of parliament at seven years

1720 South Sea Bubble: many investors ruined after speculation in the stock of the South Sea Company

1721 Walpole ministry

1726 Publication of Jonathan Swift's *Gulliver's Travels*

1727 Accession of George II

1738 Wesley's 'conversion': the start of Methodism

1745 Jacobite Rebellion led by 'Bonnie Prince Charlie'

1746 Battle of Culloden: the Duke of Cumberland routs the Jacobite army

1752 Adoption of Gregorian Calendar

1756–63 Seven Years War: Britain allied with Frederick the Great of Prussia against France, Austria, and Russia

1760 Accession of George III

1761 Publication of Laurence Sterne's *Tristram Shandy*

1769 James Watt's steam engine patented

1776 Declaration of American Independence; publication of Adam Smith's *Wealth of Nations*

1783 Younger Pitt's ministry

1789 French Revolution

1793 Outbreak of war with France

*c.***1795–1800** First steam-powered cotton mills

1801 Union with Ireland; first British census

1802 First factory legislation introduced by Peel

1805 Battle of Trafalgar: the French and Spanish fleets defeated by Nelson

1815 Battle of Waterloo: defeat of Napoleon; peace in Europe; Congress of Vienna

1819 Peterloo massacre; troops intervene at mass reform meeting, killing 11 and wounding 400

1820 Accession of George IV

1821–3 Famine in Ireland

1825 Trade Unions legalized; Stockton and Darlington railway opens

1829 Catholic Emancipation

1830 Accession of William IV

1830–32 First major cholera epidemic

1832 Great Reform Bill brings climax to period of political agitation

1833 Factory Act limits child labour

1834 Slavery abolished in the British Empire

1837 Accession of Queen Victoria

1838 Anti-Corn Law League established

1839 Chartist riots

1840 Penny post instituted

1844–5 Railway mania: 5,000 miles of track built; potato famine begins in Ireland

1851 Great Exhibition

1854–6 Crimean War

1859 Publication of Darwin's *Origin of Species*

1868 Disraeli succeeds Derby as Prime Minister (February)

1868–74 Gladstone's first Liberal government

1869 Suez Canal opened

1874–80 Disraeli's second Conservative government

1875 Disraeli buys Suez Canal shares, gaining controlling interest for Britain

1880–85 Gladstone's second Liberal government

1880–81 First Anglo-Boer War

1885 Death of Gordon at Khartoum

1886 Gladstone's third Liberal government introduces first Home Rule Bill for Ireland: Liberal Party splits

1892–4 Gladstone's fourth (minority) Liberal government

1893 Second Home Rule Bill rejected by the Lords

1899–1902 Second Anglo-Boer War

1901 Accession of Edward VII

1906 Formation of the Labour Party

1910 Accession of George V

1911 Parliament Act curtails power of the House of Lords and establishes five-yearly elections

1914–18 First World War

1916 Lloyd George succeeds Asquith as Prime Minister

1918 Lloyd George coalition government returned

1919 Treaty of Versailles establishes peace in Europe

1922 Irish Free State established

1924 Ramsay MacDonald leads first Labour government

1926 General Strike (3–12 May)

1929 General election; Ramsay MacDonald leads second Labour government

1931 Financial crisis and run on the pound; Britain abandons the gold standard; Ramsay MacDonald resigns and is returned in the election to head National Government

1936 Abdication of Edward VIII: George VI becomes king

1939–45 Second World War

1940 Churchill succeeds Chamberlain as Prime Minister

1945 General election: massive Labour victory and Attlee becomes Prime Minister

1947 Independence of India and Pakistan

1950 Outbreak of war in Korea

1951 Festival of Britain; general election: Conservatives defeat Labour, and Churchill again becomes Prime Minister

1952 Accession of Queen Elizabeth II

1956 Anglo-French invasion of Suez

1973 Entry of Britain into the European Common Market; Stormont government in Northern Ireland abolished

1979 General election won by Conservatives under Mrs Thatcher

1980 Britain becomes self-sufficient in North Sea oil

1982 Britain defeats Argentina in war over the Falkland Islands

1986 Unemployment over $3\frac{1}{4}$ million (more than 13% of the working population)

FURTHER READING

General reading on all aspects of Anglo-Saxon England:

Campbell, J., (ed.) *The Anglo-Saxons*, Phaidon 1982

Bede

Bede, *History of the English Church and People* (Trans. L. Sherley-Price), Penguin rev. edn 1968

Hunter Blair, P., *The World of Bede*, Secker and Warburg 1970

Hunter Blair, P., *Northumbria in the Days of Bede*, Gollancz 1976

King Alfred

Keynes, S., and Lapidge, M., *Alfred the Great*, Penguin 1983

Loyn, H.R., *Alfred the Great*, Oxford University Press 1967

Woodruff, D., *The Life and Times of Alfred the Great*, Weidenfeld and Nicolson 1974

William I

Barlow, F., *William I and the Norman Conquest*, English Universities Press 1965

Douglas, D. C., *William the Conqueror, The Norman Impact upon England*, Eyre and Spottiswoode 1964

Geoffrey of Monmouth

Geoffrey's History of the Kings of Britain (Trans. L. Thorpe), Penguin 1966

Tatlock, J.S.P., *The Legendary History of Britain*, University of California Press (USA) 1950

William de la Pole

Balton, J.L., *The Medieval English Economy 1150–1500*, Dent 1980

John Wyclif

Kenny, A., *Wycliffe*, Oxford University Press 1985

McFarlane, K.B., *John Wycliffe and the Beginnings of English Nonconformity*, English Universities Press 1952

Thomson, J.A.F., *The Later Lollards 1414–1520*, Oxford University Press 1965

Geoffrey Chaucer

Chaucer, *The Canterbury Tales* (Trans. N. Coghill), Penguin 1951

Kane, G., *Chaucer*, Oxford University Press 1984

Robertson, D.W., *Chaucer's London*, John Wiley 1968

William Caxton

Bennet, H.S., *English Books and Readers 1475–1557*, Cambridge University Press 1969

Painter, G.D., *William Caxton*, Chatto and Windus 1976

Margaret Beaufort

Griffiths, R.A., and Thomas, R.S., *The Making of the Tudor Dynasty*, Alan Sutton 1985

Henry VIII

Elton, G.R., *Reform and Reformation 1509–1558*, Edward Arnold 1977

Scarisbrick, J.G., *Henry VIII*, Eyre and Spottiswoode 1968

Smith, L.B., *Henry VIII, The Mask of Royalty*, Jonathan Cape 1971

Starkey, D., *The Reign of Henry VIII*, George Philip 1985

Thomas More

Chambers, R.W., *Thomas More*, Jonathan Cape 1935

Fox, A., *Thomas More: History and Providence*, Blackwell 1982

Guy, J.A., *The Public Career of Sir Thomas More*, Harvester Press 1980

Marius, R., *Sir Thomas More*, Dent 1985

Elizabeth I

Haigh, C., (ed.), *The Reign of Elizabeth I*, Macmillan Educational 1984

Hurstfield, J., *Elizabeth I and the Unity of England*, English Universities Press 1960

Neale, Sir John, *Queen Elizabeth I*, Jonathan Cape 1934

Smith, L.B., *Elizabeth Tudor, Portrait of a Queen*, Hutchinson 1976

William Shakespeare

Bentley, G.E., *Shakespeare and his Theatre*, University of Nebraska Press (USA) 1964

Bentley, G.E., *The Profession of Dramatist in Shakespeare's Time*, Princeton University Press (USA) 1971

Chambers, E.K., *The Elizabethan Stage*, 4 vols, Oxford University Press 1923

Rowse, A.L., *Shakespeare the Man*, Macmillan 1973

Rowse, A.L., (ed.), *Shakespeare's Sonnets*, Macmillan 1984

Francis Drake

Andrews, K.R., *Drake's Voyage*, Weidenfeld and Nicolson 1967

Hampden, J., *Francis Drake, Privateer*, Eyre Methuen 1972

Quinn, D.B., *England and the Discovery of America 1481–1620*, Allen and Unwin 1974

Williamson, J.A., *The Age of Drake*, A. & C. Black 1946

Francis Bacon

Bowen, C.D., *Bacon, The Temper of the Man*, Hamish Hamilton 1963

Crowther, J.D., *Francis Bacon, The First Statesman of Science*, Cresset Press 1960

Rossi, P., *Francis Bacon, From Magic to Science*, Routledge and Keagan Paul 1968

Webster, C., *The Great Instauration*, Duckworth 1975

James VI and I

Ashton, R., (ed.), *James I by his Contemporaries*, Hutchinson 1969

Lockyer, R., *Buckingham, The Life and Political Career of George Villiers, First Duke of Buckingham*, Longman 1981

Smith, A.G.R., *The Reign of King James VI and I*, Macmillan 1973

Willson, D.H., *James VI and I*, Jonathan Cape 1956

Oliver Cromwell

Carlyle, T., (ed.), *Letters and Speeches of Oliver Cromwell*, Chapman and Hall 1845

Fraser, Lady Antonia, *Cromwell, Our Chief of Men*, Weidenfeld and Nicolson 1973

Hill, C., *God's Englishman: Oliver Cromwell and the English Revolution*, Weidenfeld and Nicolson 1970

Roots, I., (ed.), *The Great Rebellion 1642–60*, Batsford 1966

Christopher Wren

Downes, K., *Christopher Wren*, Allen Lane 1971

Dutton, R., *The Age of Wren*, Batsford 1951

Furst, V., *The Architecture of Sir Christopher Wren*, Lund Humphries 1956

Summerson, J., *Christopher Wren*, Collins 1953

Samuel Pepys

Bryant, Sir Arthur, *Pepys*, 3 vols, Collins 1933–38

Latham, R., and Matthews, W., (eds) *The Diary of Samuel Pepys*, 11 vols, Bell and Hyman 1970–83

Latham, R., (ed.), *The Shorter Pepys*, Bell and Hyman 1985

Latham, R., *The Illustrated Pepys*, Bell and Hyman 1982

Ollard, R., *Pepys*, Hodder and Stoughton 1974

Isaac Newton

Cowling, T.G., *Isaac Newton and Astrology*, Leeds University Press 1977

Manuel, F., *A Portrait of Sir Isaac Newton*, Oxford University Press 1968

Palmer, R., (ed.), *The Annus Mirabilis of Sir Isaac Newton 1666–1966: A Symposium*, MIT Press (USA) 1966

Robert Walpole

Dickinson, H.T., *Walpole and the Whig Supremacy*, English Universities Press 1973

Speck, W.A., *Stability and Strife, England 1714–1760*, Edward Arnold 1977

Plumb, J.H., *Sir Robert Walpole*, 2 vols, Crescent Press 1956, 1961

John Wesley

Ayling, Stanley, *John Wesley*, Collins 1979

Green, V.H.H., *John Wesley*, Thomas Nelson and Sons Ltd 1964

Adam Smith

Campbell, R.H., and Skinner, A.S., *Adam Smith*, Croom Helm 1982

Raphael, D.D., *Adam Smith*, Oxford University Press 1985

William Pitt the Younger

Derry, John, *William Pitt*, Batsford 1962

Ehrman, John, *The Younger Pitt*, 2 vols, Constable 1969, 1983

Hannah More

Jones, Agnes, *Hannah More*, Cambridge University Press 1952

William Blake

Lindsay, Jack, *William Blake: His Life and Work*, Constable 1978

Horatio Nelson

Bradford, Ernle, *Nelson. The Essential Hero*, Macmillan 1977

Oman, Carola, *Nelson*, Hodder and Stoughton 1947

Thomas Telford

Rolt, L.T.C., *Thomas Telford*, Longmans, Green and Co., 1958

William Cobbett

Spater, George, *William Cobbett: The Poor Man's Friend*, 2 vols, Cambridge University Press 1982

Duke of Wellington

Longford, Elizabeth, *Wellington*, 2 vols, Weidenfeld and Nicolson 1969, 1972

Joseph Mallord William Turner

Lindsay, Jack, *Turner: His Life and Work*, Panther Books Ltd 1966

Robert Peel

Gash, Norman, *Peel*, Longman 1976

Alfred Tennyson

Martin, R.B., *Tennyson: The Unquiet Heart*, Oxford University Press 1980

Pinion, F.B., *A Tennyson Companion*, Macmillan 1984

Charles Dickens

Carey, John, *The Violent Effigy*, Faber 1974

Fido, Martin, *Charles Dickens*, Hamlyn 1970

Priestley, J.B., *Charles Dickens and His World*, Thames and Hudson 1969

Victoria and Albert

Auchincloss, Louis, *Queen Victoria and her Circle*, Weidenfeld and Nicolson 1979

Duff, David, *Albert and Victoria*, Muller 1972

Longford, Elizabeth, *Victoria R.I.*, Weidenfeld and Nicolson 1964

Benjamin Disraeli

Blake, Robert, *Disraeli*, Methuen 1966

Blake, Robert, *The Conservative Party from Peel to Churchill*, Eyre and Spottiswoode 1970

Hibbert, Christopher, *Disraeli and his World*, Thames and Hudson 1978

The Earl of Shaftesbury

Battiscombe, Georgina, *Shaftesbury*, Constable 1974
Best, Geoffrey, *Shaftesbury*, Batsford 1964
Hammond, J.L. and B., *Shaftesbury*, Constable 1923

William Gladstone

Bradley, Ian, *The Optimists: Themes and Personalities in Victorian Liberalism*, Faber 1980
Feuchtwanger, E.J., *Gladstone*, Allen Lane 1975
Magnus, Philip, *Gladstone*, Murray 1954

William Morris

Bradley, Ian, *William Morris and His World*, Thames and Hudson 1978
Henderson, Philip, *William Morris*, Penguin 1967
Thompson, E.P., *William Morris, Romantic to Revolutionary*, Pantheon Books (USA) 1977

Gilbert and Sullivan

Baily, Leslie, *Gilbert and Sullivan and their World*, Thames and Hudson 1973
Bradley, Ian, *The Annotated Gilbert and Sullivan*, 2 vols, Penguin 1982, 1984
Pearson, Hesketh, *Gilbert and Sullivan*, Penguin 1954

David Lloyd George

Morgan, K.O., *Lloyd George*, Weidenfeld and Nicolson 1974
Morgan, K.O., *The Age of Lloyd George*, Allen and Unwin 1972
Rowland, P., *Lloyd George*, Barrie and Jenkins 1975

Ramsay MacDonald

Marquand, David, *Ramsay MacDonald*, Jonathan Cape 1977
McKibbin, Ross, *The Evolution of the Labour Party, 1910–1924*, Oxford University Press 1974
Skidelsky, Robert, *Politicians and the Slump. The Labour Government of 1929–1931*, Penguin 1970

John Maynard Keynes

Harrod, R.F., *The Life of John Maynard Keynes*, Macmillan 1951
Moggridge, D.E., *Keynes*, Collins, Fontana 1976
Skidelsky, Robert, *John Maynard Keynes*, Macmillan 1983

Virginia Woolf

Bell, Quentin, *Virginia Woolf*, 2 vols, Hogarth Press 1972
Poole, Roger, *The Unknown Virginia Woolf*, Cambridge University Press 1978
Trombley, Stephen, '*All That Summer She Was Mad*', Junction Books 1981

Winston Churchill

Churchill, Randolph Spencer, and Gilbert, Martin, *Winston S. Churchill*, 6 vols, Heinemann 1966–1983
Manchester, William, *The Last Lion Winston Spencer Churchill: Visions of Glory 1874–1932*, Michael Joseph 1983
Pelling, Henry, *Winston Churchill*, Macmillan 1967

ACKNOWLEDGEMENTS

The pictures on pages 104, 108, 114, and 210 are reproduced by gracious permission of Her Majesty The Queen. All other photographs and illustrations are supplied by, or reproduced by kind permission of, the following:

Aberdeen Art Gallery and Museums 242
Society of Antiquaries of London 50
Worshipful Company of Apothecaries 90
Associated Press 2, 271
BBC Hulton Picture Library 34, 49, 110, 256, 267
Bibliothèque Centrale, Ghent 50
Bibliothèque Nationale, Paris 22 below, 64
Bodleian Library, Oxford 12 (MS Digby 20, f. 194 v), 17 (MS Junius 11, p. 57), 27 (MS Laud. Misc. 579, f. 1)
British Library Board 16, 22 right, 24, 26, 31, 35, 40, 46, 48, 60, 62–3, 66, 78, 81, 82, 83, 96, 102, 109, 121, 132, 142, 157, 199, 202, 216, 225, 144
Trustees of the British Museum 1, 158 (photo Bridgeman Art Library)
Collection of the Duke of Buccleuch and Queensberry, KT, at Boughton House, Kettering 84 left
The Hogarth Press 261
The Master and Fellows of Corpus Christi College, Cambridge 14 (photo Courtauld Institute of Art), 41
Christ Church College, Oxford 222
Crown Copyright. The Controller of Her Majesty's Stationary Office 191
Viscount De L'Isle, VC, KG, from his collection at Penshurst Place, Kent 76
Trustees of the Dickens House 200, 204, 205
Mr Simon Wingfield Digby, Sherborne Castle: endpapers
Keith Ellis Collection 138
Mary Evans Picture Library 192 below
The Frick Collection, New York 66 below
Guildhall Library, City of London 135
Hammersmith and Fulham Archives 228

History Today 175
The Huntington Library, San Marino, California 38, 45
Imperial War Museum 268 above right
Ironbridge Gorge Museum Trust 169, 170–71 (Elton Collection)
King's College, Cambridge 255 left
The Hon. Society of Lincoln's Inn (photo Courtauld Institute of Art) 145
Mander and Mitchenson 236
The Master and Fellows, Magdalene College, Cambridge 124, 125
Mansell Collection 192 right
The Methuen Collection 79
National Maritime Museum, London 85, 86, 88, 92, 99, 162, 164, 165
National Portrait Gallery 57, 61, 68, 84 right, 100, 127, 131, 137, 140, 146, 151, 152, 156, 165, 174, 196, 208, 219
National Trust 118 (Polesden Lacey), 215 (Hughenden Manor)
The Royal Society 115
The Master and Fellows of St John's College, Cambridge 55
Marquess of Salisbury 74
Trustees of the Science Museum, London 129
Syndication International 250–51
Tate Gallery 159 (photo Bridgeman Art Library), 184, 185, 186 (photo Bridgeman Art Library), 255 below
Earl of Verulam from the Gorhambury Collection 94 (photo Bridgeman Art Library)
Board of Trustees of the Victoria and Albert Museum 178, 207, 230
Walker Art Gallery, Liverpool 59
Weidenfeld and Nicolson Archive 20, 106, 110, 116, 119 right, 122, 149, 189, 220, 224, 232, 233, 236, 239, 244, 246, 248, 258, 262 below, 265, 268 right
His Grace the Duke of Wellington from his collection at Stratfield Saye 180

INDEX